Best Medicine:
Human Milk in the NICU

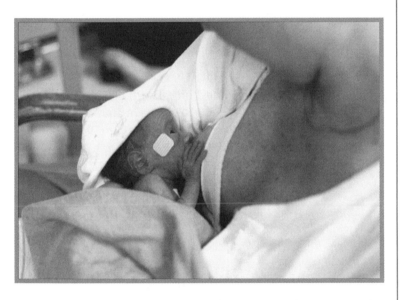

Nancy E. Wight MD, IBCLC, FABM, FAAP

Jane A. Morton MD, FABM, FAAP

Jae H. Kim MD, PhD, FRCPC, FAAP

©Copyright 2008
Hale Publishing, L.P.
1712 N. Forest St.
Amarillo, TX   79106 USA
www.iBreastfeeding.com

(806)376-9900 (phone)
(800)378-1317 (toll-free)
(806)376-9901 (fax)
(+1-806)376-9900 (International)

Printed in the USA

Managing Editor: Janet Rourke
Design Coordinator: Joyce Moore
Sales Director: Alicia Ingram
Production Services: Hale Publishing, L.P.

ISBN: 978-0-9815257-4-7

Library of Congress Number: 2008929422

Best Medicine:
Human Milk
in the NICU

Nancy E. Wight MD, IBCLC, FABM, FAAP
Jane A. Morton MD, FABM, FAAP
Jae H. Kim MD, PhD, FRCPC, FAAP

Hale Publishing

1712 N. Forest St. • Amarillo, Texas 79106

Table of Contents

Dedication

This book is dedicated to all the preterm and ill infants and their families for whom we have had the privilege to care and from whom we have learned so much.

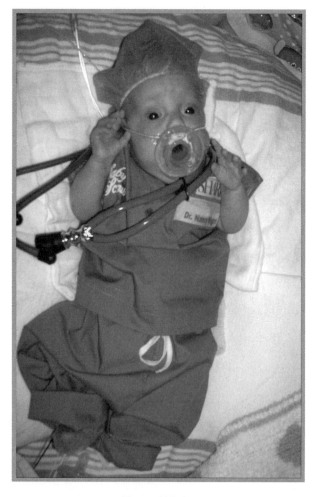

Nancy Wight
Jane Morton
Jae Kim

Foreward by Peter Hartmann

The primitive beginnings of the mammary gland can be traced back to the Pennsylvanian epoch (310 million years BP) and thus predates the origin of mammals. However, the selective advantage provided by the development of the mammary gland and its secretion (milk) is difficult to determine because fossil evidence for the development of soft tissue organs, such as the mammary gland, is very limited. Nevertheless, evidence from the function and metabolic regulation of the synthesis and secretion of milk components, as well as the anatomical and histological development of the mammary gland, provide strong evidence to suggest that lactation was associated with the facilitation of the incubation and hatching of soft (parchment) porous shelled eggs of primitive mammals, such as in monotremes (e.g., the Australian platypus). In this context, there is strong metabolic evidence to suggest that milk evolved from skin glands that originally developed from the inflammatory response of the innate immune system that protected soft skinned animals following injury. These glands developed in complexity and provided protection against dehydration and pathogenic microorganisms during the incubation of parchment shelled eggs. Subsequently, this secretion developed a nutritional function for either the hatchling or the newborn. In this context, it is of interest that the major nutritional components of milk, including lactose, milk proteins, and fat secretion, have evolved from components of the innate immune system and most nutritional components have retained anti-microbial activity. This concept of the evolution of the mammary gland and lactation has very important implications for the nourishment of the preterm infant as it emphasizes that breastmilk provides both protection and nutrition.

In the not so distant past, preterm infants did not survive. Therefore, it cannot be assumed that the milk produced by a mother who delivers preterm has been optimized by natural selection for the nourishment of the preterm infant. Nevertheless, the milk of mothers who deliver preterm is more suited to the needs of the preterm infant, with higher concentrations of protein in particular.

In this context, achieving optimal metabolic maturation, growth, and development of these most fragile humans is an enormous challenge, and it is indeed remarkable that today infants born after the completion of a little over 50% of a normal pregnancy can survive.

Best Medicine: Human Milk in the NICU emphasizes the importance of protection and nutrition derived from breastmilk for the growth and development of the preterm infant. This book extensively references and largely focuses on the science of providing human milk for premature infants. But where the science is lacking, the extensive NICU and lactation experience of the authors is drawn upon to provide best practice guidance. Although the book is extensively referenced, most of the topics have been presented in a condensed but easily readable format that is focused on the fundamentals of the respective subjects. In addition, priority areas requiring further research are clearly highlighted. No doubt this book will be a valuable resource for all health professionals interested in state of the art nourishment of the preterm infant.

Professor Peter Hartmann

The University of Western Australia

Acknowledgements

We would like to thank our colleagues and families for their support during the exciting and sometimes frustrating adventure of writing this book. We offer our sincere gratitude to Janet Rourke of Hale Publishing for her editing, coordinating, and remarkable patience during this project. We appreciate the opportunity afforded us and trust placed in us by Drs. Thomas Hale and Peter Hartmann.

We would like to thank our colleagues: physicians, nurses, lactation consultants, respiratory therapists, social workers, pharmacists, ward secretaries, medical assistants, and everyone else in the NICU and larger healthcare setting who work so hard to provide the care and environment for our fragile patients. We are proud of the progress made by our respective hospitals in supporting the use of human milk in the NICU: Sharp Mary Birch Hospital for Women, San Diego; Lucille Packard Children's Hospital at Stanford, Palo Alto; and University of California Medical Center, San Diego. We also recognize there is more we can do.

Finally, we would like to thank our patients, their mothers, and their families for being willing to be photographed during this stressful time and for the wisdom they have imparted to us.

Nancy Wight
Jane Morton
Jae Kim

𝕴ntroduction

Although advancements in neonatal intensive care have improved survival for premature infants dramatically in the last 35 years, the percent of premature and low birth weight infants continues to rise. [1, 2]

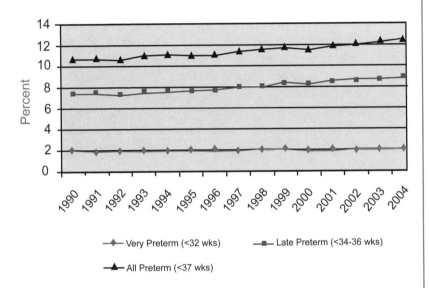

Figure 1: Preterm Birth Rates in the US 1990-2004[3]

The benefits of human milk for term infants are well recognized.[4, 5] Human milk is species-specific and has been adapted through evolution to meet the needs of the human infant, supporting growth, development, and survival.[6] It has only been in the very recent past that significantly preterm infants have survived and that attention has been paid to the crucial role of nutrition in the long-term outcome for these infants.

Current research confirms that human milk *especially* benefits the preterm infant in several areas: host defense, gastrointestinal development, special nutrition, and neurodevelopmental outcome. Indirectly, the infant benefits from having a physically and psychologically healthier mother. Ultimately, there are economic and environmental benefits for everyone.[7-9] Human milk has been rediscovered as one of the key factors in improving overall infant outcomes and is now the standard of care in the neonatal intensive care unit (NICU).[4,7,10,11]

All premature infants are not the same.[12] Infants who are born weighing less than 2500 grams (< 5 lb 8 oz) are classified as low birth weight (LBW); infants born weighing less than 1500 grams (< 3 lb 5 oz) are termed very low birth weight (VLBW); and infants born at less than 1000 grams (< 2 lb 3 oz) are termed extremely low birth weight (ELBW). Infants born at less than 37 completed weeks are considered premature.[13] Infants who are less than the 10th percentile for weight at any gestation are classified as small for gestational age (SGA). Given advances in medical technology and therapies, predominantly in the area of respiratory support, survival of preterm infants has improved significantly for all but the tiniest, most immature infants **(Table 1).**

Table 1: Preterm Births and Survival[14-16]

Estimated Births	Preterm Births: 2005	Weight at 50 % Survival (in USA)	
US (4.14 Million)	LBW (7.9%) ~ 339,000	1970	1500 g
	VLBW (1.4%) ~ 62,000	1980	1000 g
	ELBW (0.7%) ~ 31,000	1990	750 g
World (136 million)	LBW (15.5%)~21,000,000	1995	600 g
	VLBW (3%) ~ 4,000,000	2000	500 g
	ELBW (1.5%) ~ 2,000,000	2005	500 g

Nutrition appropriate for a 2000 gram preterm infant is considerably different from that needed by a 500 gram, 24 week premature infant. Optimal nutritional management, adjusted for gestational age and nutritional status at birth, is a key factor in improving the *quality* of survival, as well as survival itself.

Human milk is more than nutrition; it is medicine for both the infant and his mother: the milk for the infant and the provision of it for his mother. The benefits of human milk extend well beyond the neonatal period. The science of human milk is expanding at a rapid rate, but there is still, and will probably always be, some art involved in establishing and maintaining a mother's milk supply and transitioning an infant to full exclusive breastfeeding. As healthcare providers, we would like to recognize the mother's unique contribution to her infant's well-being and empower her to nurture her infant.

How can we help mothers succeed? Many pediatricians, neonatologists, nurses, and other ancillary professionals in the NICU were trained at a time when breastmilk was not considered adequate or even safe for the preterm infant. A mother's success depends upon the environment and the attitudes of those who care for her and her baby or babies. We must continually learn and apply what we have learned to protect the unique role of the mother and to encourage and support her decision to provide milk for her infant.

REFERENCES

1. Child Trends DataBank. 2005. (Accessed 06/16/2006, 2006, at http://www.childtrendsdatabank.org/figures/57-Figure-1.gif.)

2. Hamilton BE, Minino AM, Martin JA, Kochaneck KD, Strobino DM, Guyer B. Annual summary of vital statistics: 2005. Pediatrics 2007;119(2):345-60.

3. March of Dimes Peristats. 2007. (Accessed April 7,2008, at www.marchofdimes.com/peristats.)

4. American Academy of Pediatrics Section on Breastfeeding. Policy Statement. Breastfeeding and the use of human milk. Pediatrics 2005;115(2):496-506.

5. Cunningham AS. Chapt 9. Breastfeeding: adaptive behavior for child health and longevity. In: Stewart-Macadam P, Dettwyler KA, eds. Breastfeeding: biocultural perspectives. New York: Aldine de Gruyter; 1995.

6. Goldman AS, Chheda S, Garofalo R. Evolution of immunologic functions of the mammary gland and the postnatal development of immunity. Pediatr Res 1998;43(2):155-62.

7. California Perinatal Quality Care Collaborative PQIP. Toolkit: Nutritional support of the VLBW infant, part 1. In: California Perinatal Quality Care Collaborative, Perinatal Quality Improvement Panel, www.cpqcc.org; 2004.

8. Weimer J. The economic benefits of breastfeeding: a review and analysis. In: Food and Rural Economics Division, Economic Research Service, US Dept. of Agriculture. Food Assistance and Nutrition Research Report No. 13, 1800 M Street, NW, Washington, DC 20036-5831 www.ers.usda.gov/publications/fanrr13/; 2001.

9. Wight NE. Commentary: Donor human milk for preterm infants. J Perinatol 2001;21:249-54.

10. California Perinatal Quality Care Collaborative PQIP. Toolkit: Nutritional support of the VLBW infant, part 2. In: California Perinatal Quality Care Collaborative, Perinatal Quality Improvement Panel, www.cpqcc.org; 2005.

11. Schanler RJ, Lau C, Hurst NM, Smith EO. Randomized trial of donor human milk versus preterm formula as substitutes for mothers' own milk in the feeding of extremely premature infants. Pediatrics 2005;116(2):400-6.

12. Lawrence RA, Lawrence RM. Chapt 14: Breastfeeding the premature infant. In: Lawrence RA, Lawrence, R.M. , ed. Breastfeeding: a guide for the medical profession. 6th Ed. St. Louis, MO: Elsevier/Mosby; 2005.

13. American Academy of Pediatrics and the American College of Obstetricians and Gynecologists. Appendix E: Standard terminology for reporting of reproductive health statistics in the United States. Guidelines for perinatal care. 5th ed. Elk Grove Village, IL: American Academy of Pediatrics; 2002.

14. National Center for Health Statistics. Faststats. 2005. www.cdc.gov/nchs/fastats/birthwt.htm. Accessed 3/24/08.

15. World Health Organization. World Health Report 2005: Make every mother and child count. www.who.int/whr/2005/en. Accessed 3/24/08.

16. World Health Organization, UNICEF. Low birthweight: Country, regional and global estimates. 2004. http://www.who.int/reproductive-health/publications/low_birthweight/low_birthweight_estimates.pdf. Accessed 3/24/08.

Chapter 1
Historical Perspective

Throughout history, all civilizations have found alternatives when mothers either could not or would not breastfeed their infants.[1] Wet nursing provided better infant survival than dry nursing (animal milks or other adult foods).[2] However, up until the late 19th century, most preterm infants died, regardless of the type of feeding. The tiny infants that survived were usually close to term and small for gestational age.

Obstetricians Pierre Budin (1846-1907) and his mentor, Stephane Tarnier (1828-1897), are usually credited with the creation of perinatal medicine through their care of preterm infants ("weaklings" as they were called at the time) at L'Hôpital Maternité in Paris. Their key principles of care were: warmth, protection from infection, and nutrition, preferably breastmilk.

Figure 1: Infant incubators in operation at the Trans-Mississippi Exposition, Omaha, NE, 1898. Source: Silverman, 1979.[3] Reproduced with permission by AAP.

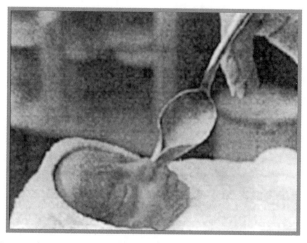

Figure 2: Nasal-spoon feeding of "Ann" (born Oct. 4, 1939, gestational age 28 weeks, birthweight 880 gm). Source: Silverman, 1979.[3] Reproduced with permission by AAP.

After visiting European premature centers, Dr. Julius H. Hess (1876-1955) started the first center for preterm infants in the United States at Michael Reese Hospital in Chicago and published the first book on the premature infant. Hess advocated human milk as the feeding of choice, starting in the second twelve hours of life, with milk provided by a wet nurse.[4] In the second version of his textbook twenty years later, he still advocated the use of breastmilk, but recommended delaying feedings for as long as four days in fear of aspiration and renal intolerance.[5] Before feedings began, the infant was to receive a physiologic salt solution subcutaneously.

Research in the 1940s noted that infants fed a diluted "half-skimmed cow's milk formula" gained weight more rapidly than those fed breastmilk, presumably due to the higher protein content of cow's milk.[6] Other studies suggested that human milk required supplementation with calcium and phosphorus for optimum bone mineralization.[7] As a result, the 1958 revision of Hess's textbook downplayed the promotion of breastmilk for preterm infants and included an expanded section on "artificial feeding."[8]

In the 1970s, research suggested that the quality, as well as the quantity, of proteins were important in preterm nutrition and that feeding too much protein (4.5 g/kg/d) could lead to azotemia, hyperammonemia, metabolic acidosis,[7] and lactobezoars[9] in some infants. Mothers' own milk was noted to provide better growth than pooled mature donor milk,[10] but no milk or formula achieved the intrauterine rate of growth. Lacking evidence that the intrauterine rate of growth was the *appropriate* standard for preterm infants ex-utero, the American Academy of Pediatrics, in its first statement on the nutritional needs of low birth weight infants, concluded that "the optimal diet for the low birth weight infant may be defined as the one that supports a rate of growth approximating that of the third trimester intrauterine life, without imposing stress on the developing metabolic or excretory systems."[11]

By the 1980s, human milk was found in almost every hospital with a neonatal intensive care unit (NICU). At that time, a crisis arose due to inconsistent practices regarding pasteurization and usage. Occasional NICU epidemics of sepsis and necrotizing enterocolitis from contaminated milk of one mother used for several NICU infants and the recognition that human immunodeficiency virus (HIV) and other viral pathogens could be transmitted through the use of fresh donor milk, caused all but a handful of milk banks in the U.S. to close.[12,13] The 1980s also saw the commercial development of preterm formulas with higher protein, calcium, phosphorus, and vitamins than term formulas,[7] resulting in more rapid growth without the metabolic complications seen in the 1970s.[14-16] Human milk alone was generally perceived to be inadequate to meet the needs of the preterm infant, although an increasing number of studies reported evidence for the benefits of human milk.

With the development of commercially available human milk fortifiers in the 1980s and 1990s, human milk with fortification became the standard of care for the low birth weight infant in the U.S.[7] Although comparative studies continued to show that infants fed special preterm formulas grew faster than those fed fortified human milk,[17-19] many other countries either could not afford or preferred not to use commercial multi-component human milk fortifiers, preferring instead to increase feeding volume and/or add specific nutrients, such as protein, calcium, and phosphorus. NICUs in the U.S. did not use higher volume feeds due to concerns regarding fluid overload aggravating pulmonary and cardiovascular status.

Although "extrauterine growth restriction" has been associated with both short-term and long-term morbidities,[20] optimal extrauterine growth rate(s) are yet to be determined. Too rapid growth in infancy, especially "catch-up" growth for in-utero growth-restricted infants, is also associated with later morbidities.[21-23]

Having established the superiority of human milk feedings, with benefits especially magnified in VLBW infants, a current barrier is the shortage of supply of mothers' own milk. Increasingly, research is

---

Timeline: Nutrition of the Premature Infant in the 20th Century
(adapted from Greer, 2001[7])

1851	First report of gavage feedings for infants
1890s	(Tarnier & Budin): Advocated breastmilk, care of "weaklings," gavage feeding
1913	(Hess): First NICU Michael Reese Hospital, Chicago
1930s	Studies confirm energy requirement of 120 kcal/kg/day
1940-1965	Feedings/fluids delayed for up to 96 hours
1943	Human milk (even with added Vit D) gives poor skeletal growth
1947	Premature infants grow faster on cow's milk formula than human milk
1960s	Delayed feedings detrimental (neurologic, developmental, hypoglycemia, hypernatremia, hyperbilirubinemia & severe weight loss). Early fluids/feeds advocated.
1968	First total parenteral nutrition (TPN) in preterm infants
1970s	Importance of protein "quality" not quantity; beginning of new interest in using human milk for preterm infants
1970s-2007+	Increasing research on the benefits of human milk for preterm infants
1980s	Development of special preterm formulas
1990s	Development of commercial multi-nutrient human milk fortifiers; emphasis on using mothers' own milk with early "trophic" feedings
1990s	Very early TPN is standard of care
1904-2007+	Not-for-profit milk banking
2005-2007+	For-profit milk banking with lacto-engineering for preterm infants

focusing on the potential to improve milk production in the pump-dependent mother [24] and the use of donor human milk.[25-27]

In the 21st century, human milk is the standard of care for *all* infants, including preterm infants:

> "Human milk is species-specific, and all substitute feeding preparations differ markedly from it, making human milk uniquely superior for infant feeding. ..... In addition, human milk-fed premature infants receive significant benefits with respect to host protection and improved developmental outcomes compared with formula-fed premature infants. ... hospitals and physicians should recommend human milk for premature and other high risk infants either by direct breastfeeding and/or using the mother's own expressed milk."[28]

REFERENCES

1. Fildes V. Breast, bottles, and babies. Edinburgh: Edinburgh University Press; 1986.

2. Baumslag N, Michels D. Milk, money and madness. Westport: Bergin & Garvey; 1995.

3. Silverman WA. Incubator-baby side shows. Pediatrics 1979;64(2):127-41, as accessed at http://www.neonatology.org/classics/silverman/silverman1.html.

4. Hess J. Premature and congenitally diseased infants. Philadelphia: Lea & Febiger; 1922.

5. Hess J, Lundeen E. The premature infant. its medical and nursing care. Philadelphia: JB Lippincott; 1941.

6. Gordon H, Levine S, Deamer W, McNamara H. Feeding of premature infants. A comparison of human and cow's milk. Am J Dis Child 1947;73:442-52.

7. Greer FR. Feeding the premature infant in the 20th century. J Nutr 2001;131(2):426-30S.

8. Lundeen E, Kunstadter R. Care of the premature infant. Philadelphia: JB Lippincott; 1958.

9. Erenberg A, Shaw RD, Yousefzadeh D. Lactobezoar in the low-birth-weight infant. Pediatrics 1979;63(4):642-6.

10. Gross SJ. Growth and biochemical response of preterm infants fed human milk or modified infant formula. N Engl J Med 1983;308(5):237-41.

11. American Academy of Pediatrics CoN. Nutritional needs of low-birthweight infants. Pediatrics 1977;60:519-30.

12. Arnold L, Erickson M. The early history of milk banking in the USA. J Hum Lact 1988;4(3):112-3.

13. Jones F. History of North American donor milk banking: One hundred years of progress. J Hum Lact 2003;19(3):313-8.

14. Cooper PA, Rothberg AD, Pettifor JM, Bolton KD, Davenhuis S. Growth and biochemical response of premature infants fed pooled preterm milk or special formula. J Pediatr Gastroenterol Nutr 1984;3:749-54.

15. Schanler RJ, Oh W. Nitrogen and mineral balance in preterm infants fed human milk or formula. J Pediatr Gastroenterol Nutr 1985;4:214-19.

16. Tyson JE, Lasky RE, Mize CE, Richards CJ, Blair-Smith N, Whyte R, Beer AE. Growth, metabolic response and development in very low birth weight infants fed banked human milk or enriched formula: 1. Neonatal findings. J Pediatr 1983;103:95-104.

17. Atkinson SA, Bryan MH, Anderson GH. Human milk feedings in premature infants: protein, fat and carbohydrate balance in the first 2 weeks of life. J Pediatr 1981;99:617-24.

18. Schanler RJ, Garza C. Improved mineral balance in very low birth weight infants fed fortified human milk. J Pediatr 1988;112(3):452-6.

19. Schanler RJ, Shulman RJ, Lau C. Feeding strategies for premature infants: beneficial outcomes of feeding fortified human milk vs preterm formula. Pediatr 1999;103:1150-7.

20. Clark RH, Wagner CL, Merritt RJ, et al. Nutrition in the neonatal intensive care unit: how do we reduce the incidence of extrauterine growth restriction? J Perinatol 2003;23: 337-44.

21. Griffin IJ. Postdischarge nutrition for high risk neonates. Clin Perinatol 2002;29(2):327-44.

22. Singhal A. Early nutrition and long-term cardiovascular health. Nutr Rev 2006;64(5 Pt 2):S44-9; discussion S72-91.

23. Lucas A. Long-term programming effects of early nutrition - implications for the preterm infant. J Perinatol 2005;25:S2-S6.

24. Mitoulas LR, Lai CT, Gurrin LC, Larsson M, Hartmann PE. Effect of vacuum profile on breast milk expression using an electric breast pump. J Hum Lact 2002;18(4):353-60.

25. Schanler RJ, Lau C, Hurst NM, Smith EO. Randomized trial of donor human milk versus preterm formula as substitutes for mothers' own milk in the feeding of extremely premature infants. Pediatrics 2005;116(2):400-6.

26. Wight NE. Commentary: Donor human milk for preterm infants. J Perinatol 2001;21:249-54.

27. Boyd CA, Quigley MA, Brocklehurst P. Donor breast milk versus infant formula for preterm infants: systematic review and meta-analysis. Arch Dis Child Fetal Neonatal Ed 2007;92:169-75.

28. American Academy of Pediatrics Section on Breastfeeding. Policy Statement. Breastfeeding and the use of human milk. Pediatrics 2005;115(2):496-506.

Chapter 2:
Preterm Developmental Physiology

Healthy, full-term infants are programmed to make the transition from receiving intrauterine continuous parenteral nutrition via the umbilical cord to extrauterine intermittent enteral support via breastmilk. Human milk is a complex fluid that simultaneously provides nutrients and bioactive components that facilitate the adaptive, functional changes required for the optimal transition from intrauterine to extrauterine life.[1] Although still immature as compared with adults, and undergoing significant postnatal growth and functional adaptation, term infants usually make the transition without much difficulty. Preterm infants, however, suffer not only from gastrointestinal immaturity, but also from functional immaturity of all organs and physiologic systems, as well as specific illnesses and complications, which further confound their transition from fetus to newborn.

DIGESTIVE TRACT DEVELOPMENT

Anatomy

The gastrointestinal (GI) tract is one of the first structures visible in the developing embryo. At six weeks gestation, the gut undergoes several critical counterclockwise rotational turns to enable efficient packing of small and large intestines into the abdominal cavity.[2] By twelve weeks gestation, the fetal intestine has all the major anatomic divisions developed.[3] The development of the fetal intestine is subdivided into four specific processes that occur during gestation: cytodifferentiation, digestion, absorption, and motility. The ontogenic timetable is complex[3] (Figure 1). The intestine grows very rapidly during the second trimester, slows down, and then continues to increase more rapidly than body length for three to four years of life.[4] Intestinal length doubles between 27 weeks gestation and full term.[5]

Cytodifferentiation

In the intestinal mucosa, villus development and cellular differentiation occur early in the second trimester.[4] What starts as global proliferation across the villus transitions to regionalization of proliferating cells into the epithelial crypt regions. The colonic architecture also becomes more specialized throughout fetal development with the transformation of villi structures to solely crypts shortly after full term birth.

Digestion

The stomach proton pump is active from 13 weeks gestation with intrinsic factor and pepsin secreted a few weeks later.[4] Gastric acid secretion is present and can lower stomach pH to less than 4.0, even in extremely preterm infants. Gastric lipase activity increases from 26 to 35 weeks of gestation and is fully active by term.[6 7] Very preterm infants also demonstrate pancreatic exocrine secretion and can digest fat, protein, and carbohydrate.[4] Although pancreatic lipase and bile salts are minimal in ELBW infants, human milk provides lipases and other digestive enzymes.[8] At the beginning of the third trimester, lactase activity is around 5% of adult levels, but feeding human milk rapidly increases this activity.[9] In addition, any undigested lactose is delivered to and fermented by the large intestine, where further energy salvage takes place.[10, 11] Nevertheless, low lactase activity can be a source of feeding intolerance in the ELBW infant.

Absorption

The presence of absorptive villi occurs early in the second trimester, but the capacity to take up nutrients is still immature with preterm infants. The ability to actively absorb glucose, one of the monosaccharides formed from lactose digestion, appears between 17 and 30 weeks.[12] The expression levels of the key glucose transporters at the luminal surface increase until term, while other glucose transporters located at the basolateral surface increase over the 17 to 30 weeks of the gestation period. The absorption of lipids requires a complex coordination of lipases, originating from the mouth, stomach, and pancreas, coupled with adequate binding to bile acids, which help orient the lipids for optimal enzyme digestion.[13] Once the triglycerides have been cleaved, the monoacyl glycerol chain or fatty acids are readily taken up and repackaged in the enterocytes to form chylomicrons, which then make their way to the liver. The fetal intestine has the ability to synthesize lipids, phospholipids, and apolipoprotein, in addition to assembling and secreting lipoproteins. Packaging and transport of chylomicrons is operational in the preterm small intestine.

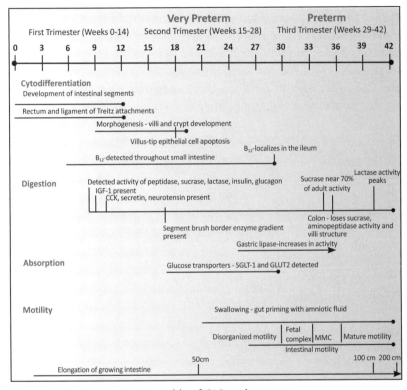

Figure 1: The Ontogenic Timetable of GI Development
Source: Adapted from Commare & Tappenden, 2007.[3] Reprinted with permission from Sage Publications Inc.

Motility

Intestinal motility develops late in gestation. Amniotic fluid provides the first luminal stimulus to the developing fetus, with the third trimester fetus receiving 10-14% of energy and protein requirements from ingested amniotic fluid.[14] Postnatally, breastmilk provides the continuum of luminal stimulation for the neonate. Slow gastric emptying is common in the preterm infant and presents as failure to tolerate milk feeds, with increased residuals. Gastric emptying is faster with human milk and is retarded by formula and by increased osmolality (Table 1).[4] Maturation of small intestinal motility and tolerance to feeds is enhanced by previous exposure to enteral nutrition.[15-17] Fortifying human milk delays gastric emptying significantly.[18, 19] Gastro-anal transit time is slower in preterm infants than in their term counterparts. Small volumes of undiluted milk lead most rapidly to a more mature feed response.[4] It is speculated that some of the pro-motility effects of human milk may be attributable to small amounts of the gut hormone motilin.[20] Stools are more varied and frequent in infants who receive human milk.[4] An overall schema for the bioactive factors in human milk is seen in Figure 2.

Table 1: Factors Affecting Gastric Emptying[4]

Faster Gastric Emptying	No Effect	Slower Gastric Emptying
Human milk	Phototherapy	Prematurity
Glucose polymers	Feed temperature	Formula milk
Starch	Nonnutritive sucking	Caloric density
Medium-chain triglycerides		Fatty acids
		Dextrose concentration
Prone position		Long-chain triglycerides
Right lateral position		Osmolality
		Illness

Source: Newell, 2000.[4] Table reprinted with permission, copyright Elsevier.

Development of the Immune System

The gut is the largest immune organ of the body. Reciprocal relationships between the production of immune factors by the lactating mammary gland and the production of those defense agents during early infancy are found in all mammalian species.[21, 22] Human milk components actively protect the infant from pathogenic infection and facilitate the establishment of the microbiota, which are necessary to activate the mucosal immune system.[1, 23, 24] As such, human milk constitutes a "communication vehicle" or link between the mother and the infant that reduces the infant's disease risk.[1, 25] Not only is human milk the appropriate "prebiotic" nutrient required to support the immune system, it is needed urgently and in high

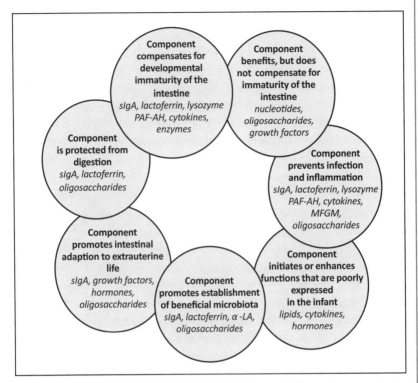

Figure 2. Strategies for beneficial effects of bioactive agents in human milk (HM). HM contains bioactive agents with overlapping and synergistic effects on intestinal development of neonates. Source: Donovan, 2006.[1] Reprinted with permission, copyright Elsevier.

volume. The longer the delay in establishing full human milk feeds, the greater the risk.[26] Yet, the capacity to tolerate rapid advancement to feedings is severely compromised in this population.

Defense factors in human milk include direct antimicrobial agents, anti-inflammatory factors, immunomodulators, and leukocytes. Protective immune factors in breastmilk coat the GI and upper respiratory tracts via mucosa-associated lymphoid tissue and prevent invasion of mucous membranes by respiratory and enteric pathogens. Inadequacies in the newborn's mucosal defenses are passively provided by protective substances in human milk or by an active, accelerated stimulation of the infant's immune system by trophic factors and cytokines secreted into human milk.[25, 27] Multiple hormones and growth-promoting peptides, such as insulin, cortisol, epidermal growth factor (EGF), and insulin-like growth factor I (IGF-1), have been found in high concentrations in maternal colostrum.[28] Since the premature infant's immune system is even more immature and his survival more precarious than that of a full-term newborn, the importance of ingesting his mother's own milk is even more apparent.[25, 29]

Formation of the Intestinal Ecosystem

The intestinal ecosystem is composed of three closely interacting components: host cells, nutrients, and microflora.[30]   Caicedo et al. describe how the developing intestinal ecosystem and the immune system work in concert. The first component, the highly immunoreactive intestinal submucosa, underlies only a fragile, single layer of epithelial cells. The second component is the intestinal flora. At birth, the intestine is sterile, but rapidly becomes colonized. In one study of infants greater than 34 weeks gestation, the most important determinants of the gut microbiotic composition in infants were the mode of delivery, type of infant feeding, gestational age, hospitalization, and antibiotic use.[31] In the preterm infant, delayed feeding, antibiotics, formula feeding, total parenteral nutrition, or nursing in incubators may delay or impair the intestinal colonization process. Instead of protecting the baby, the dysfunctional gut of the preterm infant can become a risk factor.

So-called "cross-talk" between the epithelium and commensal bacteria modulates proinflammatory mediators, preventing propagation of inflammation locally and at distal sites (lung and brain). The third component, the nutrients, not only supports the prevalence of beneficial microflora (Bifidobacterium and Lactobacilli), but also inhibits the growth of pathogenic microbes with factors such as lactoferrin and secretory IgA. As human milk contains a wide variety of live cellular and biologically active components, it can be considered a "symbiotic," a substance that has the properties of both probiotics ("good" bacteria) and prebiotics (nutritional substrates that promote the growth of probiotic bacteria). The feeding of human milk is an immediate way to promote the development of the intestinal ecosystem in both the term and preterm neonate.[30]

In addition, milk of mothers who deliver prematurely differs in composition from milk of mothers who deliver at term, both in terms of nutrients and bioactive factors.[32, 33] Preterm milk appears to have a higher concentration of growth factors, hormones, anti-inflammatory factors, immunomodulators, immunoglobulins, and live infection-fighting cells than term milk,[32, 34] thus meeting the needs of these extremely immature infants (Table 2).

Table 2: Comparison of Anti-Infective Properties in Colostrum of Preterm vs. Term Mothers

Factor	Preterm Colostrum	Term Colostrum
Total protein (g/L)	0.43 ± 1.3	0.31 ± 0.05
IgA (mg/g protein)	310.5 ± 70	168.2 ± 21
IgG (mg/g protein)	7.6 ± 3.9	8.4 ± 1
IgM (mg/g protein)	39.6 ± 23	36.1 ± 16
Lysozyme (mg/g protein)	1.5 ± 0.5	1.1 ± 0.3
Lactoferrin (mg/g protein)	165 ± 37	102 ± 25
Total cells/ ml^3	6794 ± 1946	3064 ± 424
Macrophages	4041 ± 1420	1597 ± 303
Lymphocytes	1850 ± 543	954 ± 143
Neutrophils	842 ± 404	512 ± 178

Source: Lawrence & Lawrence, 2005.[8] Table reprinted with permission, copyright Elsevier/Mosby.

Other Organs/Systems Development

Although the respiratory system is clearly the most important organ system in establishing early survival, all preterm infants experience the effects of multiple organ and system immaturities. As noted above, human milk provides some degree of mucosal immunity for the respiratory and GI systems. In addition, immunoglobulins and other antimicrobial factors can be absorbed through the immature gut mucosa to protect other organs, such as the immature urinary tract.[35, 36] Colostrum and mature milk contain high levels of vascular endothelial growth factor (VEGF), hepatic growth factor (HGF), and epidermal growth factor (EGF) to stimulate gut and other organ development.[37]

In utero, red blood cell (RBC) production is controlled exclusively by fetal erythropoietin produced in the liver. At birth, the site of erythropoietin production changes from the liver to the kidney by an unknown mechanism, and an abrupt increase in PaO2 causes serum erythropoietin to fall, shutting down RBC production for six to eight weeks, contributing to physiologic anemia and anemia of prematurity.[38] Human milk contains a significant concentration of erythropoietin, which tends to resist proteolytic degradation.[39-41] Erythropoietin receptors are widely distributed in human tissues, including the GI tract, endothelial cells, spinal cord, and brain, suggesting that erythropoietin plays a wider role in infant development.[39, 40]

Preterm infants fed maternal or banked breastmilk have significantly higher peak bilirubin concentrations and more prolonged jaundice than infants fed artificial preterm formula.[42-44] However, bilirubin has been shown to be a potent anti-oxidant,[43, 44] and modest elevations may act as relative protection against oxygen free radical-associated illness.

Environmental Issues

Preterm infants are likely to experience prolonged hospitalization, invasive procedures, and separation from their mother. The NICU environment is a source of nosocomial infections with resistant organisms and nonphysiologic treatments, as compared to the in-utero environment. Endotracheal tubes sustain life, but bypass upper airway defenses, leading to respiratory infections. Umbilical catheters and other vascular lines provide portals for bacterial entry. Hospital equipment, staff, and even the infant's family are carriers of bacterial, viral, and fungal pathogens, despite careful attention to infection control procedures.

The "enteromammary system"[32, 45, 46] produces specific IgA antibodies against antigens in the mother's environment. Through skin-to-skin contact with her preterm infant in the NICU, a lactating mother's more mature immune system can be exposed to, and make specific antibodies against, pathogens in the infant's environment. These antibodies are transferred rapidly to the mother's milk to protect her immature infant.[25, 46]

KEY CONCEPTS

- Preterm infants may have difficulty transitioning from continuous in utero parenteral nutrition to intermittent enteral nutrition.

- Components in human milk stimulate the growth and development of the preterm gastrointestinal system.

- Human milk is both a "prebiotic" (nutrition that supports normal bacteria) and a "probiotic" (good bacteria).

- The "enteromammary system" uses the mature maternal immune system to help protect the infant through antibodies in mother's milk to pathogens in the infant's environment.

REFERENCES

1. Donovan S. Role of human milk components in gastrointestinal development: current knowledge and future needs. J Pediatrics 2006;149(5):S49-S61.

2. Moore KL, Persaud VN. The developing human: clinically oriented embryology. 6th ed. Philadelphia, PA: W.B. Saunders Company; 1998.

3. Commare CE, Tappenden KA. Development of the infant intestine: Implications for nutrition support. Nutr Clin Pract 2007;22(2):159-73.

4. Newell SJ. Enteral feeding of the micropremie. Clin Perinatol 2000;27(1):221-34.

5. Touloukian RJ, Smith GJ. Normal intestinal length in preterm infants. J Pediatr Surg 1983;18(6):720-3.

6. DiPalma J, Kirk CL, Hamosh M, Colon AR, Benjamin SB, Hamosh P. Lipase and pepsin activity in the gastric mucosa of infants, children, and adults. Gastroenterology 1991;101(1):116-21.

7. Lee PC, Borysewicz R, Struve M, Raab K, Werlin SL. Development of lipolytic activity in gastric aspirates from premature infants. J Pediatr Gastroenterol Nutr 1993;17(3):291-7.

8. Lawrence RA, Lawrence RM. Chapt 14: Breastfeeding the premature infant. In: Lawrence RA, Lawrence RM (ed). Breastfeeding: a guide for the medical profession. 6th Ed. St. Louis, MO: Elsevier/Mosby; 2005.

9. Shulman RJ, Schanler RJ, Lau C, Heitkemper M, Ou CN, Smith EO. Early feeding, feeding tolerance, and lactase activity in preterm infants. J Pediatr 1998;133(5):645-9.

10. Kien CL. Digestion, absorption, and fermentation of carbohydrates in the newborn. Clin Perinatol 1996;23(2):211-28.

11. Kien CL, Liechty EA, Myerberg DZ, Mullett MD. Dietary carbohydrate assimilation in the premature infant: evidence for a nutritionally significant bacterial ecosystem in the colon. Am J Clin Nutr 1987;46(3):456-60.

12. Malo C, Berteloot A. Proximo-distal gradient of Na+-dependent D-glucose transport activity in the brush border membrane vesicles from the human fetal small intestine. FEBS Lett 1987;220(1):201-5.

13. Black DD. Development and physiological regulation of intestinal lipid absorption. I. Development of intestinal lipid absorption: cellular events in chylomicron assembly and secretion. Am J Physiol Gastrointest Liver Physiol 2007;293(3):G519-24.

14. Underwood MA, Sherman MP. Nutritional characteristics of amniotic fluid. NeoReviews 2006;7(6):e310-6.

15. Berseth CL. Gastrointestinal motility in the neonate. Clin Perinatol 1996;23:179-90.

16. Bisset WM, Watt JB, Rivers JPA, Milla PJ. Postprandial motor response of the small intestine to enteral feeds in preterm infants. Arch Dis Child 1989;64:1356-61.

17. McClure RJ, Newell SJ. Randomised controlled trial of trophic feeding and gut motility. Arch Dis Child 1999;80:F54-8.

18. Ewer AK, Yu VY. Gastric emptying in pre-term infants: the effect of breast milk fortifier. Acta Paediatr 1996;85(9):1112-5.

19. McClure RJ, Newell SJ. Effect of fortifying breast milk on gastric emptying. Arch Dis Child 1996;74:F60-2.

20. Liu J, Qiao X, Qian W, Hou X, Hayes J, Chen JD. Motilin in human milk and its elevated plasma concentration in lactating women. J Gastroenterol Hepatol 2004;19(10):1187-91.

21. Goldman A, Cheda S, Keeney S, Schmalstieg F, Schanler R. Immunologic protection of the preterm newborn by human milk. Sem Perinatol 1994;18(6):495-501.

22. Goldman AS, Chheda S, Garofalo R. Evolution of immunologic functions of the mammary gland and the postnatal development of immunity. Pediatr Res 1998;43(2):155-62.

23. Goldman AS. Modulation of the gastrointestinal tract of infants by human milk. Interfaces and interactions. An evolutionary perspective. J Nutr 2000;130:426-31S.

24. Lawrence RM, Pane CA. Human breast milk: current concepts of immunology and infectious diseases. Curr Probl Pediatr Adolesc Health Care 2007;37(1):7-36.

25. Walker WA. The dynamic effects of breastfeeding on intestinal development and host defense. Adv Exp Med Biol 2004;554:155-70.

26. Ronnestad A, Abrahamsen TG, Medbo S, et al. Late-onset septicemia in a Norwegian national cohort of extremely premature infants receiving very early full human milk feeding. Pediatrics 2005;115(3):e269-76.

27. Goldman AS, Goldblum RM, Schmalsteig Jr FC. Chapter 32: Protective properties of human milk. In: Walker DJ, Watkins J, Duggan C (eds). Nutrition in pediatrics: basic science and clinical applications. 3rd Ed. Hamilton Ontario: BC Decker Inc; 2003.

28. Xu RJ. Development of the newborn GI tract and its relation to colostrum/milk intake: a review. Reprod Fertil Dev 1996;8(1):35-48.

29. Schanler RJ, Goldblum RM, Garza C, Goldman AS. Enhanced fecal excretion of selected immune factors in very low birth weight infants fed fortified human milk. Pediatr Res 1986;20(8):711-5.

30. Caicedo RA, Schanler RJ, Li N, Neu J. The developing intestinal ecosystem: implications for the neonate. Pediatric Research 2005;58(4):625-8.

31. Penders J, Thijs C, Vink C, et al. Factors influencing the composition of the intestinal microbiota in early infancy. Pediatrics 2006;118(2):511-21.

32. Groer MW, Walker WA. What is the role of preterm human milk supplement in the host defenses of the preterm infant? Science vs. fiction. Adv Pediatr 1996;43:335-58.

33. Schanler RJ, Atkinson SA. Effects of nutrients in human milk on the recipient premature infant. J Mammary Gland Biol Neoplasia 1999;4(3):297-307.

34. Gross SJ, Buckley RH, Wakil SS, McAllister DC, David RJ, Faix RG. Elevated IgA concentration in milk produced by mothers delivered of preterm infants. J Pediatr 1981;99(3):389-93.

35. Goldblum RM, Schanler RJ, Garza C, Goldman AS. Human milk feeding enhances the urinary excretion of immunologic factors in low birth weight infants. Pediatr Res 1989;25(2):184-8.

36. Pisacane A, Graziano L, Mazzarella G, Scarpellino B, Zona G. Breast-feeding and urinary tract infection. J Pediatr 1992;120(1):87-9.

37. Kobata R, Tsukahara H, Ohshima Y, et al. High levels of growth factors in human breast milk. Early Hum Dev 2008;84(1):67-9.

38. Stockman III JA, deAlarcon PA. Chapter 134. Hematopoiesis and granulopoiesis. In: Polin RA, Fox WW (eds). Fetal and neonatal physiology. Philadelphia: WB Saunders; 1992.

39. Kling PJ. Roles of erythropoietin in human milk. Acta Paediatr Suppl 2002;91(438):31-5.

40. Semba RD, Juul SE. Erythropoietin in human milk: physiology and role in infant health. J Hum Lact 2002;18(3):252-61.

41. Kling PJ, Sullivan TM, Roberts RA, Philipps AF, Koldovsky O. Human milk as a potential enteral source of erythropoietin. Pediatr Res 1998;43(2):216-21.

42. Lucas A, Baker B. Breast milk jaundice in premature infants. Arch Dis Child 1986;61:1063-7.

43. Kumar A, Pant P, Basu S, Rao GR, Khanna HD. Oxidative Stress in neonatal hyperbilirubinemia. J Trop Pediatr 2006.

44. Mancuso C, Pani G, Calabrese V. Bilirubin: an endogenous scavenger of nitric oxide and reactive nitrogen species. Redox Rep 2006;11(5):207-13.

45. Kleinman RE, Walker WA. The enteromammary immune system: an important new concept in breast milk host defense. Dig Dis Sci 1979;24(11):876-82.

46. Goldman AS. The immune system in human milk and the developing infant. Breastfeed Med 2007;2(4):195-204.

Chapter 3:
NUTRITIONAL GOALS FOR PRETERM INFANTS

In the neonatal period, low birth weight and preterm infants have greater nutritional needs than at any other time in their lives.[1] For example, the accretion of neuronal mass is greater in the last trimester than in the first three months of a term infant's life. Without the last trimester, when many constituents, such as iron, are actively transported across the placenta to meet growth demands and fill storage organs, the preterm infant faces the most demanding growth period with a nutritional deficit. In addition, their medical condition may contribute to increased nutrient needs. The stress of common pathophysiologic events (hypotension, hypoxia, acidosis, infection, surgical intervention), and their therapies (antibiotics, corticosteroids), as well as physiologic immaturity of all organ systems are significant impediments to growth, even if full nutrition can be achieved rapidly.[1]

The goals of nutrition for the preterm infant are:
- To define and achieve a standard of short-term growth
- To meet the unique nutritional needs of prematurity
- To prevent feeding-related morbidities
- To optimize long-term outcome [2]

DEFINE AND ACHIEVE GROWTH STANDARDS

The nutritional reference standard for the term newborn is the exclusively breastfed infant. The World Health Organization (WHO) recently published growth reference standards based on optimal infant feeding (including breastfeeding), optimal health care, and optimal environmental conditions.[3] These growth charts describe how all the world's children *should* grow from birth to five years of age. Although normative data exist for longitudinal growth of infants born at various gestational ages,[4] an optimal growth standard comparable to the WHO data for term infants does not exist for preterm infants. Using longitudinal growth data from a population of immature and/or sick infants introduces inherent errors, as these graphs may underestimate the mean growth potential and require frequent updating to keep up with advances in therapies for preterm infants and preterm nutrition. Instead, the current growth

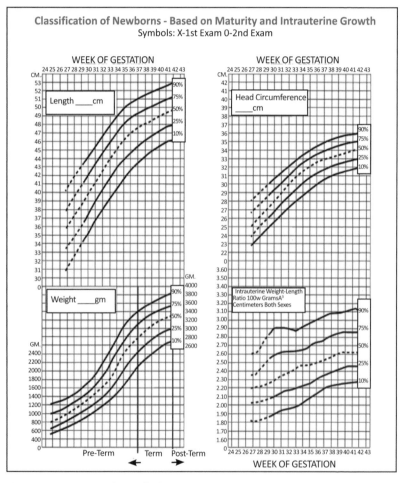

Figure 1: In Utero Growth Curves

Source: Developed by Jacob L. Kay MD, in conjunction with Mead Johnson Nutritionals. Reprinted with permission of Mead Johnson & Company.

standard used is the estimated intrauterine nutrient accretion rate at corresponding stages during the last trimester of pregnancy.[1] The currently accepted goal is to approximate the in utero growth of a normal fetus of the same postmenstrual age in both body weight and body composition, while maintaining normal concentrations of blood and tissue nutrients[5] (Figure 1).

The optimal reference standard may ultimately be different given the significant differences in the in utero and extrauterine environments, the extreme differences in condition at birth, and degrees of illness for the wide range of premature infants. The Fenton growth chart (Figure 2) is a recent preterm growth chart that combines several

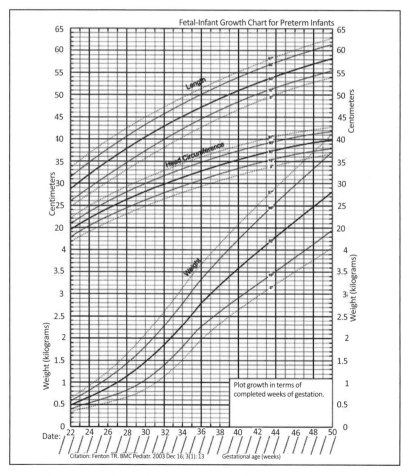

Figure 2: Preterm Growth Chart: Fenton Chart[6]

large birth datasets from multiple countries and synthesizes them into a single growth chart.[6] After term corrected age, the data merges preterm birth data with healthy term data from the Centers for Disease Control (CDC) into a single graph. The contrast between this graph and preterm longitudinal graphs is most stark at lower growth percentiles, where infants can vary in assessments from below the 3rd percentile on the Fenton chart to being closer to the 10th percentile on the NICHD charts. Optimal nutritional plans need to ensure a balance between avoiding undernutrition and excessive catch-up growth. The former may lead to poorer neurodevelopment and the latter may result in increased risk for adult onset of diseases, such as obesity, hypertension, and diabetes. Furthermore, the lack of a convenient method to measure body composition, which is more informative of ideal growth, has resulted in the absence of any reference standard for body composition.

Growth is an important health outcome for preterm infants with in-hospital growth velocity affecting both neurodevelopmental and growth outcomes at 18-22 months of age.[7] Postnatal growth failure in infants born less than 32 weeks gestation is associated with increased motor and cognitive impairment at seven years of age.[8] Despite this, National Institute of Child and Human Development (NICHD) data reveal that over 90% of infants who are less than 1000 grams at birth are discharged weighing less than the 10th percentile for corrected gestational age.[9] The term "extrauterine growth restriction" has been used to describe this phenomenon of turning appropriate for gestational age infants at birth into small for gestational age infants at discharge.[10]

MEET THE UNIQUE NUTRITIONAL NEEDS OF PREMATURITY

An infant born at term will increase his brain weight by 40% over the first eight weeks of life. A preterm infant born at 28 weeks gestation must *double* the weight of his brain (100% increase) in the first eight weeks to match in-utero growth rates. This difference in growth rate explains why nutritional deficiencies early on can be more damaging in the preterm infant compared to the term infant. The energy and nutrient requirements of preterm and LBW infants vary enormously, depending on birth weight, gestational age, degree of intrauterine growth restriction, medical complications, nutritional status, clinical management, and the model and assumptions used to establish the "requirements." In addition, the VLBW infant (less than 1500 grams) has several unique aspects of nutrition that must be considered (Table 1). Human milk alone may not meet all these special needs.

Table 1: Special Nutritional Conditions of VLBW Infants

Special Nutritional Conditions of VLBW Infants
• Less energy reserves (carbohydrate and fat)
• Higher organ:muscle mass ratio (resulting in higher metabolic rate)
• Higher energy cost due to transepidermal water loss
• More prone to hyperglycemia (despite higher energy needs for energy and brain metabolism)
• Immature gastrointestinal peristalsis
• High incidence of stressful events
• Greater oxygen consumption during growth
• Higher rate of protein synthesis and turnover (inversely proportional to gestational age)
• Higher total body water content
• Higher rate of fat deposition (despite higher EFA needs for brain and vascular development)
• Limited production of gut digestive enzymes and growth factors
• Excess urinary water and solute losses

Adapted from Hay, 1991.[11]

The recommended parenteral and enteral intakes of preterm infants for each nutrient at various weights and gestational ages are usually calculated using the factorial approach: deposition plus losses (absorption, urinary, stool, skin), and are found in many neonatal nutrition references[1, 5, 11-14] (Table 2).

Even though human milk produced by mothers who deliver prematurely is somewhat different from the milk of mothers who deliver at term, nutrient intake may be limited by milk composition, availability, and fluid volume realities or restrictions. One of the

Table 2: Comparison of Enteral Intake Recommendations for Growing Preterm Infants in Stable Clinical Condition.

Nutrients per 100 Kcal †	Consensus Recommendations*		AAPCON‡	ESPGAN-CON‡
	<1000 g	>1000 g		
Water, mL	125-167	125-167	...	115-154
Energy, kcal	100	100	100	100
Protein, g	3.0-3.16	2.5-3.0	2.9-3.3	2.25-3.1
Carbohydrate, g			9.13	7-14
Lactose, g	3.16-9.5	3.16-9.8	...	...
Oligomers, g	0-7.0	0-7.0	...	...
Fat, g			4.5-6.0	3.6-7
Linoleic acid, g	0.44-1.7	0.44-1.7	0.4+	0.5-1.4
Linolenic acid, g	0.11-0.44	0.11-0.44		>0.055
C18:2/C18:3	>5	>5	..	5-15
Vitamin A, USP units	583-1250	583-1250	75-225	270-450
With lung disease	2250-2333	2250-2333	...	...
Vitamin D, USP units	125-333	125-333	270	800-1600/d
Vitamin E, USP units			>1.1	0.6-10
Supplement, HM§	2.9	2.9	...	...
Vitamin K₁ µg	6.66-8.33	6.66-8.33	4	4-15
Ascorbate, mg	15-20	15-20	35	7-40
Thiamin, µg	150-200	150-200	>40	20-250
Riboflavin, µg	200-300	200-300	>60	60-600
Pyridoxine, µg	125-175	125-175	>35	35-250
Niacin, mg	3-4	3-4	>0.25	0.8-5.0
Pantothenate, mg	1-15	1-15	>0.30	>0.3
Biotin, µg	3-5	3-5	>1.5	>1.5
Folate, µg	21-42	21-42	33	>60
Vitamin B₁₂, µg	0.25	0.25	>0.15	>0.15
Sodium, mg	38-58	38-58	48-67	23-53
Potassium, mg	65-100	65-100	66-98	90-152
Chloride, mg	59-89	59-89	...	57-89
Calcium, mg	100-192	100-192	175	70-140
Phosphorus, mg	50-117	50-117	91.5	50-87
Magnesium, mg	6.6-12.5	6.6-12.5	...	6-12
Iron, mg	1.67	1.67	1.7-2.5	1.5
Zinc, µg	833	833	>500	550-1100
Copper, µg	100-125	100-125	90	90-120
Selenium, µg	1.08-2.5	1.08-2.5	...	.

Chromium, µg	0.083-0.42	0.083-0.42	...	..
Manganese, µg	6.3	6.3	>5	1.5-7.5
Molybdenum, µg	0.25	.25	..	...
Iodine, µg	25-50	25-50	5	10-45
Taurine, mg	3.75-7.5	3.75-7.5	.	..
Carnitine, mg	2.4	2.4	...	>1.2
Inositol, mg	27-67.5	27-67.5	...	...
Choline, mg	12-23.4	12-23.4	...	...

Source: AAP Committee on Nutrition, 2004.[5] Used with permission of the American Academy of Pediatrics.

[†] 120 kcal/kg/d was used where a conversion was made from per kg recommendations.

[‡] AAPCON indicates American Academy of Pediatrics, Committee on Nutrition; ESPGAN-CON, European Society of Pediatric Gastroenterology and Nutrition, Committee on Nutrition of the Preterm Infant.

HM§ = human milk.

most important nutritional discoveries in the last ten years has been the recognition that protein intake (both quantity and quality) and protein-energy ratio are more important in developing healthy lean body mass than just increasing caloric intake.[15,16] The smaller and more immature the infant, the higher the protein turnover and protein requirement.[14]

PREVENT FEEDING-RELATED MORBIDITIES

Preterm infants are vulnerable to both under and over-nutrition. Immaturity of the liver, kidneys, and intestine, as noted above, can predispose to significant morbidity in this area. Necrotizing enterocolitis, feeding intolerance, and prolonged hospitalization are all more common in bovine milk-based formula-fed infants[17, 18] (Figure 3), but can occur in any infant. Prolonged fasting and parenteral nutrition due to severe illness causes gut atrophy and can lead to infection and liver compromise. Restriction of calcium and phosphorus intake because of fluid restriction or inappropriate supplementation can lead to fragile bones and fractures. More importantly, inappropriate nutrition can prevent a preterm infant from reaching his full physical and intellectual potential.[19]

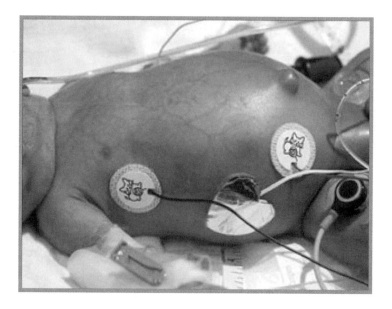

Figure 3: Necrotizing Enterocolitis in a Preterm Infant (Photo courtesy of Stacey Ziegler RNC, MN, NNP.)

OPTIMIZE LONG-TERM OUTCOMES

Whether considering in utero nutrition[20-23] or early newborn nutrition,[24-26] it is now clear that early nutrition can permanently affect long term outcomes, such as growth, glucose tolerance, insulin sensitivity, blood pressure, cardiovascular disease, allergic response, and neurocognitive development.[25-44] The term proposed for early nutritional effects on long term health is "nutritional programming."[24] New evidence suggests that early nutrition also affects gene expression ("epigenetics").[45-47]

KEY CONCEPTS

- The optimal reference standard for the growth of preterm infants is not known, but the in utero growth charts and Fenton growth chart are the current standards.

- Many preterm infants start out appropriate for gestational age (AGA), but are small for gestational age (SGA) at discharge from the NICU.

● Excessive catch-up growth may result in increased risk for obesity, hypertension, and diabetes.

● Preterm infants have unique nutritional needs that vary considerably from infant to infant.

● The most important goal is to optimize long-term outcomes.

REFERENCES

1. Schanler RJ. Chapter 28: The low birth weight infant. In: Walker W, Watkins J, Duggan C (eds). Nutrition in pediatrics: basic science and clinical applications. 3rd Ed. Hamilton, Ontario: BC Decker, Inc; 2003:491-514.

2. California Perinatal Quality Care Collaborative PQIP. Toolkit: Nutritional support of the VLBW infant, part 1. In: California Perinatal Quality Care Collaborative, Perinatal Quality Improvement Panel; 2004, www.cpqcc. org.

3. World Health Organization. WHO child growth standards: methods & development. Geneva: World Health Organization; 2006, http://www. who.int/childgrowth/en/.

4. Ehrenkranz RA, Younes N, Lemons JA, et al. Longitudinal growth of hospitalized very low birth weight infants. Pediatrics 1999; 104(2 Pt 1):280-9.

5. American Academy of Pediatrics, Committee on Nutrition. Chapter 2: Nutritional needs of the preterm infant. In: Kleinman RE (ed). Pediatric nutrition handbook. 5th Ed. Elk Grove Village, IL: American Academy of Pediatrics; 2004:23.

6. Fenton TR. A new growth chart for preterm babies: Babson and Benda's chart updated with recent data and a new format. BMC Pediatr 2003; 3:13.

7. Ehrenkranz RA, Dusick AM, Vohr BR, Wright LL, Wrage LA, Poole WK. Growth in the neonatal intensive care unit influences neurodevelopmental and growth outcomes of extremely low birth weight infants. Pediatrics 2006; 117(4):1253-61.

8. Cooke RW, Foulder-Hughes L. Growth impairment in the very preterm and cognitive and motor performance at 7 years. Arch Dis Child 2003; 88(6):482-7.

9. Dusick AM, Poindexter BB, Ehrenkranz RA, Lemons JA. Growth failure in the preterm infant: can we catch up? Semin Perinatol 2003; 27(4):302-10.

10. Clark RH, Wagner CL, Merritt RJ, et al. Nutrition in the neonatal intensive care unit: how do we reduce the incidence of extrauterine growth restriction? J Perinatol 2003; 23: 337-44.

11. Hay Jr, WW. Neonatal nutrition and metabolism. St Louis: Mosby Year Book; 1991.

12. American Academy of Pediatrics, Committee on Nutrition. Nutritional needs of low-birth-weight infants. Pediatrics 1985; 75:976-86.

13. Committee on Nutrition of the Preterm Infant - European Society of Paediatric Gastroenterology and Nutrition (ESPGAN). Nutrition and feeding of preterm infants. Oxford, England: Blackwell Scientific Publications; 1987.

14. Tsang RC, Lucas A, Uauy R, Zlotkin S (eds). Nutritional needs of the preterm infant: scientific basis and practical guidelines. Baltimore: Williams & Wilkins; 1993.

15. Anderson G, Aziz A. Multifunctional roles of dietary proteins in the regulation of metabolism and food intake: application to feeding infants. J Pediatr 2006; 149(5):S74-S9.

16. Rigo J, Senterre J. Nutritional needs of premature infants: current issues. J Pediatr 2006; 149(5):S80-8.

17. Lucas A, Cole TJ. Breast milk and neonatal necrotising enterocolitis. Lancet 1990; 336:1519-23.

18. Schanler RJ, Shulman RJ, Lau C. Feeding strategies for premature infants: beneficial outcomes of feeding fortified human milk versus preterm formula. Pediatrics 1999; 103(6 Pt 1):1150-7.

19. Martinez FE, Desai ID. Human milk and premature infants. World Rev Nutr Diet 1995; 78:55-73.

20. Barker DJ. Fetal growth and adult disease. Br J Obstet Gynaecol 1992; 99(4):275-6.

21. Barker DJ. The developmental origins of adult disease. J Am Coll Nutr 2004; 23(6 Suppl):588-95S.

22. Barker DJ, Eriksson JG, Forsen T, Osmond C. Fetal origins of adult disease: strength of effects and biological basis. Int J Epidemiol 2002; 31(6):1235-9.

23. Godfrey KM, Barker DJ. Fetal nutrition and adult disease. Am J Clin Nutr 2000; 71((Suppl 5)):1344-52S.

24. Lucas A. Does early diet program future outcome? Acta Paediatr Scand Suppl 1990; 365:58-67.

25. Lucas A. The developmental origins of adult health and well-being. Adv Exp Med Biol 2005; 569:13-5.

26. Lucas A. Long-term programming effects of early nutrition -- implications for the preterm infant. J Perinatol 2005;25 Suppl 2:S2-6.

27. Barker DJ. The fetal origins of adult hypertension. J Hypertens Suppl 1992; 10(7):S39-44.

28. Barker DJ. The fetal origins of diseases of old age. Eur J Clin Nutr 1992; 46 Suppl 3:S3-9.

29. Barker DJ. The effect of nutrition of the fetus and neonate on cardiovascular disease in adult life. Proc Nutr Soc 1992; 51(2):135-44.

30. Barker DJ. Fetal programming of coronary heart disease. Trends Endocrinol Metab 2002; 13(9):364-8.

31. Barker DJ. Commentary: Developmental origins of raised serum cholesterol. Int J Epidemiol 2003; 32(5):876-7.

32. Barker DJ. The developmental origins of chronic adult disease. Acta Paediatr Suppl 2004; 93(446):26-33.

33. Barker DJ. The developmental origins of insulin resistance. Horm Res 2005; 64 Suppl 3:2-7.

34. Barker DJ, Bagby SP. Developmental antecedents of cardiovascular disease: a historical perspective. J Am Soc Nephrol 2005; 16(9):2537-44.

35. Barker DJ, Eriksson JG, Forsen T, Osmond C. Infant growth and income 50 years later. Arch Dis Child 2005; 90(3):272-3.

36. Barker DJ, Osmond C, Forsen TJ, Kajantie E, Eriksson JG. Trajectories of growth among children who have coronary events as adults. N Engl J Med 2005; 353(17):1802-9.

37. Bhargava SK, Sachdev HS, Fall CH, et al. Relation of serial changes in childhood body-mass index to impaired glucose tolerance in young adulthood. N Engl J Med 2004; 350(9):865-75.

38. Day IN, Chen XH, Gaunt TR, et al. Late life metabolic syndrome, early growth, and common polymorphism in the growth hormone and placental lactogen gene cluster. J Clin Endocrinol Metab 2004; 89(11):5569-76.

39. Eriksson JG, Forsen TJ, Osmond C, Barker DJ. Pathways of infant and childhood growth that lead to type 2 diabetes. Diabetes Care 2003; 26(11):3006-10.

40. Kajantie E, Phillips DI, Andersson S, et al. Size at birth, gestational age and cortisol secretion in adult life: foetal programming of both hyper- and hypocortisolism? Clin Endocrinol (Oxf) 2002; 57(5):635-41.

41. Lucas A, Brooke OG, Morley R, Cole TJ, Bamford MF. Early diet of preterm infants and development of allergic or atopic disease: randomised prospective study. BMJ 1990; 300(6728):837-40.

42. Lucas A, Morley R, Cole TJ. Randomised trial of early diet in preterm babies and later intelligence quotient. BMJ 1998; 317(7171):1481-7.

43. Lucas A, Morley R, Cole TJ, Lister G, Leeson-Payne C. Breast milk and subsequent intelligence quotient in children born preterm. Lancet 1992; 339(8788):261-4.

44. Osmond C, Barker DJ. Fetal, infant, and childhood growth are predictors of coronary heart disease, diabetes, and hypertension in adult men and women. Environ Health Perspect 2000; 108(Suppl 3):545-53.

45. Feil R. Environmental and nutritional effects on the epigenetic regulation of genes. Mutat Res 2006; 600(1-2):46-57.

46. Marabou JP. 2005: Nutrition and human development. Nutr Rev 2006; 64(5 Pt 2):S1-11; discussion S72-91.

47. Waterland RA. Epigenetic mechanisms and gastrointestinal development. J Pediatr 2006; 149(5):S137-42.

Chapter 4:
NUTRITIONAL "BEST PRACTICES"
FOR THE PRETERM INFANT

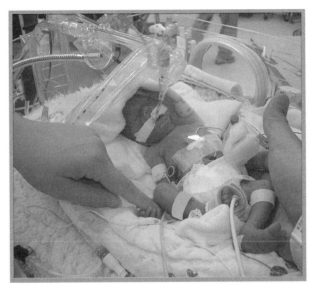

(Photo courtesy of Nancy Wight MD)

EARLY PARENTERAL NUTRITION

At birth, a preterm infant is abruptly disconnected from the ideal source of parenteral nutrition – the placenta.[1] Although intravenous (IV) fluids are standard for preterm or ill infants upon admission to the NICU, parenteral nutrition (protein, lipid, vitamins) used to be delayed for several days. Since the late 1980's, it has been clear that earlier institution of parenteral nutrition is associated with improved growth and outcome,[2] and there has been a gradual shift in favor of starting parenteral nutrition in the first day or two.[3-10] Very low birth weight infants (VLBW) lose large amounts of body protein over the first few days of life if protein is not provided immediately. This early protein loss, when added to the normal daily in utero protein accretion, produces a protein debt,[11, 12] which may never be recovered.

Early parenteral nutrition, providing a minimum of 60 to 80 non-protein kcal/kg/day and 2 gm/kg/day protein, has been shown to improve nitrogen balance, improve energy intake, improve protein synthesis, and affect better weight gain without adverse effects.[5-7, 13] Even higher amounts of protein and energy intake up to 3 gm/kg/day that approach in utero demands are well tolerated with no adverse consequences.

Similarly, early lipid intake improves nutrition by preventing essential fatty acid deficiency, acting as an energy source, a precursor for eicosanoids, and a substitute for cerebral arachadonic and docosahexaenoic acid synthesis. Lack of provision of these lipids, even as early as 72 hours, can result in increased risk for essential fatty acid deficiency.[14] Early animal studies and theoretical concerns regarding slow infusion of lipids causing pulmonary hypertension and leading to chronic lung disease have not been confirmed by recent clinical trials.[6, 13]

Minimal Enteral Nutrition (MEN) (AKA "trophic feeds" or "GI priming")

In utero, the fetal gastrointestinal tract is constantly active: swallowing amniotic fluid, absorbing fluid and some nutrition, performing rudimentary peristalsis, and forming meconium. The objective of feeding during the early days of life is to stimulate gut maturation, hormone release, motility, and support the immune system, *not* provide full enteral nutrition. Although it was never shown that prolonged withholding of feedings actually prevented necrotizing enterocolitis (NEC), some form of this strategy was widely adopted in the 1970s and 1980s.[1] Artificially starving the gut at birth leads to atrophy of the gut with multiple nutritional, morphologic, and host resistance pathologies[15] (Table 1), so that withholding feedings may actually render subsequently introduced feedings less safe.[8]

Table 1: Effects of Gut Lumenal Starvation

- Nutritional
  - Steatorrhea
  - Protein-losing enteropathy
  - Decreased circulating gut peptides
  - Decreased enzyme levels
  - Decreased nutrient transport
- Morphology/Development
  - Decreased synthesis of new epithelial cells
  - Fusion/flattening of cells
  - Edema
- Host Resistance
  - Decreased secretion of IgA, mucin
  - Increased uptake of macromolecules
  - Bacterial overgrowth
  - Direct damage to mucosal barrier

Source: Adapted from LaGamma & Browne, 1994.[15] Reprinted with permission from Elsevier.

Withholding of feedings was eventually re-evaluated with a number of trials of early introduction of feedings.[16-25] A systematic review of the results of published trials[26, 27] concluded that early introduction of feedings shortens the time to full feeds and to discharge, and does not increase the incidence of NEC, although they noted some problems with individual studies. A controlled study involving 100 LBW infants[28] confirmed these findings and found, in addition, a significant reduction in serious infections with "early" introduction of feedings. Feedings should be started with full strength, unfortified milks.[29, 30] A recent pilot trial found that feeding a sterile, isotonic, noncaloric enteral solution patterned after human amniotic fluid improved tolerance of milk feedings in infants with a history of feeding intolerance.[31] Early enteral intake appears both safe and physiologically advantageous for VLBW infants[32, 33] (Table 2).

Table 2. Effects of Early Enteral Intake on Infants Weighing Less Than 1500 Grams

- No change or decrease in NEC incidence
- Less cholestatic jaundice
- Less osteopenia
- Less physiologic jaundice
- Increased glucose tolerance
- Better weight gain
- Earlier tolerance of full enteral intake
- Increased gut hormones
- Induction of digestive enzymes
- Improved antral-duodenal coordination
- Allows gut colonization (Vit K production)
- Earlier maturation of brush border
- Prevents atrophy and starvation effects

Source: LaGamma & Browne, 1994.[15] Table reprinted with permission, copyright Elsevier.

Most infants in the GI priming studies were fed with umbilical artery catheters in place, yet the studies still noted a decreased incidence of necrotizing enterocolitis.[20, 34, 35] Although the treatment of a persistent patent ductus arteriosus (PDA) has been shown to decrease the risk for NEC due largely to the improvement in perfusion caused by a reduction in left-to-right shunting, it is less clear that there is any harm from feeding when a PDA is present or being treated.[36, 37] In fact, a recent study of feedings during indomethacin therapy for a persistent PDA found no differences in feeding tolerance and feed advancement.[38] Further research is needed to ascertain just how "unstable" an infant needs to be before feedings are withheld. Unquestionably, human milk is the safest choice for early enteral feedings, with few exceptions.

Standards/Measurement/Protocols

In light of the current variations in feeding practice, paying close attention to feeding parameters with a standardized feeding regimen appears to significantly decrease NEC and improve nutrition.[39-42] Infant weight, length, head circumference, and biochemical parameters should be followed at appropriate intervals.[1] Mother's milk volume should also be monitored. Every NICU that cares for VLBW infants should have a neonatal nutritionist as part of the team to measure infant growth and outcomes, calculate and relate parenteral nutrition and enteral intakes to current growth and medical conditions, suggest improvements in nutritional management, manage the formulary of premature infant supplements, and make nutritional plans with goals and resource referral information at discharge.[43-47]

Use of Human Milk

Research to date supports, and the consensus is growing, that human milk (with appropriate fortification for the very low birth weight infant) is the standard of care for preterm, as well as term infants.[35, 48-52] As the objective of feeding during the early days of life is to stimulate gut hormone maturation, stimulate gut hormone release, induce gut motility, and enable the growth of beneficial microflora to support the immune system, the preferred feeding is breastmilk, preferably started on day one.[8, 25, 48] Colostrum contains high concentrations of antimicrobial, anti-inflammatory, and immunomodulating factors, and prepares the gut for mature milk.[53, 54]

KEY CONCEPTS

- Parenteral nutrition with protein and lipids should be started within the first few hours of life.

- Trophic feedings with human milk should be started within the first few days of life.

- It is uncertain just how "unstable" an infant needs to be to preclude feedings.

- Simply having a feeding protocol seems to decrease feeding morbidities, including necrotizing enterocolitis.

- Human milk is the feeding of choice.

REFERENCES

1. California Perinatal Quality Care Collaborative PQIP. Toolkit: Nutritional support of the VLBW infant, part 2. In: California Perinatal Quality Care Collaborative, Perinatal Quality Improvement Panel, www.cpqcc.org; 2005.

2. Georgieff M, Mills M, Lindeke L, Iverson S, Johnson D, Thompson T. Changes in nutritional management and outcome of very-low-birthweight infants. Am J Dis Child 1989; 143(1):82-5.

3. Pauls J, Bauer K, Versmold H. Postnatal body weight curves for infants below 1000 g birth weight receiving early enteral and parenteral nutrition. Eur J Pediatr 1998; 157(5):416-21.

4. Wilson DC, Cairns P, Halliday HL, Reid M, McClure G, Dodge JA. Randomised controlled trial of an aggressive nutritional regimen in sick very low birthweight infants. Arch Dis Child Fetal Neonatal Ed 1997; 77(1):F4-11.

5. Saini J, MacMahon P, Morgan JB, Kovar IZ. Early parenteral feeding of amino acids. Arch Dis Child 1989; 64(10 Spec No):1362-6.

6. Thureen PJ, Melara D, Fennessey PV, Hay WW, Jr. Effect of low versus high intravenous amino acid intake on very low birth weight infants in the early neonatal period. Pediatr Res 2003; 53(1):24-32.

7. Porcelli Jr PJ, Sisk PM. Increased parenteral amino acid administration to extremely low-birth-weight infants during early postnatal life. J Pediatr Gastroenterol Nutr 2002; 34(2):174-9.

8. Ziegler EE, Thureen PJ, Carlson SJ. Aggressive nutrition of the very low birthweight infant. Clin Perinatol 2002; 29(2):225-44.

9. Kerner Jr JA. Chapter 57: Parenteral nutrition. In: Walker W, Watkins J, Duggan C (eds). Nutrition in pediatrics: basic science and clinical applications. 3rd Ed. Hamilton, Ontario: BC Decker Inc; 2003:957-85.

10. Simmer K. Aggressive nutrition for preterm infants--benefits and risks. Early Hum Dev 2007; 83(10):631-4.

11. Dusick AM, Poindexter BB, Ehrenkranz RA, Lemons JA. Growth failure in the preterm infant: can we catch up? Semin Perinatol 2003; 27(4):302-10.

12. Embleton NE, Pang N, Cooke RJ. Postnatal malnutrition and growth retardation: an inevitable consequence of current recommendations in preterm infants? Pediatrics 2001; 107(2):270-3.

13. Ibrahim HM, Jeroudi MA, Baier RJ, Dhanireddy R, Krouskop RW. Aggressive early total parental nutrition in low-birth-weight infants. J Perinatol 2004; 24(8):482-6.

14. Foote KD, MacKinnon MJ, Innis SM. Effect of early introduction of formula vs fat-free parenteral nutrition on essential fatty acid status of preterm infants. Am J Clin Nutr 1991; 54(1):93-7.

15. La Gamma EF, Browne LE. Feeding practices for infants weighing less than 1500 g at birth and the pathogenesis of necrotizing enterocolitis. Clin Perinatol 1994; 21(2):271-306.

16. LaGamma EF, Ostertag SG, Birenbaum H. Failure of delayed oral feedings to prevent necrotizing enterocolitis. Results of study in very-low-birth-weight neonates. Am J Dis Child 1985; 139(4):385-9.

17. Heicher D, Philip AG. Orogastric supplementation in small premature infants requiring mechanical respiration. Am J Dis Child 1976; 130(3):282-6.

18. Lucas A, Bloom SR, Aynsley-Green A. Gut hormones and 'minimal enteral feeding.' Acta Paediatr Scand 1986; 75(5):719-23.

19. Ostertag SG, LaGamma EF, Reisen CE, Ferrentino FL. Early enteral feeding does not affect the incidence of necrotizing enterocolitis. Pediatrics 1986; 77(3):275-80.

20. Dunn L, Hulman S, Weiner J, Kliegman R. Beneficial effects of early hypocaloric enteral feeding on neonatal gastrointestinal function: preliminary report of a randomized trial. J Pediatr 1988; 112(4):622-9.

21. Slagle TA, Gross SJ. Effect of early low-volume enteral substrate on subsequent feeding tolerance in very low birth weight infants. J Pediatr 1988; 113(3):526-31.

22. Berseth CL. Effect of early feeding on maturation of the preterm infant's small intestine. J Pediatr 1992; 120(6):947-53.

23. Meetze WH, Valentine C, McGuigan JE, Conlon M, Sacks N, Neu J. Gastrointestinal priming prior to full enteral nutrition in very low birth weight infants. J Pediatr Gastroenterol Nutr 1992; 15(2):163-70.

24. Thureen PJ. Early aggressive nutrition in the neonate. Pediatr Rev 1999; 20:e45-55.

25. Schanler RJ. Chapter 28: The low birth weight infant. In: Walker W, Watkins J, Duggan C (eds). Nutrition in pediatrics: basic science and clinical applications. 3rd Ed. Hamilton, Ontario: BC Decker, Inc; 2003:491-514.

26. Tyson JE, Kennedy KA. Minimal enteral nutrition for promoting feeding tolerance and preventing morbidity in parenterally fed infants. Cochrane Database Syst Rev 2000(2):CD000504.

27. Tyson JE, Kennedy KA. Trophic feedings for parenterally fed infants. Cochrane Database Syst Rev 2005(3):CD000504.

28. McClure RJ, Newell SJ. Randomised controlled study of clinical outcome following trophic feeding. Arch Dis Child Fetal Neonatal Ed 2000; 82(1): F29-33.

29. Berseth CL, Nordyke CK, Valdes MG, Furlow Bl, Go VL. Responses of gastrointestinal peptides and motor activity to milk and water feedings in preterm and term infants. Pediatr Res 1992; 31:587-90.

30. Koenig WJ, Amarnath RP, Hench V, Berseth CL. Manometrics for preterm and term infants: a new tool for old questions. Pediatrics 1995; 95:203-6.

31. Barney CK, Purser N, Christensen RD. A phase 1 trial testing an enteral solution patterned after human amniotic fluid to treat feeding intolerance. Advances in Neonatal Care 2006; 6(2):89-95.

32. Cakmak Celik F, Aygun C, Cetinoglu E. Does early enteral feeding of very low birth weight infants increase the risk of necrotizing enterocolitis? Eur J Clin Nutr 2007. Nov 28 (Epub ahead of print), doi:10.1038/sj.ejcn.160257.

33. Ronnestad A, Abrahamsen TG, Medbo S, et al. Late-onset septicemia in a Norwegian national cohort of extremely premature infants receiving very early full human milk feeding. Pediatrics 2005; 115(3):e269-76.

34. Davey AM, Wagner CL, Cox C, Kendig JW. Feeding premature infants while low umbilical artery catheters are in place: a prospective, randomized trial. J Pediatr 1994; 124(5 Pt 1):795-9.

35. Schanler RJ, Shulman RJ, Lau C. Feeding strategies for premature infants: beneficial outcomes of feeding fortified human milk versus preterm formula. Pediatrics 1999; 103(6 Pt 1):1150-7.

36. Cassady G, Crouse DT, Kirklin JW, et al. A randomized, controlled trial of very early prophylactic ligation of the ductus arteriosus in babies who weighed 1000 g or less at birth. N Engl J Med 1989; 320(23):1511-6.

37. Gersony WM, Peckham GJ, Ellison RC, Miettinen OS, Nadas AS. Effects of indomethacin in premature infants with patent ductus arteriosus: results of a national collaborative study. J Pediatr 1983; 102(6):895-906.

38. Bellander M, Ley D, Polberger S, Hellstrom-Westas L. Tolerance to early human milk feeding is not compromised by indomethacin in preterm infants with persistent ductus arteriosus. Acta Paediatr 2003; 92(9):1074-8.

39. Kamitsuka MD, Horton MK, Williams MA. The incidence of necrotizing enterocolitis after introducing standardized feeding schedules for infants between 1250 and 2500 grams and less than 35 weeks of gestation. Pediatrics 2000; 105(2):379-84.

40. Patole S, McGlone L, Muller R. Virtual elimination of necrotizing enterocolitis for 5 years - reasons? Med Hypotheses 2003; 61(5-6):617-22.

41. Patole SK, de Klerk N. Impact of standardized feeding regimens on incidence of neonatal necrotizing enterocolitis: a systematic review and meta-analysis of observational studies. Arch Dis Child Fetal Neonatal Ed 2005; 90(2):F147-51.

42. Wiedmeier SE, Henry E, Baer VL, et al. Center differences in NEC within one health-care system may depend on feeding protocol. Am J Perinatol 2008; 25(1):5-11.

43. Kuzma-O'Reilly B, Duenas ML, Greecher C, et al. Evaluation, development, and implementation of potentially better practices in neonatal intensive care nutrition. Pediatrics 2003; 111(4 Pt 2):e461-70.

44. Olsen I, Richardson D, Schmid C, Sausman L, Dwyer J. Dietitian involvement in the neonatal intensive care unit: more is better. J Am Diet Assoc 2005; 105(8):1224-123.

45. Rubin L, Richardson D, Bodarek F, McCormick M. Growth in hospital of VLBW infants. Identification of patient characteristics and inter-NICU differences. Pediatric Research 1997; 41:Abstract 239A.

46. Valentine C, Schanler R. Neonatal nutritionist intervention improves nutrition support and promotes cost containment in the management of LBW infants. J Parenter Enteral Nutr 1993(Suppl 46):466.

47. Anderson DM. Nutritional assessment and therapeutic interventions for the preterm infant. Clin Perinatol 2002; 29(2):313-26.

48. American Academy of Pediatrics Section on Breastfeeding. Policy Statement: Breastfeeding and the use of human milk. Pediatrics 2005; 115(2):496-506.

49. Schanler RJ. Fortified human milk: nature's way to feed premature infants. J Hum Lact 1998; 14(1):5-11.

50. Schanler RJ. The use of human milk for premature infants. Pediatr Clin North Am 2001; 48(1):207-19.

51. Schanler RJ, Hurst NM, Lau C. The use of human milk and breastfeeding in premature infants. Clin Perinatol 1999;26(2):379-98, vii.

52. Schanler RJ, Atkinson SA. Effects of nutrients in human milk on the recipient premature infant. J Mammary Gland Biol Neoplasia 1999; 4(3):297-307.

53. Goldman A, Cheda S, Keeney S, Schmalstieg F, Schanler R. Immunologic protection of the preterm newborn by human milk. Sem Perinatol 1994; 18(6):495-501.

54. Caicedo RA, Schanler RJ, Li N, Neu J. The developing intestinal ecosystem: implications for the neonate. Pediatric Research 2005; 58(4):625-8.

Chapter 5:
EVIDENCE FOR THE USE OF HUMAN MILK IN PRETERM INFANTS

"On the basis of findings of persistent effects of BM on cognition at 30 months' CA, we reiterate our recommendation that efforts must be made to introduce all of the mothers to the benefits of BM. Efforts should be initiated not only by the obstetrician, neonatologist, lactation consultant, and primary care provider, but should begin before pregnancy with supports after discharge from the birthing hospital. To optimize efforts, the introduction of the concept of breastfeeding can be considered in elementary school as part of healthy living education."[1]

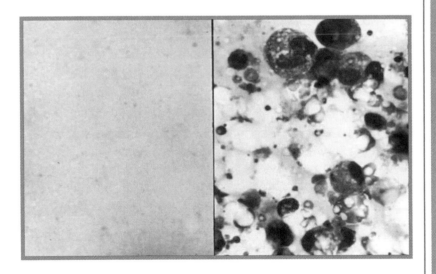

Figure 1: Artificial milk (formula) on left; centrifuged human milk on right (Photo courtesy of Becky Behre RN, IBCLC, Moscow, ID)

There are various problems associated with conducting studies on the effects of human milk on preterm infants. As preterm infants are disproportionately born to women who are less likely to breastfeed and have cultural and economic barriers to providing breastmilk for their infants, studies of the risks of not receiving human milk are often complicated and inconsistently controlled. Randomized controlled trials are either difficult or unethical. Another problem is the wide variation in the definition of a "human milk fed" infant.[2] Quantification of exposure to human milk, both in amount and timing, has been extremely difficult and highly variable. Despite these methodological problems, multiple studies have demonstrated significant benefits of human milk, both mothers' own and donor, for preterm infants.

The protective effects of human milk occur through the synergistic actions of its unique nutritional, enzymatic, hormonal, direct immunologic, immunomodulatory, anti-inflammatory, anti-oxidant, and growth factors.[2] As the mammary gland is immature with "loose" tight junctions at the time of preterm birth, all of these factors appear to be concentrated in the milk of mothers who deliver prematurely.[2,3]

SHORT-TERM PROTECTION

Host Defense

Human milk has multiple interactive factors, each of which may have multiple functions, thought to protect the preterm infant from infection.[4-6] After controlling for confounders, receiving expressed breastmilk was one of three factors significantly associated with survival in extremely low birth weight (ELBW) infants (odds ratio 57.5, 95% confidence interval 7-474, p=0.0002).[7]

Human milk reduces the incidence and severity of necrotizing enterocolitis (NEC), an acute inflammatory bowel disease, which may lead to perforation and peritonitis in preterm infants.[6, 8-25] Even partial feeding of human milk can reduce the incidence of NEC.[16, 20] In a secondary analysis of a prospective study of lactation counseling, Sisk et al.[25] found that receipt of 50% or more human milk feedings in the first 14 days was associated with a significant decrease in NEC.

Many human milk factors have been associated with the decrease in NEC, including immunoglobulins A and G,[26] epidermal growth factor,[27-29] platelet activating factor acetylhydrolase,[30-32] lactoferrin,[33] and the cytokine interleukin-10.[34]

Human milk is also associated with protection from sepsis and other infections.[14,15,20-22,35-40] Hylander et al.[40] demonstrated a significant decrease in overall infections and in the combination of sepsis and meningitis in those infants who received any human milk versus those infants exclusively formula-fed (Table 1).

Table 1: Any Human Milk Intake and Infection in VLBW Infants

	Human Milk (n=123)	Exclusive Formula (n=89)	P Value
Overall infection	36 (29.3%)	42 (47.2%)	0.01
Sepsis and/or meningitis	24 (19.5%)	29 (32.6%)	0.04

Source: Adapted from Hylander et al., 1998.[40] Reproduced with permission by the AAP.

Furman et al.[36] demonstrated that a threshold amount of at least 50 ml/kg/d of maternal milk through week four of life reduced the rate of sepsis in her cohort of VLBW preterm infants. In addition to a reduction in NEC, Schanler et al.[15] demonstrated a reduction in late-onset sepsis and a reduction in hospital length of stay with the use of fortified mothers' own milk. In a subsequent study of fortified donor human milk or preterm formula as a supplement to fortified mothers' own milk, exclusively mothers' milk fed infants had significantly fewer episodes of late onset sepsis.[14] A secondary analysis of detailed intake records of 1,433 extremely low birthweight (ELBW < 1,000g) infants from the National Institute of Child Health and Human Development (NICHD) Glutamine Trial found that 75% of the infants received some human milk during the NICU stay, but it appeared none were exclusively human milk fed.[2] The risk of sepsis during the first 35 days of life decreased as the amount of human milk intake over the first 14 days increased.[2]

Despite all these positive studies, a systematic review[41] of six cohort and three randomized controlled trials concluded that existing studies did not prove that human milk prevented infection in preterm VLBW infants because of methodological problems, including small sample size, failure to fully adjust for confounding variables, and inadequate definitions of human milk feedings and outcomes. Countering these criticisms in a letter to the editor[42] and referring to her own 2003 study,[36] Furman made a powerful argument for the validity of several of the studies and pointed out that no study had demonstrated an increased rate of infection in preterm infants fed maternal milk.

One of the major protective effects of human milk on the recipient infant operates through the "enteromammary system."[3, 43] Exposure of mothers to the NICU environment through skin-to-skin contact with their preterm infants can "induce" mothers to make specific antibodies against the nosocomial pathogens in their infants' environment.[44-46] Schanler et al.[14] found that kangaroo care was highly correlated with mothers' ability to produce milk and not correlated with any increase in infection. Rather, increased amounts of mothers' own milk decreased NEC, late-onset sepsis, chronic lung disease, retinopathy of prematurity, and length of stay.

Gastrointestinal Development

Human milk has multiple factors that stimulate growth, motility, and maturation of the intestine.[3, 44, 47, 48] Human milk is also associated with a faster decrease in intestinal permeability than artificial milks[49] and an increase in intestinal lactase activity at ten days if human milk, rather than artificial milk, is fed from four days.[50] Human milk promotes more rapid gastric emptying than formulas,[51,52] resulting in less residuals and faster realization of full enteral feedings[13, 15, 16, 39] (Table 2). Reaching full feedings faster means fewer days of IV's, less side effects from TPN, less infections and infiltrations from IV's, and less costly and fewer hospital days.[14, 15]

Special Nutrition

Milk from mothers who deliver prematurely (preterm milk) has been shown to be somewhat different from milk of mothers who deliver at term (term milk). Since the first report of higher concentrations

Table 2: Time Needed to Establish Full Enteral Feeds in 95% of Infants

Type of Feeding	Number of Days
Expressed Breastmilk	20
Standard Formula	45
Preterm Formula	48

Source: Lucas & Cole, 1990.[16] Reproduced with permission from Elsevier.

of nitrogen in preterm milk,[53] many publications have described differences in milk composition relative to gestational age at birth. Preterm milk has been noted to have increased amounts of nitrogen, total protein, immune proteins, total lipids, medium-chain fatty acids, total energy, and some vitamins and minerals, as well as trace elements.[54-62] The degree of prematurity and whether infants are born appropriate or small for gestational age may also play a role in milk composition.[55,57] Some studies did not find a difference between term and preterm milk,[63,64] but no studies have found lesser concentrations of nutrients in preterm milk at similar stages of lactation.[65] The lack of agreement between studies may reflect small sample size because of the greater inter-individual variability of milk composition in preterm milk. It may also reflect milk sample collection methods and inclusion of wide ranges of gestational age.[66]

In addition, preterm milk seems to have a higher concentration of growth factors and hormones to aid in the development of the gut and other organs. Preterm milk has more live infection fighting cells, immunoglobulins, like secretory IgA, epidermal growth factor,[29] anti-inflammatory factors, and immunomodulators than term milk.[3,67] There is a trend for nutrient and immunologic factor concentrations in preterm milk to decrease as lactation progresses, a pattern also observed in term milk.[65] The physiological basis of reported differences between preterm and term milk theoretically may be due to the immaturity of the mammary gland with increased paracellular leakage of serum proteins (e.g., immune proteins) and ions (e.g., sodium and chloride).[2, 65]

Given the innumerable protective properties of bioactive human milk concentrated in colostrum, the first feedings can be called the infant's "first immunization." The urgency and importance of reducing morbidity and mortality by providing the first small volume in the early hours of life is under investigation.[68, 69]

LONG TERM OUTCOME

Neurodevelopmental Outcome

A meta-analysis of 20 studies comparing cognitive development in breastfed and artificially-fed infants concluded that breastfeeding was associated with higher scores in all measured parameters, that developmental achievements persisted at least through adolescence, and that the benefit of human milk was strongest for children of low birth weight.[70] There is significant evidence that human milk confers neurodevelopmental advantages;[71-91] however, the direct relationship between human milk feeding and IQ has been challenged[92-94] because of the complexity of the many factors which contribute to an infant's neurodevelopmental outcome.[95, 96]

The Der et al. study[92] was in turn challenged by no less than 14 letters to the editor,[97] criticizing the age of the data, methodologies, definitions, and statistics. All researchers have made some adjustments for confounding variables between groups, especially socio-economic status and maternal education, but parenting variables are difficult to quantify.[98] Due to the ethical constraints of randomizing infants to their own mother's milk or formula, the majority of studies have been observational.[98]

Randomized allocation of infants to human milk in the form of donated milk has rarely been done,[14,83] and only Lucas et al. have followed long term neurodevelopment. In this study, infants were randomized to donor human milk or an early form of preterm formula, either as the sole source of nutrition or as a supplement to mother's own expressed breastmilk. At 18 months, there was no difference in development despite the lower nutritional content of the donor milk.[83] Further follow up of this cohort of preterm infants revealed higher IQ scores (8 points) in those infants fed their own mother's milk.[72,73 99]

In another secondary analysis of the NICHD Glutamine Trial, Vohr et al.[77] found a dose-response relationship between the amount of human milk feedings over the entire NICU stay and neurodevelopmental outcome at 18 months of age, even when adjusted for multiple cofounders. For each 10 mL/kg/day increase in human milk ingestion over the NICU stay, the Mental Development Index (MDI) score increased by 0.53 points, the Psychomotor Development Index (PDI) score increased by 0.63 points, the total Behavior Rating Scale (BRS) percentile score increased by 0.82 points, and the likelihood of rehospitalization decreased by 6% (Table 3).

Table 3: Breastmilk Intake, Developmental Outcomes, and Rehospitalization by Quintiles of Breastmilk Intake during Hospitalization

	No Breast milk (%)	Infants Receiving Percentiles of Breastmilk (%)				
		≤ 20th	20th-40th	40th-60th	60th-80th	>80th
Total breastmilk (mL/kg/d) for every day of hospitalization	0.0	1.0	7.3	24.0	63.8	110.6
Total breastmilk (mL/kg/d) on days breastmilk received	0.0	22.1	45.0	66.8	95.3	124.0
% Discharged on breastmilk	0.0	0.7	2.1	8.6	40.2	85.1
Mean MDI score	75.8	74.2	76.9	78.3	80.4	87.3*
Mean PDI score	81.3	80.6	82.7	84.2	84.4	89.4*
Mean total BRS score	45.6	44.8	52.1	50.1	51.8	58.8*
Rehospitalized < 1 yr	30.2	25.2	32.2	26.0	23.2	12.7*

See text for abbreviations. * Value different from no breastmilk at P<0.01.
Source: Adapted from Vohr et al., 2006.[77] Reproduced with permission by the AAP.

The differences associated with increased amounts of human milk held when the same infants were studied at 30 months.[1] They concluded that continued efforts must be made to offer breastmilk (BM) to all extremely low birthweight infants, both in the NICU and after discharge.

The long-chain polyunsaturated fatty acids (especially docosahexaenoic acid and arachidonic acid) found in both term and preterm milk have been implicated in optimal brain development and retinal maturation.[70, 100-102] A reduction in the incidence and severity of retinopathy of prematurity (ROP), a disease of premature infants that can cause visual impairment and blindness, has been demonstrated with the use of human milk.[14, 36, 103-105] Contrary results from a large neonatal network study did not find this effect, but the human milk intake averaged only a fifth of an infant's full intake.[106] Retrospective data suggest that human milk fed preterm infants suffer from less retinal detachment.[107]

Immunomodulation

Preterm infants fed human milk continue to benefit even after discharge. They have fewer hospital admissions in the first year of life[108] and less respiratory infections.[109] In addition, ulcerative colitis, Crohn's disease, diabetes, and allergic diseases may be reduced in breastfed preterm infants, as in full-term infants.[110]

Other Potential Benefits

Evidence is accumulating that early nutrition has long term effects on health into adulthood, including cardiovascular disease risk and bone health.[111] Adolescent blood pressure, lipid ratios, and C-reactive protein levels have been positively affected by mother's own and donor human milk given to preterm infants.[111-114] Human milk contains many antioxidants and may prevent diseases mediated by oxygen free radicals in VLBW infants.[115, 116]

A definite benefit for the preterm infant is a physically and psychologically healthier mother. Mothers of preterm infants, like mothers of full-term infants, can be expected to have a decreased risk of pre-menopausal breast cancer, ovarian cancer, and osteoporosis, reduced life-time blood loss (improved iron status), and a delay in fertility post-partum.[117] By providing an alternate focus for the mother, expressing milk for a preterm infant can help relieve the guilt of delivering an ill, preterm infant. It may also increase a mother's sense of self-competency,[117] her sense of control in a stressful situation, and her claim on her infant.[118-120] Whether breastfeeding or producing breastmilk for a preterm infant can ameliorate postpartum depression, improve maternal mood, or reduce anxiety or stress is not known. There is no evidence that breastfeeding, providing human milk, or encouraging a mother to provide human milk for her infant is harmful.[121]

The economic impact of NOT breastfeeding is significant with increased health care costs for both acute[122, 123] and chronic diseases, losses for both employees and employers, and unnecessary excess use of natural resources to make and dispose of the waste products of artificial milks.[124] If the prevalence of breastfeeding in the hospital were increased from 64% to 75%, it is estimated that over $90 million would be saved each year in excess costs for treating NEC, and many premature infant lives would be saved.[123] However, we must add back in the costs to the healthcare system and to the family of obtaining and feeding human milk to preterm infants: access to an effective breast pump, sterile and/or clean storage containers, NICU and home freezer space, and access to lactation professionals.[2, 125]

KEY CONCEPTS

● Human milk reduces infections in preterm infants, both during initial hospitalization and after discharge.

● Human milk facilitates gastrointestinal development, allowing for faster realization of full feedings.

● Most studies conclude that breastfed preterm infants have a neurodevelopmental advantage over infants fed artificial milks.

● Early nutrition may have significant effects on later health.

● Human milk can save millions in long term health care costs.

REFERENCES

1. Vohr BR, Poindexter BB, Dusick AM, et al. Persistent beneficial effects of breast milk ingested in the neonatal intensive care unit on outcomes of extremely low birth weight infants at 30 months of age. Pediatrics 2007; 120(4):e953-9.

2. Patel AL, Meier PP, Engstrom JL. The evidence for use of human milk in very low-birthweight preterm infants. NeoReviews 2007; 8(11):e459-66.

3. Groer MW, Walker WA. What is the role of preterm human milk supplement in the host defenses of the preterm infant? Science vs. fiction. Adv Pediatr 1996; 43:335-58.

4. Ogra PL, Rassin DK. Chapter 4: Human breast milk. In: Remington JS, Klein JO (eds). Infectious diseases of the fetus and newborn infant. 4th Ed. Philadelphia: WB Saunders; 1995.

5. Lawrence RM. Chapter 5: Host-resistance factors and immunologic significance of human milk. In: Lawrence RA, Lawrence RM (eds). Breastfeeding: a guide for the medical profession. Philadelphia: Elsevier-Mosby; 2005:171-214.

6. Buescher ES. Host defense mechanisms of human milk and their relations to enteric infections and necrotizing enterocolitis. Clin Perinatol 1994; 21(2):247-62.

7. Boo NY, Puah CH, Lye MS. The role of expressed breastmilk and continuous positive airway pressure as survival in extremely low birthweight infants. J Trop Pediatr 2000; 46:15-20.

8. Beeby PJ, Jeffery H. Risk factors for necrotising enterocolitis: the influence of gestational age. Arch Dis Child 1992;67(4 Spec No):432-5.

9. Santulli TV, Schullinger JN, Heird WC, et al. Acute necrotizing enterocolitis in infancy: a review of 64 cases. Pediatrics 1975; 55(3):376-87.

10. Kliegman RM, Pittard WB, Fanaroff AA. Necrotizing enterocolitis in neonates fed human milk. J Pediatr 1979; 95(3):450-3.

11. Gross SJ. Growth and biochemical response of preterm infants fed human milk or modified infant formula. N Engl J Med 1983; 308(5):237-41.

12. Guthrie SO, Gordon PV, Thomas V, Thorp JA, Peabody J, Clark RH. Necrotizing enterocolitis among neonates in the United States. J Perinatol 2003; 23(4):278-85.

13. Boo NY, Goh ES. Predictors of breastfeeding in very low birthweight infants at the time of discharge from hospital. J Trop Pediatr 1999; 45(4):195-201.

14. Schanler RJ, Lau C, Hurst NM, Smith EO. Randomized trial of donor human milk versus preterm formula as substitutes for mothers' own milk in the feeding of extremely premature infants. Pediatrics 2005; 116(2):400-6.

15. Schanler RJ, Shulman RJ, Lau C. Feeding strategies for premature infants: beneficial outcomes of feeding fortified human milk versus preterm formula. Pediatrics 1999; 103(6 Pt 1):1150-7.

16. Lucas A, Cole TJ. Breast milk and neonatal necrotising enterocolitis. Lancet 1990; 336:1519-23.

17. Schanler RJ, Garza C, Nichols BL. Fortified mothers' milk for very low birth weight infants: results of growth and nutrient balance studies. J Pediatr 1985; 107(3):437-45.

18. Pitt J, Barlow B, Heird WC. Protection against experimental necrotizing enterocolitis by maternal milk. I. Role of milk leukocytes. Pediatr Res 1977; 11(8):906-9.

19. Yu VY, Jamieson J, Bajuk B. Breast milk feeding in very low birthweight infants. Aust Paediatr J 1981; 17(3):186-90.

20. Narayanan I, Prakash K, Bala S, Verma RK, Gujral VV. Partial supplementation with expressed breast-milk for prevention of infection in low-birth-weight infants. Lancet 1980; 2(8194):561-3.

21. Narayanan I, Prakash K, Murthy NS, Gujral VV. Randomised controlled trial of effect of raw and holder pasteurised human milk and of formula supplements on incidence of neonatal infection. Lancet 1984; 2(8412):1111-3.

22. Narayanan I, Prakash K, Gujral VV. The value of human milk in the prevention of infection in the high-risk low-birth-weight infant. J Pediatr 1981; 99(3):496-8.

23. McGuire W, Anthony MY. Donor human milk versus formula for preventing necrotising enterocolitis in preterm infants: systematic review. Arch Dis Child Fetal Neonatal Ed 2003; 88(1):F11-4.

24. Henderson G, Craig S, Brocklehurst P, McGuire W. Enteral feeding regimens and necrotising enterocolitis in preterm infants: multi-centre case-control study. Arch Dis Child Fetal Neonatal Ed Sept 3, 2007 doi:101136/adc2007119560 2007.

25. Sisk PM, Lovelady CA, Dillard RG, Gruber KJ, O'Shea TM. Early human milk feeding is associated with a lower risk of necrotizing enterocolitis in very low birth weight infants. J Perinatol 2007; 27(7):428-33.

26. Eibl MM, Wolf HM, Furnkranz H, Rosenkranz A. Prevention of necrotizing enterocolitis in low-birth-weight infants by IgA-IgG feeding. N Engl J Med 1988; 319(1):1-7.

27. Dvorak B, Fituch CC, Williams CS, Hurst NM, Schanler RJ. Concentrations of epidermal growth factor and transforming growth factor-alpha in preterm milk. Adv Exp Med Biol 2004; 554:407-9.

28. Dvorak B. Epidermal growth factor and necrotizing enterocolitis. Clin Perinatol 2004; 31(1):183-92.

29. Dvorak B, Fituch CC, Williams CS, Hurst NM, Schanler RJ. Increased epidermal growth factor levels in human milk of mothers with extremely premature infants. Pediatr Res 2003; 54(1):15-9.

30. Reber KM, Nankervis CA. Necrotizing enterocolitis: preventative strategies. Clin Perinatol 2004; 31(1):157-67.

31. Moya FR, Eguchi H, Zhao B, et al. Platelet-activating factor acetylhydrolase in term and preterm human milk: a preliminary report. J Pediatr Gastroenterol Nutr 1994; 19(2):236-9.

32. Furukawa M, Lee EL, Johnston JM. Platelet-activating factor-induced ischemic bowel necrosis: the effect of platelet-activating factor acetylhydrolase. Pediatr Res 1993; 34(2):237-41.

33. Schanler RJ, Goldblum RM, Garza C, Goldman AS. Enhanced fecal excretion of selected immune factors in very low birth weight infants fed fortified human milk. Pediatr Res 1986; 20(8):711-5.

34. Dvorak B, Halpern MD, Holubec H, et al. Maternal milk reduces severity of necrotizing enterocolitis and increases intestinal IL-10 in a neonatal rat model. Pediatr Res 2003; 53(3):426-33.

35. el-Mohandes AE, Picard MB, Simmens SJ, Keiser JF. Use of human milk in the intensive care nursery decreases the incidence of nosocomial sepsis. J Perinatol 1997; 17(2):130-4.

36. Furman L, Taylor G, Minich N, Hack M. The effect of maternal milk on neonatal morbidity of very low-birth-weight infants. Arch Pediatr Adolesc Med 2003; 157(1):66-7.

37. Narayanan I, Prakash K, Prabhakar AK, Gujral VV. A planned prospective evaluation of the anti-infective property of varying quantities of expressed human milk. Acta Paediatr Scand 1982; 71(3):441-5.

38. Ronnestad A, Abrahamsen TG, Medbo S, et al. Late-onset septicemia in a Norwegian national cohort of extremely premature infants receiving very early full human milk feeding. Pediatrics 2005; 115(3):e269-76.

39. Uraizee F, Gross SJ. Improved feeding tolerance and reduced incidence of sepsis in sick very low birth weight (VLBW) infants fed maternal milk. Pediatr Res 1989; 25:298A.

40. Hylander MA, Strobino DM, Dhanireddy R. Human milk feedings and infection among very low birth weight infants. Pediatrics 1998; 102(3): E38.

41. de Silva A, Jones PW, Spencer SA. Does human milk reduce infection rates in preterm infants? A systematic review. Arch Dis Child Fetal Neonatal Ed 2004; 89:F509-F13.

42. Furman L. Yes, human milk does reduce infection rates in very low birthweight infants. Arch Dis Child Fetal Neonatal Ed 2006; 91:F78.

43. Kleinman RE, Walker WA. The enteromammary immune system: an important new concept in breast milk host defense. Dig Dis Sci 1979; 24(11):876-82.

44. Walker WA. The dynamic effects of breastfeeding on intestinal development and host defense. Adv Exp Med Biol 2004; 554:155-70.

45. Schanler RJ. The use of human milk for premature infants. Pediatr Clin North Am 2001; 48(1):207-19.

46. Goldman AS. The immune system in human milk and the developing infant. Breastfeed Med 2007; 2(4):195-204.

47. Donovan S. Role of human milk components in gastrointestinal development: current knowledge and future needs. J Pediatrics 2006; 149(5):S49-S61.

48. Martin CR, Walker WA. Intestinal immune defenses and the inflammatory response in necrotising enterocolitis. Semin Fetal Neonatal Med 2006; 11(5):369-77.

49. Catassi C, Bonucci A, Coppa GV, Carlucci A, Giorgi PL. Intestinal permeability changes during the first month: effect of natural versus artificial feeding. J Pediatr Gastroenterol Nutr 1995; 21(4):383-6.

50. Shulman RJ, Schanler RJ, Lau C, Heitkemper M, Ou CN, Smith EO. Early feeding, feeding tolerance, and lactase activity in preterm infants. J Pediatr 1998; 133(5):645-9.

51. Ewer AK, Yu VY. Gastric emptying in pre-term infants: the effect of breast milk fortifier. Acta Paediatr 1996; 85(9):1112-5.

52. Cavell B. Gastric emptying in infants fed human milk or infant formula. Acta Paediatr Scand 1981; 70:639-41.

53. Atkinson SA, Bryan MH, Anderson GH. Human milk: difference in nitrogen concentration in milk for mothers of term and premature infants. J Pediatr 1978; 93:67-9.

54. Atkinson SA. The effects of gestational age at delivery on human milk components. In: Jensen RG (ed). Handbook of milk composition. San Diego: Academic Press; 1995:222-37.

55. Barros MD, Carneiro-Sampaeio MMS. Milk composition in low birth weight infants' mothers. Acta Paediatr Scand 1983; 73:693-4.

56. Bitmar J, Wood DL, Hamosh M, Hamosh P, Mehta NR. Comparison of the lipid composition of breast milk from mothers of term and preterm infants. Am J Clin Nutr 1983; 38:300 1983;38:300-12.

57. Lepage G, Collet S, Bougle D, et al. The composition of preterm milk in relation to the degree of prematurity. Am J Clin Nutr 1984; 40(5):1042-9.

58. Anderson GH, Atkinson SA, Bryan MH. Energy and macronutrient content of human milk during early lactation from mothers giving birth prematurely and at term. Am J Clin Nutr 1981; 34(2):258-65.

59. Butte NF, Garza C, Johnson CA, Smith EO, Nichols BL. Longitudinal changes in milk composition of mothers delivering preterm and term infants. Early Hum Dev 1984; 9(2):153-62.

60. Gross SJ, Geller J, Tomarelli RM. Composition of breast milk from mothers of preterm infants. Pediatrics 1981; 68(4):490-3.

61. Gross SJ, David RJ, Bauman L, Tomarelli RM. Nutritional composition of milk produced by mothers delivering preterm. J Pediatr 1980; 96(4):641-4.

62. Schanler RJ, Oh W. Composition of breast milk obtained from mothers of premature infants as compared to breast milk obtained from donors. J Pediatr 1980; 96(4):679-81.

63. Sann L, Bienvenu F, Lahet C, Bienvenu J, Bethenod M. Comparison of the composition of breast milk from mothers of term and preterm infants. Acta Paediatr Scand 1981; 70(1):115-6.

64. Udipi SA, Kirksey A, West K, Giacoia G. Vitamin B6, vitamin C and folacin levels in milk from mothers of term and preterm infants during the neonatal period. Am J Clin Nutr 1985; 42(3):522-30.

65. Schanler RJ, Atkinson SA. Effects of nutrients in human milk on the recipient premature infant. J Mammary Gland Biol Neoplasia 1999; 4(3):297-307.

66. Atkinson SA. Human milk feeding of the micropremie. Clin Perinatol 2000; 27(1):235-47.

67. Gross SJ, Buckley RH, Wakil SS, McAllister DC, David RJ, Faix RG. Elevated IgA concentration in milk produced by mothers delivered of preterm infants. J Pediatr 1981; 99(3):389-93.

68. Edmond KM, Zandoh C, Quigley MA, Amenga-Etego S, Owusu-Agyei S, Kirkwood BR. Delayed breastfeeding initiation increases risk of neonatal mortality. Pediatrics 2006; 117(3):e380-6.

69. Rodriguez NA, Caplan MS. Abstract # 3850.10: Oropharyngeal administration of own mother's colostrum (OMC) during the first days of life: effects on immune function of extremely low birth weight (ELBW; BW < 100g) infants - a pilot study. In: APS/SPR/PAS April 29-May 2, 2006; San Francisco; 2006.

70. Anderson JW, Johnstone BM, Remley DT. Breast-feeding and cognitive development: a meta-analysis. Am J Clin Nutr 1999; 70(4):525-35.

71. Lucas A, Bishop N, King F, Cole T. Randomized trial of nutrition for preterm infants after discharge. Arch Dis Child 1992; 67: 324-7.

72. Lucas A, Morley R, Cole TJ. Randomised trial of early diet in preterm babies and later intelligence quotient. BMJ 1998; 317(7171):1481-7.

73. Lucas A, Morley R, Cole TJ, Lister G, Leeson-Payne C. Breast milk and subsequent intelligence quotient in children born preterm. Lancet 1992; 339(8788):261-4.

74. Morley R. Breast feeding and cognitive outcome in children born prematurely. Adv Exp Med Biol 2002; 503:77-82.

75. Morley R, Cole TJ, Powell R, Lucas A. Mother's choice to provide breast milk and developmental outcome. Arch Dis Child 1988; 63(11):1382-5.

76. Morley R, Lucas A. Randomized diet in the neonatal period and growth performance until 7.5-8 yr of age in preterm children. Am J Clin Nutr 2000; 71(3):822-8.

77. Vohr BR, Poindexter BB, Dusick AM, et al. Beneficial effects of breast milk in the neonatal intensive care unit on the developmental outcome of extremely low birth weight infants at 18 months of age. Pediatrics 2006; 118(1):e115-23.

78. Feldman R, Eidelman AI. Direct and indirect effects of breast milk on the neurobehavioral and cognitive development of premature infants. Dev Psychobiol 2003; 43(2):109-19.

79. Amin SB, Merle KS, Orlando MS, Dalzell LE, Guillet R. Brainstem maturation in premature infants as a function of enteral feeding type. Pediatrics 2000; 106(2 Pt 1):318-22.

80. Bier JA, Oliver T, Ferguson AE, Vohr BR. Human milk improves cognitive and motor development of premature infants during infancy. J Hum Lact 2002; 18(4):361-7.

81. Elwood PC, Pickering J, Gallacher JE, Hughes J, Davies D. Long term effect of breast feeding: cognitive function in the Caerphilly cohort. J Epidemiol Community Health 2005; 59(2):130-3.

82. Smith MM, Durkin M, Hinton VJ, Bellinger D, Kuhn L. Influence of breastfeeding on cognitive outcomes at age 6-8 years: follow-up of very low birth weight infants. Am J Epidemiol 2003; 158(11):1075-82.

83. Lucas A, Morley R, Cole TJ, Gore SM. A randomised multicentre study of human milk versus formula and later development in preterm infants. Arch Dis Child Fetal Neonatal Ed 1994; 70(2):F141-6.

84. Gale CR, Martyn CN. Breastfeeding, dummy use, and adult intelligence. Lancet 1996; 347(9008):1072-5.

85. Pollock JI. Mother's choice to provide breast milk and developmental outcome. Arch Dis Child 1989; 64(5):763-4.

86. Jacobson SW, Jacobson JL. Breastfeeding and intelligence. Lancet 1992; 339(8798):926.

87. Hart S, Boylan LM, Carroll S, Musick YA, Lampe RM. Brief report: breast-fed one-week-olds demonstrate superior neurobehavioral organization. J Pediatr Psychol 2003; 28(8):529-34.

88. Horne RS, Parslow PM, Ferens D, Watts AM, Adamson TM. Comparison of evoked arousability in breast and formula fed infants. Arch Dis Child 2004; 89(1):22-5.

89. Hagan R, French N, Evans S, et al. Breast feeding, distractibility and IQ in very preterm infants. Pediatr Res 1996; 39:266A.

90. Sacker A, Quigley MA, Kelley YJ. Breastfeeding and developmental delay: findings from the Millennium cohort study. Pediatrics 2006; 118(3):e682-9.

91. O'Connor DL, Jacobs J, Hall R, et al. Growth and development of premature infants fed predominantly human milk, predominantly premature infant formula, or a combination of human milk and premature formula. J Pediatr Gastroenterol Nutr 2003; 37(4):437-46.

92. Der G, Batty GD, Deary IJ. Effect of breast feeding on intelligence in children: prospective study, sibling pairs analysis, and meta-analysis. BMJ 2006; Nov 4;333(7575):945. Epub 2006 Oct 4.

93. Jacobson SW, Chiodo LM, Jacobson JL. Breastfeeding effects on intelligence quotient in 4- and 11-year-old children. Pediatrics 1999; 103(5):e71.

94. Furman L, Wilson-Costello D, Friedman H, Taylor HG, Minich N, Hack M. The effect of neonatal maternal milk feeding on the neurodevelopmental outcome of very low birth weight infants. J Dev Behav Pediatr 2004; 25(4):247-53.

95. Burgard P. Critical evaluation of the methodology employed in cognitive development trials. Acta Paediatr 2003; 92 (suppl.):6-10.

96. Rey J. Breastfeeding and cognitive development. Acta Paediatr 2003; 92 (suppl.):11-8.

97. Rapid Responses to: Geoff Der, G David Batty, and Ian J Deary. Effect of breast feeding on intelligence in children: prospective study, sibling pairs analysis, and meta-analysis BMJ 2006; 333: 945. (Accessed March 2008, at www.bmj.com/cgi/eletters/333/7575/945)

98. King C, Jones E. The benefits of human milk for the preterm baby. In: King C, Jones E (eds). Feeding and nutrition in the preterm infant. Edinburgh: Elsevier; 2005:1-13.

99. Lucas A, Fewtrell MS, Morley R, et al. Randomized outcome trial of human milk fortification and developmental outcome in preterm infants. Am J Clin Nutr 1996; 64(2):142-51.

100.Uauy RD, Birch DG, Birch EE, Tyson JE, Hoffman DR. Effect of dietary omega-3 fatty acids on retinal function of very-low-birth-weight neonates. Pediatr Res 1990; 28(5):485-92.

101.Carlson SE, Werkman SH, Rhodes PG, Tolley EA. Visual-acuity development in healthy preterm infants: effect of marine-oil supplementation. Am J Clin Nutr 1993; 58(1):35-42.

102.Faldella G, Govoni M, Alessandroni R, et al. Visual evoked potentials and dietary long chain polyunsaturated fatty acids in preterm infants. Arch Dis Child Fetal Neonatal Ed 1996; 75(2):F108-12.

103.DiBiasie A. Evidence-based review of retinopathy of prematurity prevention in VLBW and ELBW infants. Neonatal Netw 2006; 25(6):393-403.

104.Hylander MA, Strobino DM, Pezzullo JC, Dhanireddy R. Association of human milk feedings with a reduction in retinopathy of prematurity among very low birthweight infants. J Perinatol 2001; 21(6):356-62.

105.Hallman M, Bry K, Hoppu K, Lappi M, Pohjavuori M. Inositol supplementation in premature infants with respiratory distress syndrome. N Engl J Med 1992; 326(19):1233-9.

106.Heller CD, O'Shea M, Yao Q, et al. Human milk intake and retinopathy of prematurity in extremely low birth weight infants. Pediatrics 2007; 120(1):1-9.

107.Okamoto T, Shirai M, Kokubo M, et al. Human milk reduces the risk of retinal detachment in extremely low-birthweight infants. Pediatr Int 2007; 49(6):894-7.

108.Elder DE, Hagan R, Evans SF, Benninger HR, French NP. Hospital admissions in the first year of life in very preterm infants. J Paediatr Child Health 1999; 35(2):145-50.

109.Blaymore Bier JA, Oliver T, Ferguson A, Vohr BR. Human milk reduces outpatient upper respiratory symptoms in premature infants during their first year of life. J Perinatol 2002; 22(5):354-9.

110.American Academy of Pediatrics, Section on Breastfeeding. Policy Statement: Breastfeeding and the use of human milk. Pediatrics 2005; 115(2):496-506.

111.Lucas A. The developmental origins of adult health and well-being. Adv Exp Med Biol 2005; 569:13-5.

112.Singhal A. Early nutrition and long-term cardiovascular health. Nutr Rev 2006; 64(5 Pt 2):S44-9; discussion S72-91.

113.Singhal A, Cole TJ, Fewtrell M, Lucas A. Breastmilk feeding and lipoprotein profile in adolescents born preterm: follow-up of a prospective randomised study. Lancet 2004; 363(9421):1571-8.

114. Singhal A, Cole TJ, Lucas A. Early nutrition in preterm infants and later blood pressure: two cohorts after randomised trials. Lancet 2001; 357(9254):413-9.

115. Shoji H, Shimizu T, Shinohara K, Oguchi S, Shiga S, Yamashiro Y. Suppressive effects of breast milk on oxidative DNA damage in very low birthweight infants. Arch Dis Child Fetal Neonatal Ed 2004; 89:F136-F8.

116. Friel JK, Martin SM, Langdon M, Herzberg GR, Buettner GR. Milk from mothers of both premature and full-term infants provides better antioxidant protection than does infant formula. Pediatric Research 2002; 51(5):612-8.

117. Labbok MH. Effects of breastfeeding on the mother. Pediatr Clin NA 2001; 48(1):143-58.

118. Meier P. Supporting lactation in mothers with very low birth weight infants. Pediatric Annals 2003; 32(5):317-25.

119. Miracle DJ, Meier PP, Bennett PA. Mothers' decisions to change from formula to mothers' milk for very-low-birth-weight infants. J Obstet Gynecol Neonatal Nurs 2004; 33(6):692-703.

120. Kavanaugh K, Meier P, Zimmermann B, Mead L. The rewards outweigh the efforts: breastfeeding outcomes for mothers of preterm infants. J Hum Lact 1997; 13(1):15-21.

121. Furman LM. Does providing human milk for her very low-birthweight infant help the mother? NeoReviews 2007; 8(11):e478-84.

122. Ball TM, Wright AL. Health care costs of formula-feeding in the first year of life. Pediatrics 1999; 103(4 Part 2):870-6.

123. Weimer J. The economic benefits of breastfeeding: a review and analysis. In: Food and Rural Economics Division, Economic Research Service, US Dept. of Agriculture. Food Assistance and Nutrition Research Report No. 13, 1800 M Street, NW, Washington, DC 20036-5831 www.ers.usda.gov/publications/fanrr13/; 2001.

124. Ball TM, Bennett DM. The economic impact of breastfeeding. Pediatr Clin NA 2001; 48(1):253-62.

125. Barton AJ, Danek G, Owens B. Clinical and economic outcomes of infants receiving breast milk in the NICU. J Soc Pediatr Nurs 2001; 6(1):5-10.

Chapter 6:
CHALLENGES OF HUMAN MILK FOR PRETERM INFANTS

NUTRITIONAL CHALLENGES

Exclusive feeding of unfortified human milk in preterm infants (especially those less than 1500 grams) is associated with poorer growth rates and nutritional deficits both during and after hospitalization.[1-5] Protein nutritional status indicators are lower than with preterm formula or fortified human milk and decline over time in preterm infants fed unfortified human milk.[1,4,6] Low intakes of calcium and phosphorus in unfortified human milk result in elevated calcium and alkaline phosphatase levels and low serum phosphorous,[2,7] causing an eventual reduction in height.[8,9] Low milk sodium intake may contribute to late hyponatremia.[10]

The nutritional adequacy of human milk for preterm infants may be limited for several reasons. Premature infants are often restricted as to volume of milk, given concerns regarding chronic lung disease, the ductus arteriosus, and necrotizing enterocolitis. Variability of composition, although perfect for a full term infant feeding ad libitum, is not ideal for the preterm infant with increased nutrient needs. While the milk of mothers who deliver preterm has increased protein, IgA, and sodium, the milk changes over the first few weeks to a composition similar to term human milk (Table 1). Beyond that time, protein content continues to fall slowly over the first six months of milk production, which further compromises the adequacy of nutrients for the rapidly growing preterm graduate.[11] Unfortunately, the nutrient needs of the preterm infant, especially those less than 1500 grams, do not change nearly as fast. The content of other nutrients in preterm milk (e.g., calcium and phosphorus) do not change notably through lactation and are too low to meet the needs of many preterm infants.

Table 1: Preterm Milk Over Time Compared to Mature Term Milk

	Preterm Milk			Term Milk
Milk Component	**Colostrum**	**Transit.**	**Mature**	**Term Mature**
Total Pro, g/L	30	24	15	12
IgA, mg/g protein	109	92	64	83
NPN, % total N	15	18	17	24
Na, mmol/L	22.2	11.6	8.8	9.0
Ca, mmol/L	6.8	8	7.2	6.5

Source: Adapted from Schanler & Atkinson, 1999.[12] Reprinted with permission of Springer Science and Business Media.

In addition, loss of nutrients and other components of the milk may occur with expression, storage, and feeding methods (Figure 1).[13-18] As much of the variation in energy content is due to the fat content of milk,[19] adherence of fat to the tubing may decrease the infant's main source of energy. Three hours of light exposure can decrease the breastmilk riboflavin by 50% and vitamin A by 70%.[20]

OVERCOMING NUTRITIONAL CHALLENGES OF HUMAN MILK FOR PRETERM INFANTS

Volume

Increasing the volume of human milk is one way of increasing nutrient intake. The historic target for premature infants of 150 mL/kg/day of enteral feedings may be inadequate to overcome prior nitrogen deficits and establish optimal growth. A randomized trial of enteral feeding volumes (150 and 200 mL/kg/d) of infants born less than 30 weeks gestation, once they reached full enteral feeds, found that individual milk volume requirements for adequate weight gain without significant adverse effects varied between 150-200 mL/kg/d.[21] Increased milk intakes were associated with increased daily weight gains and a greater weight at 35 weeks, but there was no difference in morbidity or in any growth parameter at one year of

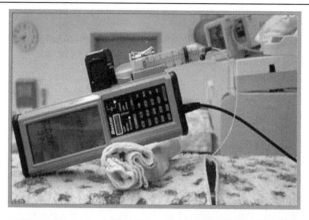

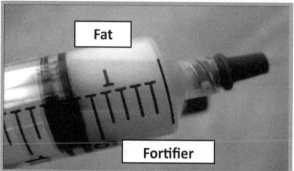

(photos courtesy of N Wight)

Figure 1: Loss of fat and fortifier by poor orientation of feeding syringe

age. Ziegler suggests that feeding volume should be increased until the infant shows signs that GI capacity has been reached, then kept at that volume through daily adjustment of the feeding volume [22].

Restricting feeding volume until a weight plateau has been identified is the most common cause of growth delay.[23] It has been suggested that fortified human milk must be fed at approximately 180 mL/kg/d if ELBW infants are to achieve adequate growth, nutrient retention, and biochemical indices of nutritional status.[23]

Hindmilk "Fortification"

As hindmilk may have a two- to three-fold greater fat content than foremilk, hindmilk can be used to increase caloric intake if the mother's milk production is in excess of the infant's needs.[24] Although one study demonstrated increased weight gain with short-term hindmilk fortification,[25] a subsequent study showed no difference in weight, length, head circumference, mid-arm circumference, or skin fold thickness after 28 days of hindmilk feeding.[26] There were no adverse effects on serum chemistries. As protein is usually the limiting nutrient, it is important to note that the protein content of foremilk and hindmilk are the same.[25] A more recent study of "well" preterm infants between 1000 grams and 1500 grams in Nigeria[27] showed significantly increased weight gain in both SGA and AGA infants fed hindmilk versus composite milk. All babies were fed with composite milk (colostrum) for the first four days of life, then randomized to hindmilk or continued composite milk at 100 mL/kg/day starting on day five of life and advanced by 15 mL/kg/day to 200 mL/kg/day for a two week total trial. Unfortunately, babies who developed abdominal distention, vomiting, apneic attacks, or who died (5/34 in the composite group and 4/34 in the hindmilk group) during the course of the study were excluded from analysis. There were no differences in length or head circumference rates of growth between the groups.

Multinutrient Fortification

Studies have repeatedly demonstrated that protein and multinutrient fortification of human milk are associated with short-term growth advantages (weight, length, and head circumference) for infants less than 34 weeks gestation or birthweight less than 1800 grams when fortified human milk is given both during and after the infant's initial hospitalization.[28-30] In addition, VLBW (less than 1500 grams) infants grow faster and have higher bone mineral content up to one year of age if provided with additional nutrients, especially protein, calcium, and phosphorus.[31, 32] However, exclusively breastfed former preterm infants tend to "catch-up" if given sufficient time (two to eight years).[33-35]

Although a weight gain of greater than 15 grams per day is recommended, the optimal growth rate (reference target) has not yet been established. It is unclear whether the rapid catch-up growth seen with aggressive supplementation is of benefit or harm for long term overall health, growth, and neurodevelopment.[36-38]

Current guidelines recommend fortification of breastmilk be initiated well before a full feeding volume is reached in VLBW (<1500g) infants[22] and may need to be continued post-discharge. Some infants between 1500-2000 grams and those infants with special nutrient needs (e.g., chronic lung disease or cardiac problems) may also require fortification. Studies of feeding types and their advancement have usually started fortifiers at enteral feeds of 100 mL/kg/d, but there is no research to suggest that starting earlier (50-75 mL/kg/day) is harmful. Also, many studies do not specify whether "full" fortification (1 packet powder per 25 mL EBM) or "half" fortification is used to start.

There is no research as to how fast to "advance" fortification, but multiple studies demonstrate no increase in feeding intolerance or NEC with multinutrient fortifiers.[28, 39-41] Care must be taken that large doses of multiple additives do not raise the osmolality of breastmilk (or formula) to unacceptable levels.[42] Osmolality increases the longer the breastmilk is in contact with the fortifier.[43] There is no general agreement as to when fortifiers should be discontinued.

VLBW infants fed human milk can benefit from vitamin supplementation, most specifically vitamins A, C, and D. Patients with, or recovering from, cholestasis may also require additional fat-soluble vitamins (A, D, E, and K). The AAP currently recommends that preterm infants (less than 1000 gram birthweight) receive 6 –12 IU/kg/day vitamin E enterally, which may be supplied either by preterm formula or by fortification of human milk.[44] When powdered commercial fortifier is used, no additional vitamin supplements are needed. Iron supplementation should be given to VLBW infants fed human milk at a dose of 2 mg/kg/d starting at one month and continuing until twelve months of age.

VLBW infants are at significant risk for chemical and clinical osteopenia due to inadequate calcium and phosphorous intake, dysfunctional vitamin D metabolism, and/or excessive renal losses of these minerals (which may be exacerbated by diuretics, especially furosemide). In one series, over half of the infants with a birthweight less than 1000 grams and nearly 25% of those with a birthweight less than 1500 grams had radiographic evidence of rickets.[45] VLBW infants receiving breastmilk that is fortified with commercially available products receive additional calcium and phosphorus, in a quantity associated with improved growth.[28,46] Supplementation of a premature's diet with vitamin D beyond 200-400 IU/day has not been found to increase later bone density.[33]

Fortification Concerns

When fortifiers are added to human milk, gastric emptying time is prolonged to equal the gastric emptying time of formulas.[47] As noted above, clinical concerns regarding feeding tolerance with fortifiers have not been verified in research. Concerns remain regarding changing the milk (altered immune function, contamination and increased bacterial growth, and bioavailability of nutrients), introduction of bovine proteins and plant oils, increasing osmolality over time, and an overall change in GI flora.

Fortification does not appear to significantly alter bacterial counts if the fortified milk is used within 24 hours.[48] This study also found that IgA content was not affected by fortification, storage temperature, or storage duration. Another study found that fortification did not decrease the total IgA content, but did decrease *E. coli*-specific IgA and lysozyme activity.[49] One study suggested that the fortifier with more iron and MCT (medium chain triglycerides) oil increased bacterial counts in human milk more than another brand of fortifier.[50] Subsequent studies demonstrated equal bacterial growth in milk fortified with the two brands of fortifiers up to six hours[51] and up to 72 hours,[52] with total bacterial colony counts declining from 0 to 72 hours in both fortified milks. Although fortifier did not affect the bacterial inhibition in another study, the addition of iron alone reduced the antimicrobial effect of human milk against *E. coli, S. aureus, P. aeruginosa* and *Candida*.[53]

Askin and Diehl-Jones[54] studied paired samples of fortified and unfortified preterm milk and found that bacterial counts were significantly increased in the fortified samples after four hours at room temperature. They also noted a 20% decrease in epidermal growth factor (EGF) titers in the same time period. EGF is believed to play a role in reducing NEC in preterm infants.

Any formula or fortifier intake will change the GI flora significantly, and for a considerable time,[55] affecting the "cross-talk" between the commensal bacteria and intestinal epithelium. At present, it does not appear that fortification of human milk increases necrotizing enterocolitis.[40,56]

At present, there are liquid and powdered fortifiers; both essentially preterm formulas to be added to human milk. The powdered products have the advantage of not diluting the human milk and appear to be preferred by parents.[57] A comparison of the two products suggests the liquid preparation results in lower protein, calcium, phosphorus, and zinc intakes.[40]

New Directions in Fortification

Ideally, each sample of human milk should be analyzed for macro- and micro-nutrient content and fortified with only the nutrients required by that infant. Such individualized lactoengineering is not practical or cost-effective at this time. However, commercial efforts are underway to tailor donated human milk to more closely meet the needs of preterm infants, and to produce a human milk fortifier made from donated human milk. Research to determine the benefits of this type of fortifier is currently underway with results expected in a few years.

Probiotics are live non-pathogenic microbial preparations that colonize the intestine and provide benefit to the host.[58] "They normalize intestinal microflora, increase mucosal barrier function, reduce intestinal permeability, enhance immune defenses, and improve enteral nutrition."[58] Probiotics appear to enhance feeding tolerance in preterm infants[59] and may have an additive effect with breastfeeding on gut immunity.[60] Several studies have suggested that use of probiotics in preterm infants may reduce the incidence and severity of NEC.[61,62] Because of the immunocompromised status of preterm infants, systemic infection as a result of probiotic treatment is a possibility.[62] More research as to the safety and efficacy of each strain is necessary before probiotics are widely used in preterm infants.

INFECTION CONCERNS REGARDING HUMAN MILK FOR PRETERM INFANTS

While human milk has considerable host defense properties, it can still be contaminated with pathogenic microorganisms during expression, storage, and feeding. Human milk can also transmit many different maternal bacterial and viral illnesses.[63] Group B streptococcal disease and methicillin-resistant staphylococcus aureus have been implicated in morbidity and mortality in preterm infants fed contaminated milk.[64-67] Infectious mastitis does not pose a risk for the full-term healthy infant, but may increase risk to the VLBW infant. The risk of using breastmilk from a mother with a potentially transmittable illness or medication must be weighed against both the short-term and long-term risks of withholding human milk from the preterm infant.

AAP 2006 Red Book

1. Outbreaks from gram negative bacterial infections in NICUs occasionally have been attributed to contaminated human milk specimens that have been collected or stored improperly.

2. Milk from other than the biologic mother should be treated according to Human Milk Banking Association of North America (HMBANA) guidelines.

3. Routine culturing or heat treatment of mother's milk fed to her infant has not been demonstrated to be necessary or cost-effective.

(American Academy of Pediatrics, 2006[63] p. 125.)

Current infectious contraindications to using mother's milk in developed countries include human immunodeficiency virus (HIV/AIDS), Human T-Lymphotrophic virus types 1 and 2 (HTLV 1 & 2), and active tuberculosis prior to treatment. Other maternal illnesses may require the mother to temporarily "pump and dump" her milk until the mother is no longer infectious (varicella-zoster, measles, herpes on the breast). Although infants of women with Hepatitis B virus (HBV) may breastfeed, the infant should receive hepatitis B vaccine and immunoglobulin. Transmission of Hepatitis C is theoretically possible, but transmission through breastfeeding has not been documented.[63]

The most common source of angst for neonatologists is the very preterm infant of a mother who is positive for cytomegalovirus (CMV) or whose CMV status is unknown.[68] CMV is shed intermittently in human milk (along with the antibody) and transmission is common, although active disease is rare, except in VLBW infants in some studies.[69-92] The use of fresh colostrum may pose less of a concern than milk pumped after the first week.[91] Decisions about using breastmilk from CMV positive mothers should balance the risk of active CMV disease and the risks of not receiving human milk. Freezing may decrease CMV infectivity, but does not reliably eliminate it.[93] Interventions to screen breastmilk or render it non-infectious have met with variable success.[94-96]

CONCLUSIONS

Constituents of human milk have three main functions: provide nutrition, give immune protection, and promote development. Some constituents accomplish all three.[97] Unfortunately, for the preterm infant, especially the VLBW infant, nutritional adequacy may be limited. In addition, as the milk is not taken directly at breast until relatively late in the infant's hospital course, there are opportunities for infectious challenges as well. There are ways around these challenges, however, so that preterm infants may benefit from their own mother's milk immediately and throughout the hospital course and beyond.

KEY CONCEPTS

● Although preterm human milk is different from the milk of mothers who deliver at term, it changes to mature milk faster than the needs of the VLBW infant change.

● The most significant nutritional inadequacies for VLBW infants are protein, calcium, and phosphorus.

● The method of feeding can affect the nutritional quality of human milk.

● Increasing volume and multinutrient fortification can overcome the nutritional problems, but may also raise infectious disease concerns.

- The risk of cytomegalovirus infection in the VLBW infant must be carefully weighed against the risks of not receiving his own mother's milk.

REFERENCES

1. Atkinson SA, Bryan MH, Anderson GH. Human milk feeding in premature infants: protein, fat, and carbohydrate balances in the first two weeks of life. J Pediatr 1981; 99(4):617-24.

2. Atkinson SA, Radde IC, Anderson GH. Macromineral balances in premature infants fed their own mothers' milk or formula. J Pediatr 1983; 102(1):99-106.

3. Cooper PA, Rothberg AD, Pettifor JM, Bolton KD, Devenhuis S. Growth and biochemical response of premature infants fed pooled preterm milk or special formula. J Pediatr Gastroenterol Nutr 1984; 3(5):749-54.

4. Kashyap S, Schulze KF, Forsyth M, Dell RB, Ramakrishnan R, Heird WC. Growth, nutrient retention, and metabolic response of low-birth-weight infants fed supplemented and unsupplemented preterm human milk. Am J Clin Nutr 1990; 52(2):254-62.

5. Gross SJ. Growth and biochemical response of preterm infants fed human milk or modified infant formula. N Engl J Med 1983; 308(5):237-41.

6. Polberger SK, Axelsson IE, Raiha NC. Urinary and serum urea as indicators of protein metabolism in very low birthweight infants fed varying human milk protein intakes. Acta Paediatr Scand 1990; 79(8-9):737-42.

7. Pettifor JM, Rajah R, Venter A, et al. Bone mineralization and mineral homeostasis in very low-birth-weight infants fed either human milk or fortified human milk. J Pediatr Gastroenterol Nutr 1989; 8(2):217-24.

8. Fewtrell MS, Cole TJ, Bishop NJ, Lucas A. Neonatal factors predicting childhood height in preterm infants: evidence for a persisting effect of early metabolic bone disease? J Pediatr 2000; 137(5):668-73.

9. Lucas A, Brooke OG, Baker BA, Bishop N, Morley R. High alkaline phosphatase activity and growth in preterm neonates. Arch Dis Child 1989; 64(7 Spec No):902-9.

10. Roy RN, Chance GW, Radde IC, Hill DE, Willis DM, Sheepers J. Late hyponatremia in very low birthweight infants (less than 1.3 kilograms). Pediatr Res 1976; 10(5):526-31.

11. Saarela T, Kokkonen J, Koivisto M. Macronutrient and energy contents of human milk fractions during the first six months of lactation. Acta Paediatr 2005; 94(9):1176-81.

12. Schanler RJ, Atkinson SA. Effects of nutrients in human milk on the recipient premature infant. J Mammary Gland Biol Neoplasia 1999; 4(3):297-307.

13. Ogundele MO. Effects of storage on the physicochemical and antibacterial properties of human milk. Br J Biomed Sci 2002; 59(4):205-11.

14. Fidler N, Sauerwald TU, Demmelmair H, Koletzko B. Fat content and fatty acid composition of fresh, pasteurized, or sterilized human milk. Adv Exp Med Biol 2001; 501:485-95.

15. Stocks RJ, Davies DP, Allen F, Sewell D. Loss of breast milk nutrients during tube feeding. Arch Dis Child 1985; 60(2):164-6.

16. Narayanan I, Singh B, Harvey D. Fat loss during feeding of human milk. Arch Dis Child 1984; 59(5):475-7.

17. Mehta NR, Hamosh M, Bitman J, Wood DL. Adherence of medium-chain fatty acids to feeding tubes during gavage feeding of human milk fortified with medium-chain triglycerides. J Pediatr 1988; 112(3):474-6.

18. Greer FR, McCormick A, Loker J. Changes in fat concentration of human milk during delivery by intermittent bolus and continuous mechanical pump infusion. J Pediatr 1984; 105(5):745-9.

19. Schanler RJ. The use of human milk for premature infants. Pediatr Clin North Am 2001; 48(1):207-19.

20. Bates CJ, Liu DS, Fuller NJ, Lucas A. Susceptibility of riboflavin and vitamin A in breast milk to photodegradation and its implications for the use of banked breast milk in infant feeding. Acta Paediatr Scand 1985; 74(1):40-4.

21. Kuschel CA, Evans N, Askie L, Bredemeyer S, Nash J, Polverino J. A randomized trial of enteral feeding volumes in infants born before 30 weeks' gestation. J Paediatr Child Health 2000; 36(6):581-6.

22. Ziegler EE, Thureen PJ, Carlson SJ. Aggressive nutrition of the very low birthweight infant. Clin Perinatol 2002; 29(2):225-44.

23. Hay WW, Jr., Lucas A, Heird WC, et al. Workshop summary: Nutrition of the extremely low birth weight infant. Pediatrics 1999; 104(6):1360-8.

24. Schanler RJ. Human milk supplementation for preterm infants. Acta Paediatrica 2005; 94(Suppl 449):64-7.

25. Valentine C, Hurst N, Schanler R. Hindmilk improves weight gain in low-birth-weight infants fed human milk. J Pediatr Gastroenterol Nutr 1994; 18(4):474-7.

26. Payanikli P, et al. Hindmilk feeding in VLBW infants. In: Pediatric Academic Societies. San Francisco, Abstract # 2526 & # 2194; 2004.

27. Ogechi AA, William O, Fidelia BT. Hindmilk and weight gain in preterm very low-birthweight infants. Pediatr Int 2007; 49(2):156-60.

28. Kuschel CA, Harding JE. Multicomponent fortified human milk for promoting growth in preterm infants. Cochrane Database Syst Rev 2004(1):CD000343.

29. Schanler RJ. Fortified human milk: nature's way to feed premature infants. J Hum Lact 1998; 14(1):5-11.

30. Schanler RJ. Chapter 28: The low birth weight infant. In: Walker W, Watkins J, Duggan C (eds). Nutrition in pediatrics: basic science and clinical applications. 3rd Ed. Hamilton, Ontario: BC Decker, Inc; 2003:491-514.

31. Friel J, Andrews W, Matthew Jea. Improved growth of very low birthweight infants. Nutr Res 1993; 13:611-20.

32. Worrell L, Thorp J, Tucker Rea. The effects of the introduction of a high-nutrient transitional formula on growth and development of very-low-birth-weight infants. J Perinatol 2002; 22:112-9.

33. Backstrom M, Maki R, Kuusela A, et al. The long-term effect of early mineral, vit D, and breast milk intake on bone mineral status in 9-to 11-year-old children born prematurely. J Pediatr Gastroenterol Nutr 1999; 29:575-82.

34. Morley R, Lucas A. Randomized diet in the neonatal period and growth performance until 7.5-8 yr of age in preterm children. Am J Clin Nutr 2000; 71(3):822-8.

35. Schanler R, Burns P, Abrams S, Garza C. Bone mineralization outcomes in human milk-fed preterm infants. Pediatr Res 1992; 31(6):583-6.

36. Griffin IJ. Postdischarge nutrition for high risk neonates. Clin Perinatol 2002; 29(2):327-44.

37. Hall RT. Nutritional follow-up of the breastfeeding premature infant after hospital discharge. Pediatr Clin North Am 2001; 48(2):453-60.

38. Singhal A, Cole TJ, Fewtrell M, et al. Promotion of faster weight gain in infants born small for gestational age: is there an adverse effect on later blood pressure? Circulation 2007; 115(2):213-20.

39. Lucas A, Fewtrell MS, Morley R, et al. Randomized outcome trial of human milk fortification and developmental outcome in preterm infants. Am J Clin Nutr 1996; 64(2):142-51.

40. Schanler RJ, Shulman RJ, Lau C. Feeding strategies for premature infants: beneficial outcomes of feeding fortified human milk versus preterm formula. Pediatrics 1999; 103(6 Pt 1):1150-7.

41. Moody GJ, Schanler RJ, Lau C, Shulman RJ. Feeding tolerance in premature infants fed fortified human milk. J Pediatr Gastroenterol Nutr 2000; 30(4):408-12.

42. Srinivasan L, Bokiniec R, King C, Weaver G, Edwards AD. Increased osmolality of breast milk with therapeutic additives. Arch Dis Child Fetal Neonatal Ed 2004; 89(6):F514-7.

43. De Curtis M, Candusso M, Pieltain C, Rigo J. Effect of fortification on the osmolality of human milk. Arch Dis Child Fetal Neonatal Ed 1999; 81(2): F141-3.

44. American Academy of Pediatrics, Committee on Nutrition. Chapter 2: Nutritional needs of the preterm infant. In: Kleinman RE (ed). Pediatric nutrition handbook. 5th Ed. Elk Gove Village, IL: American Academy of Pediatrics; 2004:23.

45. Backstrom MC, Kuusela AL, Maki R. Metabolic bone disease of prematurity. Ann Med 1996; 28(4):275-82.

46. Wauben IP, Atkinson SA, Grad TL, Shah JK, Paes B. Moderate nutrient supplementation of mother's milk for preterm infants supports adequate bone mass and short-term growth: a randomized, controlled trial. Am J Clin Nutr 1998; 67(3):465-72.

47. Ewer AK, Yu VY. Gastric emptying in pre-term infants: the effect of breast milk fortifier. Acta Paediatr 1996; 85(9):1112-5.

48. Jocson MAL, Mason EO, Schanler RJ. The effects of nutrient fortification and varying storage conditions on host defense properties of human milk. Pediatrics 1997; 100:240-3.

49. Quan R, Yang C, Rubinstein S, Lewiston NJ, Stevenson DK, Kerner JA, Jr. The effect of nutritional additives on anti-infective factors in human milk. Clin Pediatr (Phila) 1994; 33(6):325-8.

50. Chan GM. Effects of powdered human milk fortifiers on the antibacterial actions of human milk. J Perinatol 2003; 23(8):620-3.

51. Telang S, Berseth CL, Ferguson PW, Kinder JM, DeRoin M, Petschow BW. Fortifying fresh human milk with commercial powdered human milk fortifiers does not affect bacterial growth during 6 hours at room temperature. J Am Diet Assoc 2005; 105(10):1567-72.

52. Santiago MS, Codipilly CN, Potak DC, Schanler RJ. Effect of human milk fortifiers on bacterial growth in human milk. J Perinatol 2005; 25(10):647-9.

53. Ovali F, Ciftci I, Cetinkaya Z, Bukulmez A. Effects of human milk fortifier on the antimicrobial properties of human milk. J Perinatol 2006; 26(12):761-3.

54. Askin DF, Diehl-Jones W. Effects of human milk fortifier on bacterial growth and cytokines in breast milk. In: Proceedings of the Annual Meeting. Am Soc Cell Biol. San Francisco, CA; 2002.

55. Rubaltelli FF, Biadaioli R, Pecile P, Nicoletti P. Intestinal flora in breast- and bottle-fed infants. J Perinat Med 1998; 26(3):186-91.

56. Schanler RJ, Lau C, Hurst NM, Smith EO. Randomized trial of donor human milk versus preterm formula as substitutes for mothers' own milk in the feeding of extremely premature infants. Pediatrics 2005; 116(2):400-6.

57. Fenton TR, Tough SC, Belik J. Breast milk supplementation for preterm infants: parental preferences and postdischarge lactation duration. Am J Perinatol 2000; 17(6):329-33.

58. Schanler RJ. Probiotics and necrotising enterocolitis in premature infants. Arch Dis Child Fetal Neonatal Ed 2006; 91:F395-7.

59. Kitajima H, Sumida Y, Tanaka R, et al. Early administration of Bifidobacterium breve to preterm infants: randomised controlled trial. Arch Dis Child 1997; 76:F101-7.

60. Rinne M, Kalliomaki M, Arvilommi H, et al. Effect of probiotics and breastfeeding on the Bifidobacterium and Lactobacillus/Enterococcus microbiota and humeral immune responses. J Pediatr 2005; 147:186-91.

61. Bin-Nun A, Bromiker R, Wilschanski M, et al. Oral probiotics prevent necrotizing enterocolitis in very low birth weight neonates. J Pediatr 2005; 147(2):192-6.

62. Land HM, Rouster-Stevens K, Woods CR, et al. Lactobacillus sepsis associated with probiotic therapy. Pediatrics 2005; 116:517-8.

63. American Academy of Pediatrics. Human milk. In: Pickering LK, Baker CJ, Long SS, McMillan JA (eds). Red Book: 2006 report of the committee on infectious diseases. 27th Ed. Elk Grove Village, IL: American Academy of Pediatrics; 2006:123-30.

64. Arias-Camison JM. Late onset group B streptococcal infection from maternal expressed breast milk in a very low birth weight infant. J Perinatol 2003; 23(8):691-2.

65. Godambe S, Shah PS, Shah V. Breast milk as a source of late onset neonatal sepsis. Pediatr Infect Dis J 2005; 24(4):381-2.

66. Olver WJ, Bond DW, Boswell TC, Watkin SL. Neonatal group B streptococcal disease associated with infected breast milk. Arch Dis Child Fetal Neonatal Ed 2000; 83(1):F48-9.

67. Gastelum DT, Dassey D, Mascola L, Yasuda LM. Transmission of community-associated methicillin-resistant Staphylococcus aureus from breast milk in the neonatal intensive care unit. Pediatr Infect Dis J 2005; 24(12):1122-4.

68. Schanler RJ. CMV acquisition in premature infants fed human milk: reason to worry? J Perinatol 2005; 25(5):297-8.

69. Ekema G, Pedersini P, Milianti S, Ubertazzi M, Minoli D, Manciana A. Colonic stricture mimicking Hirschsprung's disease: a localized cytomegalovirus infection. J Pediatr Surg 2006; 41(4):850-2.

70. Kerrey BT, Morrow A, Geraghty S, Huey N, Sapsford A, Schleiss MR. Breast milk as a source for acquisition of cytomegalovirus (HCMV) in a premature infant with sepsis syndrome: detection by real-time PCR. J Clin Virol 2006; 35(3):313-6.

71. Hamprecht K, Goelz R, Maschmann J. Breast milk and cytomegalovirus infection in preterm infants. Early Hum Dev 2005; 81(12):989-96.

72. Doctor S, Friedman S, Dunn MS, et al. Cytomegalovirus transmission to extremely low-birthweight infants through breast milk. Acta Paediatr 2005; 94(1):53-8.

73. Morgan MA, el-Ghany el SM, Khalifa NA, Sherif A, Rasslan LR. Prevalence of cytomegalovirus (CMV) infection among neonatal intensive care unit (NICU) and healthcare workers. Egypt J Immunol 2003;10(2):1-8.

74. Mussi-Pinhata MM, Yamamoto AY, do Carmo Rego MA, Pinto PC, da Motta MS, Calixto C. Perinatal or early-postnatal cytomegalovirus infection in preterm infants under 34 weeks gestation born to CMV-seropositive mothers within a high-seroprevalence population. J Pediatr 2004; 145(5):685-8.

75. Cheong JL, Cowan FM, Modi N. Gastrointestinal manifestations of postnatal cytomegalovirus infection in infants admitted to a neonatal intensive care unit over a five year period. Arch Dis Child Fetal Neonatal Ed 2004; 89(4):F367-9.

76. Vollmer B, Seibold-Weiger K, Schmitz-Salue C, et al. Postnatally acquired cytomegalovirus infection via breast milk: effects on hearing and development in preterm infants. Pediatr Infect Dis J 2004; 23(4):322-7.

77. Iwanaga M, Zaitsu M, Ishii E, et al. Protein-losing gastroenteropathy and retinitis associated with cytomegalovirus infection in an immunocompetent infant: a case report. Eur J Pediatr 2004; 163(2):81-4.

78. Bradshaw JH, Moore PP. Perinatal cytomegalovirus infection associated with lung cysts. J Paediatr Child Health 2003; 39(7):563-6.

79. Bryant P, Morley C, Garland S, Curtis N. Cytomegalovirus transmission from breast milk in premature babies: does it matter? Arch Dis Child Fetal Neonatal Ed 2002; 87(2):F75-7.

80. Sharland M, Khare M, Bedford-Russell A. Prevention of postnatal cytomegalovirus infection in preterm infants. Arch Dis Child Fetal Neonatal Ed 2002; 86(2):F140.

81. Maschmann J, Hamprecht K, Dietz K, Jahn G, Speer CP. Cytomegalovirus infection of extremely low-birth weight infants via breast milk. Clin Infect Dis 2001; 33(12):1998-2003.

82. Vochem M, Hamprecht K, Jahn G, Speer CP. Transmission of cytomegalovirus to preterm infants through breast milk. Pediatr Infect Dis J 1998; 17(1):53-8.

83. Neuberger P, Hamprecht K, Vochem M, et al. Case-control study of symptoms and neonatal outcome of human milk-transmitted cytomegalovirus infection in premature infants. J Pediatr 2006; 148(3):326-31.

84. Schleiss MR. Role of breast milk in acquisition of cytomegalovirus infection: recent advances. Curr Opin Pediatr 2006; 18(1):48-52.

85. Schleiss MR. Acquisition of human cytomegalovirus infection in infants via breast milk: natural immunization or cause for concern? Rev Med Virol 2006; 16(2):73-82.

86. Meier J, Lienicke U, Tschirch E, Kruger DH, Wauer RR, Prosch S. Human cytomegalovirus reactivation during lactation and mother-to-child transmission in preterm infants. J Clin Microbiol 2005; 43(3):1318-24.

87. Miron D, Brosilow S, Felszer K, et al. Incidence and clinical manifestations of breast milk-acquired Cytomegalovirus infection in low birth weight infants. J Perinatol 2005; 25(5):299-303.

88. Jim WT, Shu CH, Chiu NC, et al. Transmission of cytomegalovirus from mothers to preterm infants by breast milk. Pediatr Infect Dis J 2004; 23(9):848-51.

89. Willeitner A. Transmission of cytomegalovirus (CMV) through human milk: are new breastfeeding policies required for preterm infants? Adv Exp Med Biol 2004; 554:489-94.

90. Gessler P, Bischoff GA, Wiegand D, Essers B, Bossart W. Cytomegalovirus-associated necrotizing enterocolitis in a preterm twin after breastfeeding. J Perinatol 2004; 24(2):124-6.

91. Yasuda A, Kimura H, Hayakawa M, et al. Evaluation of cytomegalovirus infections transmitted via breast milk in preterm infants with a real-time polymerase chain reaction assay. Pediatrics 2003; 111(6 Pt 1):1333-6.

92. Hamprecht K, Maschmann J, Vochem M, Dietz K, Speer CP, Jahn G. Epidemiology of transmission of cytomegalovirus from mother to preterm infant by breastfeeding. Lancet 2001; 357(9255):513-8.

93. American Academy of Pediatrics Committee on Infectious Diseases. 2006 Red Book: Report of the committee on infectious diseases. 27th Ed. American Academy of Pediatrics; 2006.

94. Maschmann J, Hamprecht K, Weissbrich B, Dietz K, Jahn G, Speer CP. Freeze-thawing of breast milk does not prevent cytomegalovirus transmission to a preterm infant. Arch Dis Child Fetal Neonatal Ed 2006; 91(4):F288-90.

95. Curtis N, Chau L, Garland S, Tabrizi S, Alexander R, Morley CJ. Cytomegalovirus remains viable in naturally infected breast milk despite being frozen for 10 days. Arch Dis Child Fetal Neonatal Ed 2005; 90(6): F529-30.

96. Forsgren M. Cytomegalovirus in breast milk: reassessment of pasteurization and freeze-thawing. Pediatr Res 2004; 56(4):526-8.

97. Jones E, King C. Feeding and nutrition in the preterm infant. Philadelphia: Elsevier Churchill Livingstone; 2005.

Chapter 7:
DONOR HUMAN MILK FOR PRETERM INFANTS

Photo courtesy of HMBANA

WHO/UNICEF Joint Statement[1]
"Where it is not possible for the biologic mother to breastfeed, the first alternative, if available, should be the use of human milk from other sources. Human milk banks should be made available in appropriate situations."

Figure 1: Donor Human Milk and the WHO/UNICEF

Although mothers' own milk is clearly best, human milk banking has a long tradition (more than 100 years) in many countries and a recognized role in the care of preterm and ill infants[2-4] (Figure 1). The American Academy of Pediatrics established its first formal guidelines for human milk banks in 1943.[5] Initially, milk was dispensed unprocessed from approximately 50 U.S. milk banks, but with the threat of HIV, the return of tuberculosis, and drug abuse, by 2000, all but five of the milk banks had closed. Those that remained formed the Human Milk Banking Association of North America (HMBANA) in 1985 and adopted strict procedures for donor screening, milk processing (pasteurization), milk storage, and shipping.[6]

With the explosion of research on the possible medical uses of human milk components and the recognition of the benefits of human milk for preterm infants, more attention has been focused on donor human milk. By the end of 2007, the U.S. had eleven non-profit milk banks and one for-profit milk bank (Figure 2). During 2003, North American milk banks processed more than 500,000 ounces of donated human milk that was used for individuals with a variety of diagnoses.[7] Brazil leads the world with over 180 milk banks, processing more than 215,000 liters of donated milk for over 300,000 premature and low birth weight infants, saving the country's Ministry of Health more than $540 million per year.[4, 8] In 2002, the World Health Assembly unanimously endorsed the Global Strategy for Infant and Young Child Feeding, which recommends banked donor milk as an option when an infant cannot breastfeed or mother's expressed breastmilk is unavailable.[9]

Figure 2: Milk Bank Locations[10]

Donor Milk Recipients

While the largest *number* of recipients of heat-treated donor human milk are preterm infants, the largest *volume* of milk is used by older infants and adults. The usual recipients of banked donor milk are VLBW (<1500g) infants whose mothers cannot provide breastmilk for various reasons: maternal illness, medications, substance abuse, or poor social support and resources.[11] Other potential recipients are infants with severe allergies, feeding intolerance, short gut syndrome, malabsorption, and other GI problems who cannot tolerate artificial milks. Post-surgical infants may have feedings advanced more quickly when human milk is used as the initial feeding.[12, 13] As pasteurized milk is devoid of any functional cells, infants with immune deficiencies may benefit from the immunoglobulins and other immune factors without the fear of graft versus host disease.[11, 14]

Donor milk has been used to supply IgA to adult liver transplant patients who were IgA deficient,[15] in patients in immune suppression because of chemotherapy or bone marrow transplant,[16] and in a young adult male with severe gastro-esophageal reflux.[17] Human milk components are under active investigation regarding their ability to induce apoptosis in cancer cells and decrease viral replication (papilloma virus). Human milk has been used for centuries in the treatment of conjunctivitis, otitis externa, and wound healing.

Milk Donors

Human milk donors are usually mothers of healthy term infants between the ages of two and six months,[19] but mothers of preterm infants (less than 32 weeks) also donate excess milk. In Norway, the average amount of milk donated per woman is 29 liters, with two-thirds of the donors CMV-IgG positive.[19] The donors' mean

---

AAP: Breastfeeding and the Use of Human Milk[18]

"Banked human milk may be a suitable feeding alternative for infants whose mothers are unable or unwilling to provide their own milk."

"Fresh human milk from unscreened donors is not recommended because of the risk of transmission of infectious agents."

---

age, number of pregnancies, and education vary by country and region,[19-22] but when questioned, the most common reasons for donation are altruistic.[21-24] Experience has shown that donors do not wish to waste the milk they worked so hard to pump, and they wish to help some other infant or child.[23] Mothers of infants who die may wish to donate milk as a contribution to other infants and as a component of their own grief resolution. Heath care professionals play an important role in introducing milk donation and motivating mothers to donate.[22]

Donor Milk Processing/Banking

There are currently no federal regulations governing milk banks in the United States. Guidelines were first established by the HMBANA,[10] written in cooperation with the U.S. Centers for Disease Control (CDC), the Food and Drug Administration (FDA), and the American Academy of Pediatrics (AAP). Two states (California and New York) require milk banks to hold a tissue bank license, similar to eye and sperm banks. Proprietary procedures have been established by the one commercial milk bank in accordance with FDA regulations governing food facilities.[25]

Whether donating to a HMBANA milk bank or a commercial concern, milk donors receive a full health and lifestyle risk screening, as well as serologic screening for HIV 1 and 2, HTLV 1 and 2, hepatitis B and C, and syphilis. Some populations are also screened for tuberculosis. Medical release forms are obtained to allow the milk bank to contact the prenatal and infant care providers.[7] The mother is given a unique donor identification number and delivers her frozen expressed milk to the milk bank or a collection depot. The commercial milk bank also screens for five drugs of abuse and does DNA "fingerprinting" to identify the donor.[25]

In the milk bank, the milk is carefully logged in, thawed to slurry, and cultured for pathogens. Milk testing positive for staphylococcus aureus, methicillin-resistant staphylococcus aureus, pseudomonas, bacillus species, or an excess of normal stool flora is discarded without further processing. HMBANA milk banks then pasteurize the milk (62.5°C for 30 minutes), while other milk banks may use a variant of the high-temperature short time (HTST) process (72°C for

5-15 seconds). A second culture is obtained after the heating process for quality control, and milk with *any* bacterial growth is discarded. The commercial process also screens for viral activity by polymerase chain reaction (PCR).[25] The milk is given lot numbers and expiration dates, stored, and shipped frozen upon receipt of a prescription to the hospital or patient.

Changes in Human Milk with Processing

The effects of freezing, heating, and handling of human milk are cumulative and affect both the immunologic and nutritional qualities of the milk, as well as the bacterial and viral content. Heat treatment at 56°C (133°F) or greater for 30 minutes reliably eliminates all functional white blood cells and bacteria, inactivates human immunodeficiency virus (HIV)[26] and human T-lymphotrophic virus,[27] and decreases the titers of other viruses. Holder pasteurization [62.5°C (144.5°F) for 30 minutes] reliably inactivates HIV and CMV, and will eliminate or significantly decrease titers of most other viruses.[3, 28] HTST heat treatment for 5 seconds destroys all bacteria and for 15 seconds makes CMV activity undetectable.[29]

Immunologic factors are variously affected by heat treatment, and many studies have found different values for different milk components based on differing milk specimens, handling techniques, and assays. With Holder pasteurization, a significant amount of the IgA, bifid growth factor, and lysozyme remain, lipids are unaffected, but 57% of the lactoferrin and most of the IgG are destroyed.[3, 30-33] Transforming growth factors α and β2, present in human milk, are involved in growth, differentiation, and repair of human intestinal epithelial cells and are unchanged after pasteurization[34] (Table 1, Table 2).

Table 1: Effects of Heat Treatment on Human Milk Components (% Retention)

Component	56 C° X 30 min	62.5 C° X 30 min	72 C° X 15 sec	Preterm formula
S. aureus	100% killed	100% killed	100% killed	?
E. coli	100% killed	100% killed	100% killed	?
S. agalactiae			100% killed	?
CMV		No infectivity	No infectivity	0
Lactoferrin	72%	22%	No change	0
IgA	84%	51%	No change	0
Lysozyme	123%	100%	293%	0
Phosphatase	25%	1.4%		0
Vits B_1, B_2, B_6, Folic acid, C	No change	No change	No change	Adequate

Adapted from: Arnold et al., 1993;[35] Goldblum et al., 1984;[29] Hamprecht et al., 2004;[36] and Terpstra et al., 2007[37]

In general, nutritional components may be altered somewhat, but Holder pasteurization does not appear to influence nitrogen retention in LBW infants.[38] Vitamins A, D, E, B_2, and B_6, choline, niacin, and pantothenic acid are only slightly affected by pasteurization, while thiamine was reduced up to 25%, biotin up to 10%, and vitamin C up to 35%.[39] The essential fatty acids found naturally in human milk, arachadonic acid and docosahexaenoic acid, are not affected by pasteurization.[40-42]

Table 2: Impact of Processing on Immunologic Properties

Factor (NC = No Change)	Storage 0-4°C	Storage -20°C	Heat-Treatment 56°C X 30 min
IgA	NC	NC	Stable ($\downarrow$@ 62.5°C)
SIgA	NC	NC	Stable ($\downarrow$@ 62.5°C)
Lactoferrin	NC	NC	NC ($\downarrow$@ 62.5°C)
Lysozyme	NC	NC	NC ($\downarrow$@ 62.5°C)
C3 Complement	NC	NC	NC
Bifidum Factor	NC	NC	Stable

Source: Adapted from Lawrence, 1999.[32] Reprinted with permission from Wiley-Blackwell Publishing.

Refrigeration of fresh milk beyond 72 hours lowers the bacteriocidal activity.[43] Freezing affects lipids in human milk by breaking down fat globules, thereby increasing the surface available for lipase activity[44] and lessening the palatability of the milk to the infant. Microwaving clearly decreases the anti-infective properties of human milk; the higher the temperature, the greater the effect.[45] Readers are referred to a helpful review article with many further references regarding the contents of processed donor human milk.[46] To better preserve the immunologic and nutrient components of human milk, yet preclude transmission of pathogens, experiments are underway using varying heating techniques, lyophilization, and irradiation.[4]

Benefits of Donor Human Milk for Preterm Infants

Donor human milk is species-specific and as noted above, even when processed, retains much of its nutritional and immunologic value,[47] while preterm formulas provide only basic nutrition. Protective effects of human milk on infection rates have been observed with the use of *both* fresh and pasteurized milk.[48-50] Lucas and Cole[48] found a dose-response decrease in NEC with both mother's own and pasteurized donor human milk. In a randomized, controlled trial of 226 high-risk neonates, Narayanan et al.[50] demonstrated that infants given only raw human milk or pasteurized human milk had similar (10.5% versus 14.3%) infection rates. However, when formula was added to each, the heat-treated milk had less protective effect than the raw human milk on infection rates (33% versus 16%) (see below). In Norway, where fresh and pasteurized donor human milk are used routinely for VLBW infants, late-onset sepsis was reduced by early feeding of both mothers' own and donor milk.[51] Two meta-analyses of the limited available literature prior to 2005[52, 53] found significant reductions in NEC with pasteurized donor human milk. A more recent study of three hospitals within a single healthcare system found the two centers which used standardized feeding protocols and heat-treated donor human milk had significantly less NEC.[54]

CONCERNS REGARDING DONOR HUMAN MILK FOR PRETERM INFANTS

Nutritional Concerns

As donor human milk is usually milk from mothers of term infants, the nutritional content may be of more concern than mothers' own milk, with insufficient protein, calcium, phosphorus, and sodium for optimal growth. Variability of composition, alteration of nutrients with processing, and loss of nutrients during storage and feeding are also concerns. Although caloric content is not significantly different, lower protein levels in term donor milk result in slower growth.[2, 38, 55-57] This can be overcome with fortification, just as with mothers' own milk (Table 3).

Table 3: Pooled Pasteurized Breast Milk and Untreated Mother's Own Milk (MOM) in the Feeding of VLBW Babies: a RCT.

	MOM	Pooled Term	P Value
Days to regain birth weight	11.5	17.2	< 0.0001
Days from regained birth weight to 1800 grams	32	44	< 0.0001
Growth (gm/d)	16	12	< 0.0001
Increase in head circumference (cm/wk)	0.77	0.74	0.8
Increase in length (cm/wk)	0.77	0.76	0.5

MOM = Mothers' Own Milk
Source: Adapted from: Stein et al., 1986[56] Reprinted with permission from Lippincott, Williams & Wilkins, Inc.

In a randomized, blinded trial of pasteurized donor human milk used as a supplement to mother's own milk, when not enough mother's own milk was available for 23-29 week infants, Schanler et al.[55] found that donor milk offered little short-term advantage over preterm formula for feeding extremely preterm infants. Weight gain was less with donor milk supplementation, and length of stay and retinopathy of prematurity were similar to the preterm formula supplemented group. There was a decrease in NEC and a small decrease in late onset sepsis in the donor milk supplemented group, which were not statistically significantly different from the preterm formula group, possibly due to lower than expected rates of these illnesses in all groups. There was a significant decrease in chronic lung disease with both mothers' own and donor human milk. Importantly, use of mothers' own milk was associated with a significant decrease in length of stay, NEC, late-onset sepsis, chronic lung disease, and retinopathy of prematurity.[55] In this study, only 27% of the mothers who intended to breastfeed had enough milk to meet their infant's needs, and all infants in the study received at least 50% of their intake as mothers' own milk. An interesting finding was that mothers who did the most kangaroo care had the best milk supply, and there was no increase in infant infection with kangaroo care.

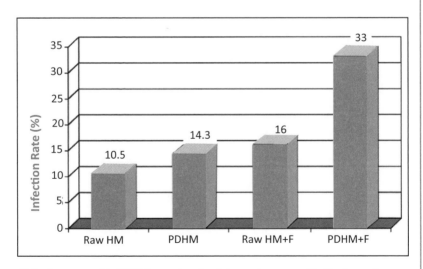

HM = human milk; PDHM = pasteurized donor human milk; F = formula

Figure 3: Infection Rates in High Risk Infants

Source: Adapted from Narayanan et al., 1984.[50] Figure reprinted with permission of Elsevier.

Infection Concerns

As noted above, adding fortifier or formula may change the immune competence of human milk. Narayanan[50] found a significant increase in infection when formula was added to pasteurized donor milk, but not when it was added to raw milk (Figure 3). A recent study demonstrated that the antibacterial activity of preterm human milk was affected by the addition of bovine-based fortifier, but not by the addition of a human breastmilk-based fortifier.[58]

Pasteurized donor human milk is sterile when shipped from the milk bank. Although bacterial contamination during storage and feeding is a possibility, bacterial contamination with processing has not been reported in the U.S.

Neonatologists' Concerns

A survey study of California neonatologists' attitudes and knowledge base of human milk and donor human milk for preterm infants[59] found strong support for mothers' own milk use in the NICU, but a significant lack of basic knowledge about human milk and donor milk. Few neonatologists were aware that breastmilk is not normally sterile or that pasteurized donor milk is. Most neonatologists had no experience with donor milk in their training or clinical practice. Key concerns identified were: accessibility and logistics of obtaining milk; safety and infection control issues; social acceptability and legal issues; and nutritional adequacy and efficacy issues. Obviously, more research and education are needed in this area.

Use of Pasteurized Donor Human Milk in the NICU

The use of heat-treated donor human milk is increasing in U.S. NICUs (Figure 4). Indications for pasteurized donor human milk were tracked in one NICU[61] (Table 4). Amounts used were also tallied (Figure 5). The most common indication was prematurity, and the most common uses were for trophic feedings before mother's own colostrum was available and when a mother's milk supply was insufficient to meet her VLBW infant's needs.

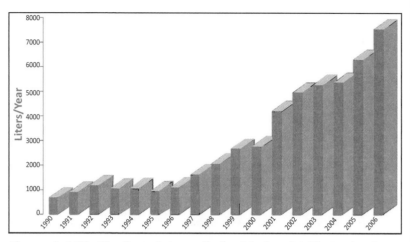

Figure 4: Milk Distributed Annually by Mothers' Milk Bank of San Jose. Source: Cohen, 2007.[60] Reprinted with permission from AAP.

Table 4: Indications for Donor Milk[61]

Primary Indication	2004 (%)	2005 (%)	2006 (%)	2007 (%)
Prematurity/VLBW	67	71	68	71
Feeding intolerance	16.5	14	15	8
IUGR	5.5	3	-	2
Post-NEC	2.5	3.3	3	1
Post GI surgery	2.5	4.3	3	5
Surrogate pregnancy	2.5	1.1	3	5
ISAM*	1.5	-	-	1
Parental request	1.5	-	6	6
Interval delivery	0.5	-	-	-
Other	-	3.3	2	1
*ISAM - infant of substance-abusing mother				

Logistics

As with any medication or procedure in the hospital, the use of donor human milk should be regulated with appropriate policies, procedures, and quality control. Surrogate mothers' milk is used routinely, but it is recommended that fresh milk from a relative or

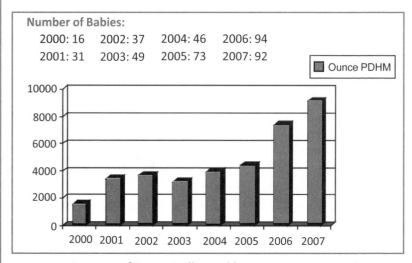

Figure 5: Amount of Donor Milk Used by Year in One 61-Bed Level 3 NICU[61] (PDHM = pasteurized donor human milk)

friend be screened the same as a donor to a milk bank.[62] Just as with mothers' own milk, appropriate procedures for monitoring freezer temperature and handling donor milk are essential.

Donor milk can be ordered as needed for individual infants or a supply can be kept on hand in the NICU for immediate use when ordered by the physician. Lot numbers of the milk are recorded when the infant is fed. Some NICUs use informed consent forms, others information sheets, and in others, it is simply the standard of care.

Commercial Development of Donor Human Milk Products

Commercial milk banking can be compared to commercial blood banking, with individuals donating their milk, the milk bank processing the milk into various components or products, then selling the products back to the hospital or individual. Benefits of this approach are the possibility of decreased cost of the donor milk with economies of scale (not yet realized), lactoengineering of components or mixtures for special populations (e.g., the premature infant or cancer therapy), and most importantly, the recognition of the economic value of human milk. Possible concerns include mothers or collection depots selling milk with potential falsification of screening or harm to the mother's own infant, and a competing system for milk donation, with no guarantee that those who need the milk will receive it. Processes for producing many components of human milk are already patented. Research is in progress regarding the risks and benefits of commercially developed human milk products for preterm infants.

KEY CONCEPTS

● Human milk banking has been around, in one form or another, for a very long time.

● The largest number of donor milk recipients are preterm and low birth weight infants, although the greatest volume of milk is dispensed to older infants and children.

● Human milk donors are generally mothers of healthy term infants, and as such, their unfortified milk may not be appropriate for VLBW infants without fortification.

● Various forms of heat treatment alter the components of human milk, usually reducing the immunologic factors to various degrees. (Preterm formula has none of these factors, however!)

● Although research is limited, it appears heat-treated donor human milk does reduce necrotizing enterocolitis and late-onset sepsis.

● The use of donor human milk in NICUs is increasing, as is the commercial development of nutritional products made from donor human milk.

● Much more research is needed in order to be assured of the safest and most effective method(s) of processing human milk for all of its recipients.

REFERENCES

1. WHO/UNICEF. WHO/UNICEF Joint Statement. Meeting on infant and young child feeding. J Nurse-Midwifery 1980; 25:31-8.

2. Williamson S, Hewitt JH, Finucane E, Gamsu HR. Organisation of bank of raw and pasteurised human milk for neonatal intensive care. Br Med J 1978; 1(6110):393-6.

3. Lawrence RA, Lawrence RM. Breastfeeding: a guide for the medical profession. 6th Ed. St. Louis, MO.: Elsevier/Mosby; 2005.

4. Arnold LDW. Chapter 14: Donor human milk banking. In: Riordan J (ed). Breastfeeding and human lactation. 3rd Ed. Boston: Jones and Bartlett; 2005:409-34.

5. American Academy of Pediatrics, Committee on Mother's Milk. Operation of mother's milk bureaus. J Pediatr 1943; 23:112.

6. Human Milk Banking Association of North America. Best practice for expressing, storing and handling human milk in hospitals, homes and child care settings. Raleigh: Human Milk Banking Association of North America; 2005.

7. Updegrove K. Human milk banking in the United States. Newborn and Infant Nursing Reviews 2005; 5(1):27-33.

8. IBFAN. Brazil leads the world in human milk banks. IBFAN INFO November 2001; 3(4):5.

9. World Health Organization, UNICEF. Global strategy for infant and young child feeding. Geneva, http://whqlibdoc.who.int/ publications/2003/9241562218.pdf: WHO; 2003.

10. Human Milk Banking Association of North America. 2008. (Accessed March 29, 2008, at http://www.hmbana.org.)

11. Wight NE. Commentary: donor human milk for preterm infants. J Perinatol 2001; 21:249-54.

12. Rangecroft L, de San Lazaro C, Scott J. A comparison of the feeding of the post-operative newborn with banked breastmilk or cow's milk feeds. J Pediatr Surg 1978; 13:11-2.

13. Riddell D. Use of banked human milk for feeding infants with abdominal wall defects. In: Annual meeting of the Human Milk Banking Association of North America, 1989. Vancouver, BC, Canada, Oct 15; 1989.

14. Tully MR. Banked human milk and the treatment of IgA deficiency and allergy symptoms. J Hum Lact 1990; 6(2):75.

15. Merhav HJ, Wright HI, Mieles LA, Van Thiel DH. Treatment of IgA deficiency in liver transplant recipients with human breast milk. Transpl Int 1995; 8(4):327-9.

16. Asquith MT, Pedrotti PW, Stevenson DK, Sunshine P. Clinical uses, collection, and banking of human milk. Clin Perinatol 1987; 14(1):173-85.

17. Wiggins PK, Arnold LD. Clinical case history: donor milk use for severe gastroesophageal reflux in an adult. J Hum Lact 1998; 14(2):157-9.

18. American Academy of Pediatrics, Section on Breastfeeding. Policy Statement: Breastfeeding and the use of human milk. Pediatrics 2005; 115(2):496-506.

19. Lindemann PC, Foshaugen I, Lindemann R. Characteristics of breast milk and serology of women donating breast milk to a milk bank. Arch Dis Child Fetal Neonatal Ed 2004; 89:F440-1.

20. Almeida SG, Dorea JG. Quality control of banked milk in Brasilia, Brazil. J Hum Lact 2006; 22(3):335-9.

21. Azema E, Callahan S. Breast milk donors in France: a portrait of the typical donor and the utility of milk banking in the French breastfeeding context. J Hum Lact 2003; 19(2):199-202.

22. Pimenteira Thomaz AC, Maia Loureiro LV, da Silva Oliveira T, et al. The human milk donation experience: motives, influencing factors, and regular donation. J Hum Lact 2008; 24(1):69-76.

23. Arnold LD, Borman LL. What are the characteristics of the ideal human milk donor? J Hum Lact 1996; 12(2):143-5.

24. Osbaldiston R, Mingle LA. Characterization of human milk donors. J Hum Lact 2007; 23(4):350-7; quiz 8-61.

25. Milk safety and processing. Prolacta Bioscience, 2008. (Accessed March 29, 2008, at www.prolacta.com.)

26. Orloff SL, Wallingford JC, McDougal JS. Inactivation of human immunodeficiency virus type I in human milk: effects of intrinsic factors in human milk and of pasteurization. J Hum Lact 1993; 9(1):13-7.

27. Yamato K, Taguchi H, Yoshimoto S, et al. Inactivation of lymphocyte-transforming activity of human T-cell leukemia virus type I by heat. Jpn J Cancer Res 1986; 77(1):13-5.

28. American Academy of Pediatrics, Committee on Infectious Diseases. 2006 Red Book: Report of the committee on infectious diseases. 27th Ed. American Academy of Pediatrics; 2006.

29. Goldblum RM, Dill CW, Albrecht TB, Alford ES, Garza C, Goldman AS. Rapid high-temperature treatment of human milk. J Pediatr 1984; 104(3):380-5.

30. Evans TJ, Ryley HC, Neale LM, Dodge JA, Lewarne VM. Effect of storage and heat on antimicrobial proteins in human milk. Arch Dis Child 1978; 53(3):239-41.

31. Ford JE, Law BA, Marshall VM, Reiter B. Influence of the heat treatment of human milk on some of its protective constituents. J Pediatr 1977; 90(1):29-35.

32. Lawrence RA. Storage of human milk and the influence of procedures on immunological components of human milk. Acta Paediatr Suppl 1999; 88(430):14-8.

33. Welsh JK, May JT. Anti-infective properties of breast milk. J Pediatr 1979; 94(1):1-9.

34. McPherson RJ, Wagner CL. The effect of pasteurization on transforming growth factor alpha and transforming growth factor beta 2 concentrations in human milk. Adv Exp Med Biol 2001; 501:559-66.

35. Arnold LD, Larson E. Immunologic benefits of breast milk in relation to human milk banking. Am J Infect Control 1993; 21(5):235-42.

36. Hamprecht K, Maschmann J, Muller D, et al. Cytomegalovirus (CMV) inactivation in breast milk: reassessment of pasteurization and freeze-thawing. Pediatr Res 2004; 56(4):529-35.

37. Terpstra FG, Rechtman DJ, Lee ML, et al. Antimicrobial and antiviral effect of high-temperature short-time (HTST) pasteurization applied to human milk. Breastfeed Med 2007; 2(1):27-33.

38. Schmidt E. Effects of varying degrees of heat treatment on milk protein and its nutritional consequences. Acta Paediatr Scand Suppl 1982; 296:41-3.

39. Van Zoeren-Grobben D, Schrijver J, Van den Berg H, Berger HM. Human milk vitamin content after pasteurisation, storage, or tube feeding. Arch Dis Child 1987; 62(2):161-5.

40. Fidler N, Sauerwald TU, Demmelmair H, Koletzko B. Fat content and fatty acid composition of fresh, pasteurized, or sterilized human milk. Adv Exp Med Biol 2001; 501:485-95.

41. Fidler N, Sauerwald TU, Koletzko B, Demmelmair H. Effects of human milk pasteurization and sterilization on available fat content and fatty acid composition. J Pediatr Gastroenterol Nutr 1998; 27(3):317-22.

42. Luukkainen P, Salo MK, Nikkari T. The fatty acid composition of banked human milk and infant formulas: the choices of milk for feeding preterm infants. Eur J Pediatr 1995; 154(4):316-9.

43. Martinez-Costa C, Silvestre MD, Lopez MC, Plaza A, Miranda M, Guijarro R. Effects of refrigeration on the bactericidal activity of human milk: a preliminary study. J Pediatr Gastroenterol Nutr 2007; 45(2):275-7.

44. Garza C, Hopkinson JM, Schanler RJ. Human milk banking. In: Howell RR, Morriss RH, Pickering LK (eds). Human milk in infant nutrition and health. Springfield, IL: Charles C. Thomas; 1986:225-55.

45. Quan R, Yang C, Rubinstein S, et al. Effects of microwave radiation on anti-infective factors in human milk. Pediatrics 1992; 89(4 Pt 1):667-9.

46. Tully DB, Jones F, Tully MR. Donor milk: what's in it and what's not. J Hum Lact 2001; 17(2):152-5.

47. Goes HC, Torres AG, Donangelo CM, Trugo NM. Nutrient composition of banked human milk in Brazil and influence of processing on zinc distribution in milk fractions. Nutrition 2002; 18(7-8):590-4.

48. Lucas A, Cole TJ. Breast milk and neonatal necrotising enterocolitis. Lancet 1990; 336:1519-23.

49. Narayanan I, Prakash K, Bala S, Verma RK, Gujral VV. Partial supplementation with expressed breast-milk for prevention of infection in low-birth-weight infants. Lancet 1980; 2(8194):561-3.

50. Narayanan I, Prakash K, Murthy NS, Gujral VV. Randomised controlled trial of effect of raw and holder pasteurised human milk and of formula supplements on incidence of neonatal infection. Lancet 1984; 2(8412):1111-3.

51. Ronnestad A, Abrahamsen TG, Medbo S, et al. Late-onset septicemia in a Norwegian national cohort of extremely premature infants receiving very early full human milk feeding. Pediatrics 2005; 115(3):e269-76.

52. McGuire W, Anthony MY. Donor human milk versus formula for preventing necrotising enterocolitis in preterm infants: systematic review. Arch Dis Child Fetal Neonatal Ed 2003; 88(1):F11-4.

53. Boyd CA, Quigley MA, Brocklehurst P. Donor breast milk versus infant formula for preterm infants: a systematic review and meta-analysis. Arch Dis Child Fetal Neonatal Ed 2007; 92(3):F169-75.

54. Wiedmeier SE, Henry E, Baer VL, et al. Center differences in NEC within one health-care system may depend on feeding protocol. Am J Perinatol 2008; 25(1):5-11.

55. Schanler RJ, Lau C, Hurst NM, Smith EO. Randomized trial of donor human milk versus preterm formula as substitutes for mothers' own milk in the feeding of extremely premature infants. Pediatrics 2005; 116(2):400-6.

56. Stein H, Cohen D, Herman AA, et al. Pooled pasteurized breast milk and untreated own mother's milk in the feeding of very low birth weight babies: a randomized controlled trial. J Pediatr Gastroenterol Nutr 1986; 5(2):242-7.

57. Williamson S, Finucane E, Ellis H, Gamsu HR. Effect of heat treatment of human milk on absorption of nitrogen, fat, sodium, calcium, and phosphorus by preterm infants. Arch Dis Child 1978; 53(7):555-63.

58. Chan GM, Lee ML, Rechtman DJ. Effects of a human milk-derived human milk fortifier on the antibacterial actions of human milk. Breastfeed Med 2007; 2(4):205-8.

59. Wight NE. Neonatologists' attitudes and practice on the use of mother's own and pasteurized donor human milk in the NICU. Academy of Breastfeeding Medicine News and Views 2003; 9(4):32-3; Abstract P21.

60. Cohen RS. Current issues in human milk banking. NeoReviews 2007; 8(7):e289.

61. Wight NE. Personal communication: NICU donor milk statistics 2004-2007. 2008.

62. California Perinatal Quality Care Collaborative PQIP. Toolkit: Nutritional support of the VLBW infant, part 2. In: California Perinatal Quality Care Collaborative, Perinatal Quality Improvement Panel, www.cpqcc.org; 2005.

Chapter 8:
MANAGING BREASTFEEDING IN THE NICU

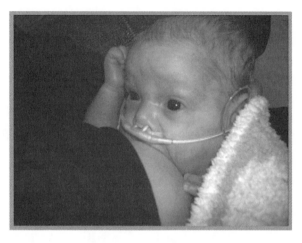

Breastfeeding premature infant on nasal cannula oxygen in NICU
(Photo courtesy of Nancy Wight MD)

There are two major barriers that undermine successful lactation management in the NICU. The first is the misconception that management of lactation can be postponed until the mother has recovered and the baby is deemed stable. The other is the prevalent attitude that the responsibility for lactation support rests with a small number of specialized care providers and/or the mother versus a collaborative team that includes physicians.[1, 2] To overcome these barriers, specific guidelines need to be in place to avoid unnecessary delays and to enlist a team approach.

For a mother, the decision to provide milk for a VLBW infant is quite distinct from the decision to breastfeed a healthy, term infant.[2] First, the decision is usually made based on health-related issues (i.e., the vulnerability of the infant puts him at greater risk of diseases from which breastmilk may protect him). Socioeconomic factors associated with initiation rates for term mothers may not influence those preterm mothers who learn of the protective benefits of their milk.[3] Second, mothers who did not intend to breastfeed, often decide to pump, while not planning to feed at the breast.[4] Third, mothers are highly influenced by the advice of professionals who care for the infant, feeling thankful for (not coerced by) their guidance and even resentful if misinformed about formula being equally acceptable [5] (see Chapter 11).

Establishing Maternal Milk Supply

The volume of milk produced by a pump-dependent mother is the strongest determinant of the duration and exclusivity of breastfeeding the very low birth weight (VLBW, < 1500 g) infant. Mothers of full-term infants produce 550-700 grams of milk by day six post-partum[6-8] (Table 1). In a study by Hill et al.,[9] milk output reached a maximum at two weeks post-partum, then gradually declined over the next three weeks, and milk production was lower in mothers of VLBW infants compared to mothers of term infants.

Table 1: Expected Milk Volumes at Term

Hours post birth	Volume mL (SD)/24 hrs	Volume mL per pumping
24	50 (± 100)	5-15
36	120 (± 20)	5-15
48	180 (± 20)	15-25
60	340 (± 30)	30-45
72	440 (± 50)	45-60
96	600 (± 60)	45-75
Day 10-14 Post-partum		
Ideal	> 750 mL/24 hrs	90 mL/pumping
Borderline	350-500mL/24 hrs	
Low	< 350 mL/24 hrs	

Source: Adapted from Hurst & Meier, 2005[21] and Neville, 1995.[22]

The average baseline milk production on days six to seven postpartum is highly predictive of adequacy of milk volume (defined as ≥ 500 mL/d) at six weeks post-partum.[9-11] Mothers of preterm infants are 2.8 times more at risk of not producing adequate milk than term mothers who fully breastfeed, although a better comparison group would be mothers of full-term infants who are exclusively pumping and not breastfeeding.

It is not clear to what extent, if any, preterm birth contributes to limitation of milk supply in mothers of VLBW infants. Lactogenesis I (the hormonal preparation and growth of breast tissue) starts during pregnancy.[12] Some experts suggest that the mother of an extremely preterm infant may be at a disadvantage regarding milk production, as she has not had sufficient time for breast growth and development. Based on the usual changes in lactogenesis II markers (milk citrate, lactose, sodium, and total protein), Cregan et al.[13] concluded that 82% of preterm women had a compromised initiation of lactation. Also, lactogenesis II may be delayed in mothers of very preterm infants.[13,14]

In one study,[15] milk production in the first week of breast pumping was not related to gestational age at delivery and was similar to milk production after a full-term pregnancy. In other studies,[9, 11, 16] infant gestational age was inversely related to onset of lactogenesis and milk volume. Mothers with extremely preterm births had both delayed lactogenesis and reduced milk volumes compared to those with birth between 28 to 34 weeks. Stress and fatigue may also affect the milk ejection reflex,[17] although one study found that perceived stress, sleep difficulty, and fatigue during the first six weeks postpartum were not related to milk volume.[18]

Lack of maternal-infant contact, as experienced by mothers of breastfeeding term infants, may reduce the neuro-hormonal stimulus of oxytocin and prolactin.[19, 20] Establishing a daily milk volume of 800-1000 mL by ten to fourteen days post delivery ensures that even if a mother's milk supply drops by 50% during the infant's hospitalization, the mother will still have enough milk to feed her preterm infant at the time of discharge.[21]

Mechanical Milk Expression

Early, frequent, and effective breastfeeding or milk expression, usually using an electric pump, has been shown to be the most important factor in establishing normal lactation.[23-25] Prolactin bursts associated with infant suckling or the mother breast pumping may support the continued growth of secretory tissue in the maternal breast for several weeks or months after birth.[26] Initiating early expression (within the first day) is associated with higher levels of milk production.[23-25, 27, 28] Recommendations for the ideal frequency of pumping (8-10 times every 24 hours) are based on the frequency of breastfeeding a term infant, but research has demonstrated most mothers pump five to six times/24 hours.[23,29] An individual mother may need to pump more or less frequently depending on her breast storage capacity and rate of milk synthesis.[30,31] The object is to maximize each mother's milk supply while minimizing the number of minutes per day she needs to spend on milk expression.[31]

Early initiation of expression is also recommended, within the first six hours post-partum[23] or as soon after delivery as the mother is stable (not "recovered").[2] A recent study of mothers with infants less than 30 weeks demonstrated increased milk volumes by two weeks post-partum in mothers who used frequent hand expression (greater than five times per day), in addition to electric pumping in the first three post-partum days.[32] Despite pumping with the same frequency, the mean milk output on day 14 was 780 mL/day versus 443mL/day for those who used hand expression greater than five times/day versus less than two times/day in the first three days (p <0.01).

The initiation and maintenance of lactation for mothers of VLBW infants is best accomplished with a hospital grade, automatic-cycling electric "double" pump (Figure 1).[33-35] In contrast to sequential pumping, the double pump results in higher milk yield, reduced time, and a higher prolactin level.[33-35] Current research is attempting to improve the efficiency of available pumps.[36,37] A rental grade "double," electrical pump, enabling a mother to pump both breasts simultaneously, should be consistently available to the mother during her hospital stay and at discharge. In addition, staff should be available and committed to assisting mothers with a regular pumping schedule, as frequently these mothers are physically compromised by medications or illness.

Several recommendations based on expert experience are provided to increase the percent of expressed milk. Mothers are to be encouraged to pump at their infant's bedside where they can see, touch, or hold their infants while expressing milk,[38] possibly facilitating oxytocin release. Additionally, mothers are advised to pump until milk droplets stop flowing, plus another two minutes to promote greater emptying. Although maximal milk expression usually takes 10-15 minutes in mothers of term infants, the time is extremely variable from woman to woman and at various times during lactation.[37] Creamatocrit monitoring may be a tool to

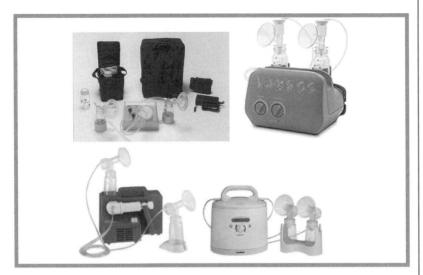

Figure 1: Examples of Breast Pumps (Image rights courtesy of Limerick, Inc. (top left), Ameda, Inc. (top right), and Medela, Inc. (bottom)

---

ensure complete emptying, as degree of breast fullness is inversely proportional to fat content of the milk.[37,39]

Keeping Score

For the mother of the VLBW infant, keeping a pumping diary of milk production is the equivalent of charting lactation vital signs. In centers with successful implementation of lactation support, a NICU-designed log for mothers to record their pumping history cues mothers to visit, pump, and hold their infants frequently[38,40] (Figure 2). Such charting, if regularly recognized by the NICU staff, may encourage pumping and skin-to-skin care. Ongoing monitoring of a mother's milk supply via a pumping log and lactation vital signs can provide opportunity for intervention before the milk supply is irretrievably low.

Early Colostrum Feeds

Aside from the health advantages for the infant of initiating early feedings with colostrum, there are benefits for the mother and staff as well. The use of human milk for trophic feeds in VLBW infants

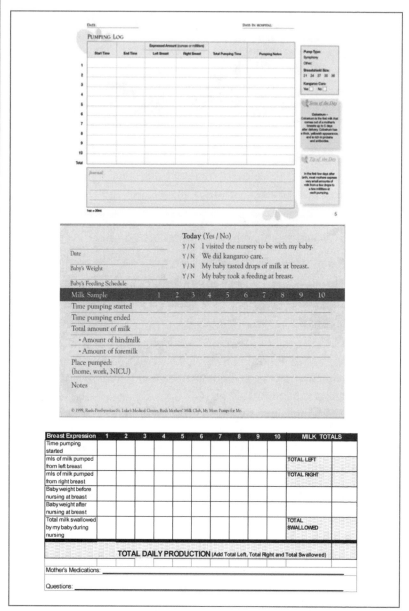

Figure 2: Examples of Milk Expression Logs: Top - Medela Pumping Log (Image rights granted by Medela, Inc.); Middle - Rush Mothers' Milk Club® (All Rights Reserved, Rush-Presbyterian St. Luke's Medical Center); Bottom - Lucile Packard Children's Hospital at Stanford (Courtesy of Jane Morton MD)

is associated with improved milk production.[41] This may be related to a subtle psychological benefit mothers experience in knowing their own milk is being utilized. In addition, the use of human milk provides protection, similar to a live vaccination, as well as nutrition that is superior to preterm formula.

Other Non-Pharmacologic Methods

Early non-pharmacological means to stimulate milk production include expressing milk while relaxed at the bedside (or in proximity to the infant),[38,42] skin-to-skin care,[43,44] and non-nutritive tasting at the breast.[45] In many nurseries, skin-to-skin care is practiced when the infant is stable, on or off the ventilator[46] (Figure 3). Non-nutritive tasting may be accomplished while the baby is on nasal-CPAP.[47] These interventions may stimulate both prolactin and oxytocin as mothers become conditioned to readily let down with psychological and tactile stimulants. Oxytocin promotes energy storage, calmness, and socialization.[48] Psychological inhibitors of the neuro-endocrine let-down reflex include fear, pain, and embarrassment, while positive stimuli include the sight, sound, or feel of the infant.[49] The average pumped milk yield without letdown is less than 4% of available milk.[36, 50] The key to milk production is milk removal, which is partially dependent on the let-down reflex.

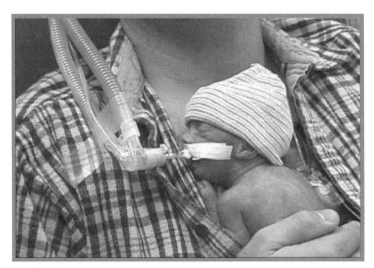

Figure 3: Kangaroo care with Dad on Ventilator (Photo courtesy of Graham Bernstein MD).

Breast Massage/Hand Expression

Breast massage has been shown to improve milk production, both in mothers who double pump (both breasts simultaneously), as well as those who pump sequentially.[34,51] Effective emptying is critical to maximizing milk production and preventing engorgement and mastitis.[30] Massage of the areolar-nipple area, immediately prior to pumping, may help stimulate a let-down reflex, a prerequisite to effective emptying. In one study, the continuous co-action of vacuum and compression stimuli in a novel breast pump seemed to enhance milk secretion.[52] Manual expression, used in conjunction with electric pumping, may facilitate the collection of small volumes of colostrum and help initiate milk flow when the breasts are engorged.

A recent study of preterm mothers with infants less than 30 weeks, demonstrated a beneficial influence on milk volume in mothers who used two practices: hand expression of colostrum and "hands-on pumping" once the milk comes in.[29] Despite pumping with the same frequency as other study mothers, those who used hand expression of colostrum more than five times per day in the first three postpartum days demonstrated sustained high output over the eight-week study (Figure 4). Once milk came in, mothers were taught "hands-on pumping." Instead of passively relying only on pump suction during the expression session, mothers were taught to use breast compression, massage, and, if needed, hand expression

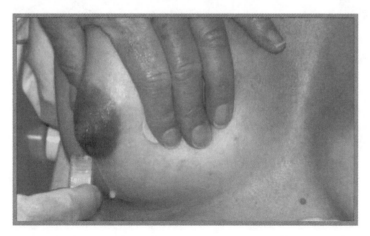

Figure 4: Hand expressing colostrum into a 1 mL collecting vial. (Photo courtesy of Jane Morton MD)

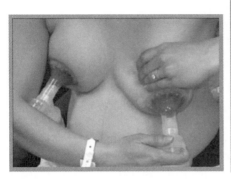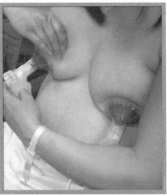

Figure 5: Practicing "hands-on pumping," a mother alternates from one breast to the other and back while applying breast compression over areas that maximize the sprays in the collecting chamber. (Photo courtesy of Jane Morton MD)

(Figure 5). The overall increase in milk volume for 42 mothers was 63%. To achieve this, the mean duration of pumping sessions increased by two minutes. However, the longest unpumped interval (sleeping time) significantly increased and the frequency of daily pumping decreased. By week eight, mothers who used frequent, early hand expression, as well as hands-on pumping, had a mean daily milk volume of over 950 mL/day. The duration for expression ranged from 15 to 45 minutes, averaging 25 minutes, suggesting the risks in advising time limits.

Recent ultrasound studies observing duct dilatation with milk ejection demonstrate several clinically important points:

- mothers have multiple let-downs over the course of the feed/ expression

- the major fraction of milk is released after the first let-down

- at the end of the feed/expression, there is retrograde flow of milk in the milk ducts.[53, 54]

Taking maximal advantage of emptying both breasts immediately after the first let down is important. Possibly, the triple combination of external manual breast compression, pump suction (double pumping), and the milk ejection reflex results in a greater fraction of milk removal from individual alveoli and/or from a greater percentage of alveoli than hands-free pumping.

These results suggest that mothers of preterm infants of any gestational age may be able to attain and sustain high production levels by combining the use of electric pumps with manual techniques. While the availability of high quality pumps is clearly important, reliance on electric pumping alone may compromise milk production potential in pump-dependent mothers. Although the advice to improve output by increasing pumping frequency is standard, it may be equally, if not more, important to improve the effectiveness of expression. Future controlled studies must consider the long-term impact on milk production of sole reliance on pump suction versus "hands-on pumping" in pump-dependent mothers.

Maintaining Maternal Milk Supply

Mothers of preterm infants typically must express milk for weeks before the infant can be put to breast, and for several weeks after discharge, before full exclusive breastfeeding is achieved, if ever.[23, 25] It is very common for a mother of a preterm infant to have her milk supply decrease after four to six weeks of pumping, as she resumes her normal daily routine or returns to work.[55, 56] As milk production is positively related to feeding frequency and degree of emptying,[30, 57, 58] treatment of insufficient milk is centered on increasing the frequency and thoroughness of milk removal. The underlying cause must be ascertained and treated. If impaired let-down is a problem, relieving pain with analgesics and topical treatment of sore nipples may help. Forcing fluids has been shown to have no benefit in increasing a milk supply.[59-61] Mothers need to be educated that they do not need to drink milk to make milk.

Galactogogues

Many medications and herbal therapies have been recommended as galactogogues (a material that stimulates the production of milk).[62,63] Growth hormone,[64] chlorpromazine,[65] thyrotropin-releasing hormone,[66-70] and sulpiride[68-70] have all been shown to induce lactation. Metoclopramide (Reglan®) is most frequently used in the United States due to its safety, efficacy, availability, and relative lack of side effects when compared to the other known galactogogues.[55, 71-77]

Domperidone (Motilium™) is widely used in Canada and Mexico and has fewer side effects because it does not cross the blood-brain barrier, but it is not currently available in the United States.[78-80] A more recent randomized controlled trial of domperidone did not show any difference in milk supply from placebo.[81] The most recent placebo-controlled randomized controlled trial of domperidone (10 mg po three times daily for 14 days) studied 46 mothers (< 31 week preterm infants) with insufficient milk volumes (173 mL/day domperidone group v. 195 mL/day in placebo group) at or after 3 weeks postpartum and found an increase in breast milk volume of 283% in the domperidone group vs. 14% in the placebo group. Serum prolactin also increased significantly in the domperidone group. A surprising finding was significant increases in breastmilk calcium in the domperidone group vs. control group (62% increase vs. 4.4% decrease, p=0.02). There were no significant adverse events in either group.[82] Although oxytocin has traditionally been used to trigger milk ejection, not increase volume, an early study demonstrated an increased supply of colostrum with its use.[83] This outcome was not confirmed by a later clinical study[84] in which dosing was different. More recent data from the rabbit suggests that oxytocin has a role in both secretory activity of the lactating mammary gland and myoepithelial contraction.[85]

More than thirty herbs are considered to be powerful galactogogues.[86,87] Fenugreek (Trigonella Foenum-graecum) is one of the oldest medicinal plants, dating back to Hippocrates and ancient Egyptian times.[88] As fenugreek is a food additive, it is felt to be safe, although mothers' perspiration and milk often smell of maple syrup. Galactogogues are generally prescribed along with recommendations regarding the frequency and thoroughness of expression.

Expressed Breastmilk Storage and Handling

Although human milk has remarkable antibacterial properties, it is not sterile and should be handled and stored properly to maintain its nutritional, developmental, and immunological potential, and prevent transmission of infection.[89-91] Detailed, evidence-based recommendations for all phases of breastmilk collection, storage, thawing, and feeding are available.[90] Close attention to hand washing before expressing or pumping and cleaning of pumping equipment can minimize colonization by pathogens.[91] Glass or hard plastic (food

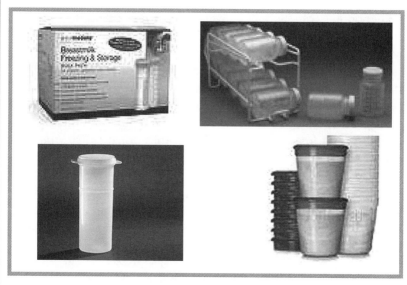

Figure 6: Examples of breastmilk storage containers.

grade polypropylene) containers are preferred for preterm infants, and whenever possible, expressing directly into the final storage containers helps to minimize contamination of the milk (Figure 6). Caregivers handling the milk should pay close attention to hand hygiene and may wear gloves to protect the milk. Surfaces used to prepare the milk for feeding should be cleaned before and after the preparation.

Milk storage recommendations vary for full-term, healthy infants, but all agree that conservative practices are indicated for preterm and ill infants. Evidence-based guidelines are summarized in Table 2.

Table 2: Guidelines for Collection, Storage and Handling of Mothers' Own Milk for Preterm, Hospitalized Infants[21, 89, 90]

Milk Collection
• Wash hands before expressing (gloves not necessary).
• Perform normal body hygiene (no need to wash breasts before pumping).
• Provide initial sterile pump kit for each mother.

- Disassemble pump kit & wash all pieces in contact with milk with hot, soapy water, and rinse with hot water (can use dishwasher) after each use.

- Some experts recommend sterilizing pump kit parts in boiling water for 15-20 minutes each 24 hours.

- Label each bottle with name, Medical Record #, date, and time of pumping.

- Collect milk in hard plastic (polypropylene) or glass with tight lid (NOT nipple).

- Store each collection in a separate container.

- No need for bacteriologic screening (unless possible sepsis or NEC).

Milk Storage

- Use or refrigerate freshly pumped milk within ~ 1 hour of expression.

- May refrigerate for 48 hours before using or freezing.

- Transport milk frozen.

- Freeze for less than 12 months (less than 3 months optimal).

- Do not refreeze any thawed milk.

Thawing

- Thaw milk quickly in warm water bath (maximum 20 minutes).

- Ensure bottle caps are tight to prevent contamination.

- Never thaw in microwave.

- Use thawed milk within 24 hours (48 hours for pasteurized donor milk).

Milk Preparation/Fortification/Warming

- Designate clean space for milk preparation.

- Clean area before and after milk preparation.

- May wear gloves to avoid contaminating milk.

- Add fortifier to room temperature human milk.

- Avoid vigorous shaking.

- Store fortified human milk in refrigerator and use within 24 hours of fortification.

- Warm to room temperature (27°C) before feeding.

- Never microwave to warm.

Feeding
• For continuous milk infusions, limit infusion time to 4 hours.
• Use shortest feeding tubes.
• Use colostrum and milk in order pumped unless freshly pumped is milk available.*
• Use syringe pump upright.
• Give bolus feeds where tolerated.
• Minimize milk exposure to sunlight and phototherapy lights.
• If milk supply is limited, feed milk and formula separately.
* Fresh breastmilk may not be appropriate for very low birth weight infants whose mother's are CMV positive. Freezing reduces CMV activity.

Bacteriologic screening of a mother's own milk for her infant has not been shown to be necessary or cost-effective.[89] Contact with human milk does not constitute an occupational exposure.[92, 93]

"Whereas **universal precautions DO NOT APPLY** to human breast milk, gloves may be worn by health care workers in situations where exposures to breast milk might be frequent, for example in breast milk banking."

■ Centers for Disease Control. MMWR 1988; 37:377-82

"Contact with breast milk **does not constitute an occupational exposure** risk as defined by OSHA standards."

■ Committee on Pediatric AIDS, AAP. Pediatrics 1995; 96:977-79

Appropriate steps should be taken to ensure an individual mother's milk is given only to her own child, unless the milk has been heat-treated under standardized conditions.[89] There are several protocols available in case the wrong mother's milk is given to an infant.[90,94,95] All involve a review of or obtaining appropriate laboratory studies for specific infectious diseases (HIV, Hep B, Hep C, etc.) on the donor mother, and some follow-up of the infant. Fortunately, the risk of transmission of ANY infectious disease is extremely small with a single or a few feedings of the wrong mother's milk.

Strategies to Facilitate Breastfeeding in the NICU

Conceptualizing a strategy to assist the preterm infant to transition from tube or bottle feeding to breastfeeding is easier if one considers what the normal prenatal learning process involves. During the last trimester, the fetus is held so tightly the bones become molded, the skin constantly pressed by this confinement. Warm fluid bathes the surface and inner linings of the body, stimulating growth, behavior, such as swallowing, and the senses, including smell. With each kick, the mother, without reading a book, without lifting a finger, (with effortless learning) becomes increasingly aware that her body is working to support life.

Without the last trimester, the preterm infant spends his hospital life with his extremities extended, touched more by tapes and tubes than by skin. Without his kicks, his mother misses the constant reminders of her carriage, the growing trust in her body, and the mysterious attachment that develops for someone you feel but cannot see.

Any system that supports breastfeeding must address this reality. Instead of focusing on the volume of milk transferred from the breast to the infant, the "baby steps" of learning to breastfeed involve "catch-up" learning. Numerous studies support the benefits of initiating this process early, when the infant is stable and developmentally ready, rather than using gestational age and/or weight as a qualifier (Table 3).

Table 3: Readiness for Feeding Practices

Feeding Practice	Readiness
Skin-to-skin	Safely transfers to and from bed
Non-nutritive breastfeeds	Sucks on pacifier
Early nutritive breastfeeds	Takes ~ 5 ml (test weights)
Semi-demand breastfeeds	Takes ~ 50% of a feed
Full breastfeeds	Wakes for all feeds

Skin-to-skin (Kangaroo) Care

Skin-to-skin care has been shown to be safe and effective in promoting physiologic stability and breastfeeding in preterm infants[96] (Table 4). It is the first step towards a mother being comfortable holding her preterm infant for feeding. There are benefits for both mother and infant from skin-to-skin care.

Skin-to-skin care may be practiced when the infant is stable, on or off the ventilator [47, 116-118] (Figure 7). The duration of skin-to-skin care should depend on maternal availability, not infant criteria unless the infant shows evidence of physiologic instability. The infant should be placed upright between the mother's breasts with the mother reclined.

Non-Nutritive Breastfeeding

Clinical trials of non-nutritive sucking on a pacifier have been shown to decrease length of stay and facilitate transition to oral feeding for preterm infants.[47] A natural extension of kangaroo care, non-nutritive breastfeeding ("dry" breastfeeding or "tasting") offers the mother and infant the chance to practice positioning for breastfeeding and infant suckling before the infant is ready to fully coordinate suck, swallow, and breathing. A mother pumps her breasts before putting the infant to breast, so the infant may get a drop or two of milk while licking, nuzzling, or briefly latching on to the breast. The infant can be orogastric or nasogastric tube fed while suckling on the emptied breast to associate the smell and taste of mother's milk and the feeling of fullness with breastfeeding. Non-nutritive breastfeeding can begin as soon as the infant is extubated.[38] The mother benefits from visualizing her infant's behaviors at the breast and from an increased milk supply and longer breastfeeding post-discharge.[45] As the infant matures, the mother can pump off lesser amounts of milk before breastfeeding, allowing the infant to gradually adapt to a larger and stronger milk flow.

Nutritive Breastfeeding

Nyqvist and colleagues[119] and Lau[120] have described the development of preterm infants' breastfeeding behavior in detail. Irrespective of gestational age, infants demonstrated rooting and sucking behaviors with the first contact at the breast.[119] Infants should be transitioned

Table 4: Benefits of Skin-to-Skin (Kangaroo) Care

Mother	Infant
Increases mother's milk production and prolongs duration of breastfeeding[23, 44, 97, 98]	Improves physiologic stability in terms of heart rate, respiratory rate, oxygen saturation, apnea, and bradycardia spells[98-102]
Fosters parental relaxation, minimizes stress, and improves parental bonding [46, 99-101, 103]	Regulates body temperature[101, 104-107]
Enhances parent's confidence and competence[108]	Increases time in deep sleep and reduces agitation[101, 102, 107]
Stimulates the maternal entero-mammary system. Antigens (e.g., viruses, bacteria, fungi) stimulate lymphocytes in a mother's intestine, which then "home" to her breasts, and there stimulate the production of specific antibodies targeted against those antigens.[109, 110]	Results in higher mean daily weight gain[106] and earlier discharge home[97, 106, 111]
	Decreases pain from heel sticks[112] and other painful procedures[113]
	Fosters neurologic development [101, 114]
	Is associated with fewer infections[97, 111, 115]

to oral feedings when physiologically capable, not based on arbitrary weight or gestational age criteria.[119-122] In a survey of 420 U.S. neonatal intensive care units,[123] fewer than 50% identified a specific feeding policy and 75% used either gestational age or weight criteria in determining when to initiate oral feedings.

There are no minimum gestational age or weight requirements.[123] Infants have been shown capable of breast or bottle-feeding much sooner than previously believed, with some breastfeeding as early as 28 weeks, and achieving full nutritive breastfeeding at 36 weeks.[119, 124-128] The most recent study of 15 infants born at gestational ages of 26 to 31 weeks from Uppsala, Sweden,[128] with breastfeeding initiated as early as 29 weeks corrected age, and use of the Preterm Infant

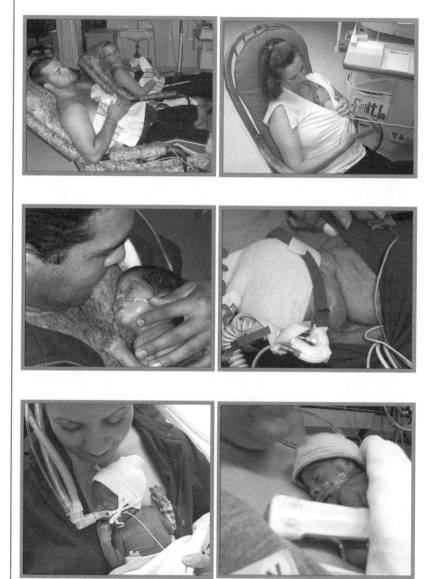

Figure 7: Skin-to-skin (kangaroo) care in many forms (Photos courtesy of Nancy Wight MD)

Breastfeeding Behavior Scale (PIBBS) and semi-demand feeding, revealed full direct breastfeeding (with appropriate weight gain) attained at a mean of 35 weeks (range 32 to 38 weeks). Parent rooms were available in the NICU and mothers roomed-in with their infants, performed PIBBS scores, and did tube and cup feeding as well as breastfeeding. The infants were discharged to "home care" at an average of 35.4 weeks and formally discharged from the hospital at an average of 37 weeks.[128]

Infants can be introduced to the breast (or bottle) as soon as the infant is deemed stable. An infant is deemed stable for the introduction of the breast or bottle when the infant does not have a persistent physiologic decompensation, such as bradycardia or desaturation when handled, the infant is handling his/her own secretions, and shows sucking behavior on a finger, pacifier, or the emptied breast. Introducing the infant to breastfeeding *before* introducing a bottle may facilitate breastfeeding.[129] There is current evidence that early attempts at oral feeding may facilitate more rapid maturation of sucking characteristics.[130]

There is no reason to "test" a preterm infant on a bottle before offering the breast. Controlled studies confirm that breastfeeding infants have more stable oxygen saturation and body temperature as compared to bottle-feeding infants,[131-133] although less milk is transferred with breastfeeding.[131,134-137] The mechanism for this improved stability with breastfeeding seems to be less interruption in breathing with breastfeeding. Bottle-fed preterm infants frequently do not breathe during sucking bursts, instead they breathe rapidly during pauses in sucking.[135,137] In contrast, the same preterm infants integrated breathing within sucking bursts, approximating a suck-breathe pattern of 1:1 as they reached 34-35 weeks gestation. It appears a self-paced[138] or restricted flow[139] system improves duration and efficiency of oral feedings for infants with immature suck-swallow-breathe patterns.

Transitioning directly from gavage to breastfeeding is possible and may prolong both exclusive and any breastfeeding,[140] but requires the mother to be continuously present, which may not be possible because of physical limitations of many NICUs and mothers' outside commitments. Mothers of preterm infants in the U.S., in contrast to other countries (e.g., Sweden), are not expected or facilitated to remain with their infants to encourage earlier breastfeeding competence or to enable the use of at-the-breast supplementation methods, such as a supplemental nursing system. Transported infants' mothers may not be available for frequent feeding practice. The increasing use of individual room NICU care, enabling parents to remain with their ill infants, may well facilitate earlier and increased direct breastfeeding.[94]

Semi-Demand Breastfeeds (Cue-Based Feeds)

Preterm infants allowed to self-regulate intake are at risk for under nutrition until approximately term corrected age.[38] One method of ensuring adequate intake while taking advantage of the preterm infant's developing hunger cues is semi-demand or "cue" based feedings. When an infant demonstrates the ability to take greater than or equal to 50% of his feeds orally (by breast or combination of breast and bottle), scheduled three hour feedings are replaced by an eight hour minimum intake (e.g., 100 mL) which allows the infant his own regulation of sleep and feeding.[141] Test weights can be performed each cue feeding or at the end of the eight hours, and the balance of the needed volume is given by gavage, cup, or bottle. As the infant matures, the period can be changed to 12, 18, or 24 hours to allow for even more self-regulation of sleep and feeding. This plan can be continued at home using small portable electronic scales.[141] A randomized trial of semi-demand feedings versus standard advancement of oral feedings demonstrated a more rapid (by five days) achievement of full oral feedings in the semi-demand group with no difference in weight gain (both acceptable) between the groups.[124]

Test-Weighing

Despite the development of clinical scoring systems,[119, 142] maternal and health care professional clinical estimates of milk intake in preterm breastfeeding infants are unreliable.[143,144] Test

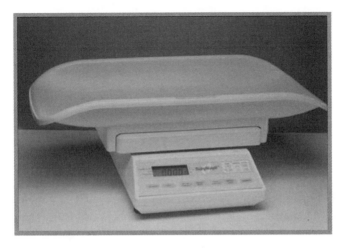

Figure 8: Electronic scale for test-weights (Photo courtesy Medela, Inc.)

---

weighing, done by standard protocol, appears to be a valid measure of intake at the breast and can be used to determine need for supplementation[145,146] (Figure 8). Mothers can test weigh accurately[145,147] and without stress,[148] although there were no significant differences in infant weight gain over the first four weeks post-discharge between the infants who were test-weighed and those who were not.[148] There is some evidence that test-weighing may underestimate intake due to insensible water loss.[149]

Alternative Feeding Methods

Alternative feeding methods have been sought for both term and preterm infants with the presumption that bottle-feeding would interfere with the establishment of breastfeeding. "Nipple preference" is not a new concept. Radiographic and ultrasound studies show a distinct difference between tongue and jaw movements of breast and bottle-feeding full-term infants.[63,150] Given the limitations of feeding ability in preterm infants, it has been common for NICU caregivers to assume (without any evidence) that a nipple with a larger hole and rapid flow would be "easier" for preterm infants. As noted above, slow, restricted flow may be more appropriate to facilitate the development of oral feeding skills and prevent apnea and bradycardia during feedings (Figure 9).

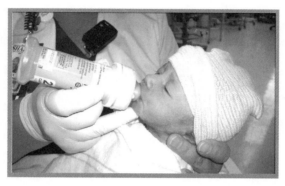

Figure 9: Bottle feeding a preterm infant – an "alternative" feeding method (to breastfeeding) (Photo courtesy of Nancy Wight MD)

Although research as to efficacy is limited, **cup-feeding** appears safe for preterm infants[151-157] and may facilitate longer breastfeeding post-discharge,[158,159] although it may necessitate a somewhat longer hospital stay[158] (Figure 10). A significant amount of milk is spilled on the bib (36-38%) during cup feedings.[157,160]

A variant of cup-feeding, the "paladai," a small gravy-boat shaped container with a spout, has been used successfully for preterm infants in India,[157] although it is not clear as to whether the infant sips the milk or it is poured, in small aliquots, into the mouth (Figure 11). A recent pilot study designed to evaluate paladi cup feeding in breastfed infants found that the paladai feedings resulted in increased spillage, increased feeding times, and more stress cues than bottle feeding.[161]

Clinical experience suggests other methods of feeding may be appropriate for specific infants (Figure 12). **Finger-feeding** has been suggested for neurologically impaired infants and all preterm infants.[63,162] In one study, finger-feeding was credited with an improved rate of breastfeeding at discharge, from 44% to 71% in one Australian hospital's special care nursery.[162] **Supplemental nursing systems** at the breast are often used for mothers with insufficient milk supply. Supplemental nursing systems have the advantage of supplying appropriate supplement while simultaneously stimulating the breast to produce more milk. The tubing is taped to the breast, with the end at the nipple. The infant latches on to the breast and

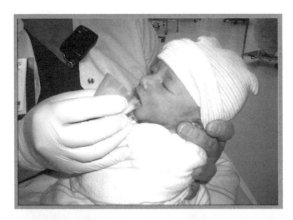

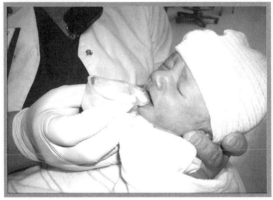

Figure 10: Cup-feeding with medicine cup (top) and Foley Cup Feeder (bottom) (Photos courtesy of Nancy Wight MD)

Figure 11: Paladai feeder (Photo courtesy of Chele Marmet)

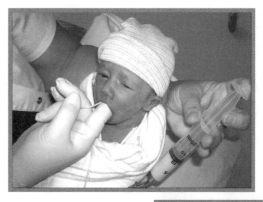

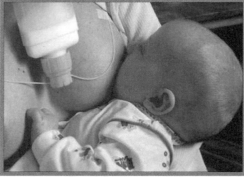

Figure 12: Finger-feeding with feeding tube and syringe (top); SNS in use (bottom) [Photos courtesy of Nancy Wight (top left) and Medela, Inc. (below)]

tube and siphons the supplement from a reservoir. There are various commercial versions (Lact-Aid, Medela SNS), and homemade versions are easy to make. Supplementing at the breast encourages latch-on because of the immediate reward, encourages correct infant suckling technique, and allows baby-led pacing of the feeding, as well as measurement of the amount taken.[63] Unfortunately, supplemental nursing systems may be awkward to use, hard to clean, expensive, and require moderately complex learning.

Droppers, spoons and syringes have been used to supplement preterm infants and have the advantage of being inexpensive, easy to clean, and easy to learn to use. However, they are time consuming, messy, imprecise, and extremely impractical for long-term use. At

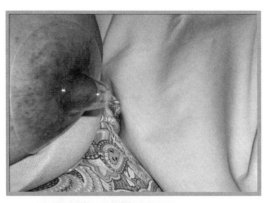

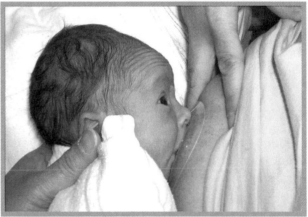

Figure 13: Nipple shield (top) and infant latched on with nipple-shield (bottom). Experts will notice the infant's lower lip is not ideally positioned. Despite this, the infant took 27 mL. (Photos courtesy of Nancy Wight MD)

present, there is no available research on the efficacy of any of these devices. In the absence of additional research, every effort should be made to accommodate mothers' preferences as to feeding methods, as long as appropriate weight gain is maintained.

Weak sucking pressures found in preterm infants may result in difficulty maintaining attachment to the breast and, therefore, ineffective milk transfer.[139] **Nipple shields** (Figure 13) can be used, when appropriate, to maximize milk transfer at the breast.[163,164] Meier et al. found over four times the average milk intake with nipple shield use for those infants not achieving or maintaining effective attachment to the breast or for those infants quickly falling asleep at the breast. There was no significant association between duration of nipple use and duration of breastfeeding.[164]

Furman studied 105 former VLBW infants at 35 weeks corrected age with a standard feeding observation: 35 breastfeeding and 70 bottle-feeding. Breastfeeding infants, as compared to bottle-feeding infants, took in smaller volumes, fed less efficiently, and spent less time with sucking bursts.[136] These data support the clinical impression of many caregivers in the NICU that weight gain, full oral feeds, and therefore discharge home, are more reliably achieved with bottle-feeding. Bottle-feeding is not physiologically "easier," but it appears more efficient, especially given the following observation. "To successfully breastfeed, the infant must be an "active" participant in the process. In contrast, bottle-feeding can be encouraged or even forced by the caregiver."[165]

Conclusion

Referencing the World Health Organization's Baby Friendly Hospital Initiative's "Ten Steps" for full term infants,[166] Spatz[167] summarized best practices and proposed ten steps to promote and protect breastfeeding in vulnerable infants:

- Informed decision
- Establishment and maintenance of milk supply
- Breastmilk management
- Feeding of breast milk
- Skin-to-skin care
- Nonnutritive sucking at the breast
- Transition to breast
- Measuring milk transfer
- Preparation for discharge
- Appropriate follow-up

KEY CONCEPTS

- Establishing and maintaining a mother's milk supply is a key factor in transitioning to direct breastfeeding.

- All caregivers should send the unequivocal message that mother's own milk is best for baby.

- Encourage mothers to begin milk expression, both hand expression and electric pumping, immediately and make the choice about breastfeeding later.

- Once the milk "comes in," suggest mothers use "hands-on pumping" instead of reliance on pump suction alone.

- Adjust pumping recommendations to the physiology of the individual mother whenever possible.

- "Keeping score" – i.e., documenting the time, duration, and amount of milk expressed provides useful information for the mother and the NICU staff for maintenance of milk volume

- Although preterm birth may not limit milk production, factors surrounding the birth may adversely affect milk volume. Recent studies suggest these factors can be mitigated by techniques supporting effective and frequent milk removal.

- Kangaroo care and non-nutritive suckling at the emptied breast facilitate transition to full breastfeeding.

- Clinical estimates of milk intake at the breast are unreliable. Test-weighing is accurate, informative, and NOT stressful for mothers.

- Although safe, no "alternate" feeding method has been shown to increase the likelihood of transitioning preterm infants from tube/bottle feeding to breastfeeding.

REFERENCES

1. Powers N, Gwyn L, Bloom B, et al. Process differences related to breastmilk use at NICU discharge. Conference Abstract P11. ABM News and Views 2002; 8(3):25.

2. California Perinatal Quality Care Collaborative PQIP. Toolkit: Nutritional support of the VLBW infant, part 1. In: California Perinatal Quality Care Collaborative, Perinatal Quality Improvement Panel, www.cpqcc.org; 2004.

3. Sisk PM, Lovelady CA, Dillard RG, Gruber KJ. Lactation counseling for mothers of very low birth weight infants: effect on maternal anxiety and infant intake of human milk. Pediatrics 2006; 117(1):e67-75.

4. Meier P, Engstrom J, Spanier-Mingolelli S, et al. Dose of own mothers' milk provided by low-income and non-low income mothers of very low birthweight infants (abstract). Pediatric Research 2000; 47:292A.

5. Miracle DJ, Meier PP, Bennett PA. Mothers' decisions to change from formula to mothers' milk for very-low-birth-weight infants. J Obstet Gynecol Neonatal Nurs 2004; 33(6):692-703.

6. Arthur PG, Smith M, Hartmann PE. Milk lactose, citrate, and glucose as markers of lactogenesis in normal and diabetic women. J Pediatr Gastroenterol Nutr 1989; 9(4):488-96.

7. Saint L, Smith M, Hartmann PE. The yield and nutrient content of colostrum and milk of women from giving birth to 1 month post-partum. Br J Nutr 1984; 52(1):87-95.

8. Hartmann P, Sherriff J, Kent J. Maternal nutrition and the regulation of milk synthesis. Proc Nutr Soc 1995; 54(2):379-89.

9. Hill PD, Aldag JC, Chatterton RT, Zinaman M. Comparison of milk output between mothers of preterm and term infants: the first 6 weeks after birth. J Hum Lact 2005; 21(1):22-30.

10. Hill PD, Aldag JC. Milk volume on day 4 and income predictive of lactation adequacy at 6 weeks of mothers of nonnursing preterm infants. J Perinat Neonatal Nurs 2005; 19(3):273-82.

11. Hill PD, Aldag JC, Chatterton RT, Zinaman M. Primary and secondary mediators' influence on milk output in lactating mothers of preterm and term infants. J Hum Lact 2005; 21(2):138-50.

12. Neville M, Morton J, Umemura S. Lactogenesis. Pediatric Clinics of North America 2001; 48(1):35-52.

13. Cregan MD, De Mello TR, Kershaw D, McDougall K, Hartmann PE. Initiation of lactation in women after preterm delivery. Acta Obstet Gynecol Scand 2002; 81(9):870-7.

14. Henderson J, Simmer K, Newnham J, Doherty D, Hartmann P. Impact of very preterm delivery on the timing of lactogenesis II in women. Poster #34. In: 12th International Conference of the International Society for Research in Human Milk and Lactation 2004; Queen's College, Cambridge, UK; 2004.

15. Chatterton RT, Jr., Hill PD, Aldag JC, Hodges KR, Belknap SM, Zinaman MJ. Relation of plasma oxytocin and prolactin concentrations to milk production in mothers of preterm infants: influence of stress. J Clin Endocrinol Metab 2000; 85(10):3661-8.

16. Henderson JJ, Hartmann PE, Newnham JP, Simmer K. Effect of preterm birth and antenatal corticosteroid treatment on lactogenesis II in women. Pediatrics 2008; 121(1):e92-100.

17. Dewey KG. Maternal and fetal stress are associated with impaired lactogenesis in humans. J Nutr 2001; 131(11):3012-5S.

18. Hill PD, Aldag JC, Chatterton RT, Zinaman M. Psychological distress and milk volume in lactating mothers. West J Nurs Res 2005; 27(6):676-93; discussion 94-700.

19. Carter CS, Altemus M. Integrative functions of lactational hormones in social behavior and stress management. Ann N Y Acad Sci 1997; 807:164-74.

20. Uvnas-Moberg K. Physiological and endocrine effects of social contact. Ann N Y Acad Sci 1997; 807:146-63.

21. Hurst N, Meier P. Chapter 13: Breastfeeding the preterm infant. In: Riordan J (ed). Breastfeeding and human lactation. 3rd Ed. Boston: Jones and Bartlett; 2005:367-408.

22. Neville MC. Lactogenesis in women. In: Jensen RG. Handbook of Milk Composition. San Diego: Academic Press; 1995, p. 88.

23. Furman L, Minich N, Hack M. Correlates of lactation in mothers of very low birth weight infants. Pediatrics 2002; 109(4):e57 www.pediatrics. org/cgi/content/full/109/4/e57.

24. Smith MM, Durkin M, Hinton VJ, Bellinger D, Kuhn L. Initiation of breastfeeding among mothers of very low birth weight infants. Pediatrics 2003; 111(6 Pt 1):1337-42.

25. Wooldridge J, Hall W. Posthospitalization breastfeeding patterns of moderately preterm infants. J Perinat Neonat Nurs 2003 2003; 17(1):50-64.

26. Cox DB, Kent JC, Casey TM, Owens RA, Hartmann PE. Breast growth and the urinary excretion of lactose during human pregnancy and early lactation: endocrine relationships. Exp Physiol 1999;84(2):421-34.

27. Flacking R, Nyqvist KH, Ewald U, Wallin L. Long-term duration of breastfeeding in Swedish low birth weight infants. J Hum Lact 2003; 19(2):157-65.

28. Hill PD, Aldag JC, Chatterton RT. Effects of pumping style on milk production in mothers of non-nursing preterm infants. J Hum Lact 1999; 15(3):209-16.

29. Morton J, Hall J, Wong R, Rhine W. Combining hand techniques with electric pumping increases milk production in preterm mothers. Submitted for publication 2008.

30. Daly SE, Kent JC, Owens RA, Hartmann PE. Frequency and degree of milk removal and the short-term control of human milk synthesis. Exp Physiol 1996; 81(5):861-75.

31. Jones E, King C. Feeding and nutrition in the preterm infant. Philadelphia: Elsevier Churchill Livingstone; 2005.

32. Morton JA, Hall JY, Thairu L, et al. Early hand expression affects breastmilk production in pump-dependent mothers of preterm infants, Abstract # 7720.9. In: Pediatric Academic Societies; 2007; May 5-8, Toronto, Canada; 2007.

33. Hill PD, Aldag JC, Chatterton RT. The effect of sequential and simultaneous breast pumping on milk volume and prolactin levels: a pilot study. J Hum Lact 1996; 12(3):193-9.

34. Jones E, Dimmock PW, Spencer SA. A randomised controlled trial to compare methods of milk expression after preterm delivery. Arch Dis Child Fetal Neonatal Ed 2001; 85(2):F91-5.

35. Slusher T, Slusher I, Biomdo M, Bode-Thomas F, Redd B, Meier P. Electric breast pump use increases maternal milk volume and decreases time to onset of adequate maternal milk volume in African nurseries. In: Pediatric Academic Societies Meeting, ; 2004; San Francisco, CA, May 1-4, Abstract #2530; 2004.

36. Mitoulas LR, Lai CT, Gurrin LC, Larsson M, Hartmann PE. Effect of vacuum profile on breast milk expression using an electric breast pump. J Hum Lact 2002; 18(4):353-60.

37. Mitoulas LR, Lai CT, Gurrin LC, Larsson M, Hartmann PE. Efficacy of breast milk expression using an electric breast pump. J Hum Lact 2002; 18(4):344-52.

38. Meier PP. Breastfeeding in the special care nursery. Prematures and infants with medical problems. Pediatr Clin North Am 2001; 48(2):425-42.

39. Daly SE, Di Rosso A, Owens RA, Hartmann PE. Degree of breast emptying explains changes in the fat content, but not fatty acid composition, of human milk. Exp Physiol 1993; 78(6):741-55.

40. Meier PP, Engstrom JL, Mingolelli SS, Miracle DJ, Kiesling S. The Rush Mothers' Milk Club: breastfeeding interventions for mothers with very-low-birth-weight infants. J Obstet Gynecol Neonatal Nurs 2004; 33(2):164-74.

41. Schanler RJ, Shulman RJ, Lau C. Feeding strategies for premature infants: beneficial outcomes of feeding fortified human milk versus preterm formula. Pediatrics 1999; 103(6 Pt 1):1150-7.

42. Feher SD, Berger LR, Johnson JD, Wilde JB. Increasing breast milk production for premature infants with a relaxation/imagery audiotape. Pediatrics 1989; 83(1):57-60.

43. Fewtrell MS, Lucas P, Collier S, Singhal A, Ahluwalia JS, Lucas A. Randomized trial comparing the efficacy of a novel manual breast pump with a standard electric breast pump in mothers who delivered preterm infants. Pediatrics 2001; 107(6):1291-7.

44. Hurst NM, Valentine CJ, Renfro L, Burns P, Ferlic L. Skin-to-skin holding in the neonatal intensive care unit influences maternal milk volume. J Perinatol 1997; 17(3):213-7.

45. Narayanan I. Sucking on the "emptied" breast--a better method of non-nutritive sucking than the use of a pacifier. Indian Pediatr 1990; 27(10):1122-4.

46. Kirsten G, Bergman N, Hann F. Kangaroo mother care in the nursery. Pediatr Clin NA 2001; 48(2):443-52.

47. Pinelli J, Symington A. Non-nutritive sucking for promoting physiologic stability and nutrition in preterm infants. Cochrane Database Syst Rev 2005(4):CD001071.

48. Uvnas-Moberg K, Johansson B, Lupoli B, Svennersten-Sjaunja K. Oxytocin facilitates behavioural, metabolic and physiological adaptations during lactation. Appl Anim Behav Sci 2001; 72(3):225-34.

49. Newton N, Newton M. Psychologic aspects of lactation. N Engl J Med 1967; 277(22):1179-88.

50. Kent JC, Ramsay DT, Doherty D, Larsson M, Hartmann PE. Response of breasts to different stimulation patterns of an electric breast pump. J Hum Lact 2003; 19(2):179-86; quiz 87-8, 218.

51. Morton JA, Hall JY, Thairu L, et al. Breast massage maximizes milk volumes of pump-dependent mothers. Abstract. In: Society for pediatric rsearch; 2007; Toronto Canada; 2007.

52. Alekseev NP, Ilyin VI, Yaroslavski VK, et al. Compression stimuli increase the efficacy of breast pump function. Eur J Obstet Gynecol Reprod Biol 1998; 77(2):131-9.

53. Kent JC, Mitoulas LR, Cregan MD, et al. Importance of vacuum for breastmilk expression. Breastfeed Med 2008; 3(1):11-9.

54. Ramsay DT, Mitoulas LR, Kent JC, et al. Milk flow rates can be used to identify and investigate milk ejection in women expressing breast milk using an electric breast pump. Breastfeed Med 2006; 1(1):14-23.

55. Ehrenkranz RA, Ackerman BA. Metoclopramide effect on faltering milk production by mothers of premature infants. Pediatrics 1986; 78(4):614-20.

56. Hill PD, Aldag JC, Chatterton RT, Jr. Breastfeeding experience and milk weight in lactating mothers pumping for preterm infants. Birth 1999; 26(4):233-8.

57. Daly SE, Hartmann PE. Infant demand and milk supply. Part 2: The short-term control of milk synthesis in lactating women. J Hum Lact 1995; 11(1):27-37.

58. Daly SE, Hartmann PE. Infant demand and milk supply. Part 1: Infant demand and milk production in lactating women. J Hum Lact 1995; 11(1):21-6.

59. Dusdieker LB, Stumbo PJ, Booth BM, Wilmoth RN. Prolonged maternal fluid supplementation in breast-feeding. Pediatrics 1990; 86(5):737-40.

60. Stumbo PJ, Booth BM, Eichenberger JM, Dusdieker LB. Water intakes of lactating women. Am J Clin Nutr 1985; 42(5):870-6.

61. Dusdieker LB, Booth BM, Stumbo PJ, Eichenberger JM. Effect of supplemental fluids on human milk production. J Pediatr 1985; 106(2):207-11.

62. Wight N, Montgomery A. Use of galactogogues in initiating or maintaining maternal milk supply (Protocol #9). In: Academy of Breastfeeding Medicine; 2004.

63. Wight NE. Management of common breastfeeding issues. Pediatric Clinics of North America 2001; 48(2):321-44.

64. Caron RW, Jahn GA, Deis RP. Lactogenic actions of different growth hormone preparations in pregnant and lactating rats. J Endocrinol 1994; 142(3):535-45.

65. Brown RE. Relactation: an overview. Pediatrics 1977; 60(1):116-20.

66. Bose CL, D'Ercole AJ, Lester AG, Hunter RS, Barrett JR. Relactation by mothers of sick and premature infants. Pediatrics 1981; 67(4):565-9.

67. Tyson JE, Perez A, Zanartu J. Human lactational response to oral thyrotropin releasing hormone. J Clin Endocrinol Metab 1976; 43(4):760-8.

68. Aono T, Aki T, Koike K, Kurachi K. Effect of sulpiride on poor puerperal lactation. Am J Obstet Gynecol 1982; 143(8):927-32.

69. Ylikorkala O, Kauppila A, Kivinen S, Viinikka L. Sulpiride improves inadequate lactation. Br Med J (Clin Res Ed) 1982; 285(6337):249-51.

70. Ylikorkala O, Kauppila A, Kivinen S, Viinikka L. Treatment of inadequate lactation with oral sulpiride and buccal oxytocin. Obstet Gynecol 1984; 63(1):57-60.

71. Budd SC, Erdman SH, Long DM, Trombley SK, Udall JN, Jr. Improved lactation with metoclopramide. A case report. Clin Pediatr (Phila) 1993; 32(1):53-7.

72. Ertl T, Sulyok E, Ezer E, Sarkany I, Thurzo V, Csaba IF. The influence of metoclopramide on the composition of human breast milk. Acta Paediatr Hung 1991; 31(4):415-22.

73. Gupta AP, Gupta PK. Metoclopramide as a lactogogue. Clin Pediatr (Phila) 1985; 24(5):269-72.

74. Guzman V, Toscano G, Canales ES, Zarate A. Improvement of defective lactation by using oral metoclopramide. Acta Obstet Gynecol Scand 1979; 58(1):53-5.

75. Lewis PJ, Devenish C, Kahn C. Controlled trial of metoclopramide in the initiation of breast feeding. Br J Clin Pharmacol 1980; 9(2):217-9.

76. Sousa PL, Barros FC, Pinheiro GN, Gazalle RV. Breast feeding in Brazil. J Trop Pediatr Environ Child Health 1975; 21(4):209-19.

77. Anderson PO, Valdes V. A critical review of pharmaceutical galactagogues. Breastfeed Med 2007; 2(4):229-42.

78. da Silva OP, Knoppert DC, Angelini MM, Forret PA. Effect of domperidone on milk production in mothers of premature newborns: a randomized, double-blind, placebo-controlled trial. CMAJ 2001; 164(1):17-21.

79. Hofmeyr GJ, Van Iddekinge B, Blott JA. Domperidone: secretion in breast milk and effect on puerperal prolactin levels. Br J Obstet Gynaecol 1985; 92(2):141-4.

80. Petraglia F, De Leo V, Sardelli S, Pieroni ML, D'Antona N, Genazzani AR. Domperidone in defective and insufficient lactation. Eur J Obstet Gynecol Reprod Biol 1985; 19(5):281-7.

81. Hansen W, McAndrew S, Harris K, Zimmerman M. Metoclopramide effect on breastfeeding the preterm infant: a randomized trial. Obstet Gynecol 2005; 105(2):383-9.

82. Campbell-Yeo ML, Allen AC, Joseph KS et al. A Double Blind Placebo Controlled Randomized Trial of the Effect of Domperidone on the Composition of Human Breast Milk. Abstract # 4315.1, May 2-6, 2008, Honolulu, Hawaii.

83. Ruis H, Rolland R, Doesburg W, Broeders G, Corbey R. Oxytocin enhances onset of lactation among mothers delivering prematurely. Br Med J (Clin Res Ed) 1981; 283(6287):340-2.

84. Fewtrell MS, Loh KL, Blake A, Ridout DA, Hawdon J. Randomised, double blind trial of oxytocin nasal spray in mothers expressing breast milk for preterm infants. Arch Dis Child Fetal Neonatal Ed 2006; 91(3):F169-74.

85. Lollivier V, Marnet P, Delpal S, et al. Oxytocin stimulates secretory processes in lactating rabbit mammary epithelial cells. J Physiology 2006; 570(1):125-40.

86. Fleiss PM. Herbal remedies for the breastfeeding mother. Mothering 1988; 48:68.

87. Low Dog T, Micozzi M. Womens' health in complementary and integrative medicine - a clinical guide. New York: Churchill Livingstone; 2005.

88. Huggins K. Fenugreek: One remedy for low milk production. Medela Rental Roundup 1998; 15:16.

89. American Academy of Pediatrics, Committee on Infectious Diseases. 2006 Red Book: Report of the committee on infectious diseases. 27th Ed. American Academy of Pediatrics; 2006.

90. Human Milk Banking Association of North America. Best practice for expressing, storing and handling human milk in hospitals, homes and child care settings. Raleigh: Human Milk Banking Association of North America; 2005.

91. Tully M. Recommendations for handling of mother's own milk. J Hum Lact 2000; 16(2):149-51.

92. Centers for Disease Control and Prevention. Update: Universal precautions for prevention of transmission of human immunodeficiency virus, hepatitis B virus, and other bloodborne pathogens in health-care settings. MMWR Morb Mortal Wkly Rep 1988; 37(24):377-82, 87-8.

93. Committee on Pediatric AIDS. Human milk, breastfeeding, and transmission of human immunodeficiency virus in the United States. American Academy of Pediatrics, Committee on Pediatric AIDS. Pediatrics 1995; 96(5 Pt 1):977-9.

94. California Perinatal Quality Care Collaborative PQIP. Toolkit: Nutritional support of the VLBW infant, part 2. In: California Perinatal Quality Care Collaborative, Perinatal Quality Improvement Panel, www.cpqcc.org; 2005.

95. Warner B, Sapsford A. Misappropriated human milk: fantasy, fear, and fact regarding infectious risk. Newborn & Infant Nursing Reviews 2004; 4(1):56-61.

96. DiMenna L. Considerations for implementation of a neonatal kangaroo care protocol. Neonatal Network 2006; 25(6):405-12.

97. Charpak N, Ruiz-Pelaez JG, Figueroa de CZ, Charpak Y. A randomized, controlled trial of kangaroo mother care: results of follow-up at 1 year of corrected age. Pediatrics 2001; 108(5):1072-9.

98. Bier JA, Ferguson AE, Morales Y, et al. Comparison of skin-to-skin contact with standard contact in low-birth-weight infants who are breast-fed. Arch Pediatr Adolesc Med 1996; 150(12):1265-9.

99. Clifford P, Barnsteiner J. Kangaroo care and the very low birthweight infant: is it an appropriate practice for all premature babies? Journal of Neonatal Nursing 2001; 7(1):14-8.

100. Hosseini R, Hashimi M, Ludington-Hoe S. Preterm infants and fathers: physiologic and behavioral effects of skin-to-skin contact. Ursus Medicus 1992; 2:47-55.

101. Ludington-Hoe SM, Anderson GC, Simpson S, et al. Skin-to-skin contact beginning in the delivery room for Colombian mothers and their preterm infants. J Hum Lact 1993; 9(4):241-2.

102. Messmer PR, Rodriguez S, Adams J, et al. Effect of kangaroo care on sleep time for neonates. Pediatr Nurs 1997; 23(4):408-14.

103. Anderson GC, Dombrowski MA, Swinth JY. Kangaroo care: not just for stable preemies anymore. Reflect Nurs Leadersh 2001; 27(2):32-4, 45.

104. Bauer J, Sontheimer D, Fischer C, Linderkamp O. Metabolic rate and energy balance in very low birth weight infants during kangaroo holding by their mothers and fathers. J Pediatr 1996; 129(4):608-11.

105. Bauer K, Uhrig C, Sperling P, Pasel K, Wieland C, Versmold HT. Body temperatures and oxygen consumption during skin-to-skin (kangaroo) care in stable preterm infants weighing less than 1500 grams. J Pediatr 1997; 130(2):240-4.

106. Cattaneo A, Davanzo R, Bergman N, Charpak N. Kangaroo mother care in low-income countries. International Network in Kangaroo Mother Care. J Trop Pediatr 1998; 44(5):279-82.

107. Chwo MJ, Anderson GC, Good M, Dowling DA, Shiau SH, Chu DM. A randomized controlled trial of early kangaroo care for preterm infants: effects on temperature, weight, behavior, and acuity. J Nurs Res 2002; 10(2):129-42.

108. Anderson GC. Current knowledge about skin-to-skin (kangaroo) care for preterm infants. J Perinatol 1991; 11(3):216-26.

109. Hanson LA. Immunobiology of human milk: How breastfeeding protects babies. Amarillo: Pharmasoft Publishing; 2004.

110. Kleinman RE, Walker WA. The enteromammary immune system: An important new concept in breast milk host defense. Dig Dis Sci 1979; 24(11):876-82.

111. Charpak N, Ruiz-Pelaez JG, Figueroa de CZ, Charpak Y. Kangaroo mother versus traditional care for newborn infants </=2000 grams: a randomized, controlled trial. Pediatrics 1997; 100(4):682-8.

112. Johnston CC, Stevens B, Pinelli J, et al. Kangaroo care is effective in diminishing pain response in preterm neonates. Arch Pediatr Adolesc Med 2003; 157(11):1084-8.

113. American Academy of Pediatrics, Committee on Fetus and Newborn and Section on Surgery, Canadian Paediatric Society Fetus and Newborn Committee. Prevention and management of pain in the neonate: an update. Pediatrics 2006; 118(5):2231-41.

114. Feldman R, Eidelman AI. Skin-to-skin contact (kangaroo care) accelerates autonomic and neurobehavioural maturation in preterm infants. Dev Med Child Neurol 2003; 45(4):274-81.

115. Sloan NL, Camacho LW, Rojas EP, Stern C. Kangaroo mother method: randomised controlled trial of an alternative method of care for stabilised low-birthweight infants. Maternidad Isidro Ayora Study Team. Lancet 1994; 344(8925):782-5.

116. Banagale RC. Serum thyroxine values in breast-fed infants. Am J Dis Child 1984; 138(4):410.

117. Legault M, Goulet C. Comparison of kangaroo and traditional methods of removing preterm infants from incubators. J Obstet Gynecol Neonatal Nurs 1995; 24(6):501-6.

118. Tornhage CJ, Stuge E, Lindberg T, Serenius F. First week kangaroo care in sick very preterm infants. Acta Paediatr 1999; 88(12):1402-4.

119. Nyqvist KH, Sjoden PO, Ewald U. The development of preterm infants' breastfeeding behavior. Early Hum Dev 1999; 55(3):247-64.

120. Lau C. Oral feeding in the preterm infant. NeoReviews 2006; 7(1):e19-e27, Accessed September 2, 2006.

121. Lau C, Hurst N. Oral feeding in infants. Curr Probl Pediatr 1999; 29(4):105-24.

122. Medoff-Cooper B. Multi-system approach to the assessment of successful feeding. Acta Paediatr 2000; 89(4):393-4.

123. Siddell EP, Froman RD. A national survey of neonatal intensive-care units: criteria used to determine readiness for oral feedings. J Obstet Gynecol Neonatal Nurs 1994; 23(9):783-9.

124. McCain G, Gartside P, Greenberg J, Lott J. A feeding protocol for healthy preterm infants that shortens time to oral feeding. J Pediatrics 2001; 139(3):74-9.

125. Nyqvist KH, Farnstrand C, Eeg-Olofsson KE, Ewald U. Early oral behaviour in preterm infants during breastfeeding: an electromyographic study. Acta Paediatr 2001; 90(6):658-63.

126. Simpson C, Schanler R, Lau C. Early introduction of oral feeding in preterm infants. Pediatrics 2002; 110:517-22.

127. Nyqvist K. The development of preterm infants' milk intake during breastfeeding. J Neonatal Nursing 2001; 7(2):48-52.

128.Nyqvist KH. Early attainment of breastfeeding competence in very preterm infants. Acta Paediatrica 2008; 97:776-781.

129.Auer C, Steichen J, Fargo J. The relationship between first oral feeding (breast versus bottle) and pre- and post-discharge feeding in an NICU population. In: Pediatric Academic Societies Meeting (PAS). San Francisco, CA, May 1-4, 2004, http://www.abstracts2view.com/pasall/view.php?nu=PAS4L1_1949; 2004.

130.Pickler R, Best A, Reyna B, Gutcher G, Wetzel P. Predictors of nutritive sucking in preterm infants. J Perinatology 2006; 26:693-9.

131.Blaymore Bier JA, Ferguson AE, Morales Y, Liebling JA, Oh W, Vohr BR. Breastfeeding infants who were extremely low birth weight. Pediatrics 1997; 100(6):E3.

132.Meier P. Bottle- and breast-feeding: effects on transcutaneous oxygen pressure and temperature in preterm infants. Nurs Res 1988; 37(1):36-41.

133.Meier P, Anderson GC. Responses of small preterm infants to bottle- and breast-feeding. MCN Am J Matern Child Nurs 1987; 12(2):97-105.

134.Martell M, Martinez G, Gonzalez M, Diaz Rossello JL. Suction patterns in preterm infants. J Perinat Med 1993; 21(5):363-9.

135.Meier P, Brown L. State of the science: breastfeeding for mothers and low birthweight infants. Nursing Clinics of North America 1996; 31:351-65.

136.Furman L, Minich N. Efficiency of breastfeeding as compared to bottle-feeding in very low birth weight (VLBW, <1.5 kg) infants. J Perinatol 2004; 24(11):706-13.

137.Meier P. Suck-breathe patterning during bottle and breast feeding for preterm infants. British Journal of Clinical Practice (International Congress and Symposium Series 215, Major controversies in infant nutrition, TJ David, Ed, London: Royal Society of Medicine Press) 1996: pp 9-20.

138.Lau C, Schanler RJ. Oral feeding in premature infants: advantage of a self-paced milk flow. Acta Paediatr 2000; 89(4):453-9.

139.Lau C, Sheena HR, Shulman RJ, Schanler RJ. Oral feeding in low birth weight infants. J Pediatr 1997; 130(4):561-9.

140.Kliethermes PA, Cross ML, Lanese MG, Johnson KM, Simon SD. Transitioning preterm infants with nasogastric tube supplementation: increased likelihood of breastfeeding. J Obstet Gynecol Neonatal Nurs 1999; 28(3):264-73.

141.Meier P. Supporting lactation in mothers with very low birth weight infants. Pediatric Annals 2003; 32(5):317-25.

142. Nyqvist KH, Rubertsson C, Ewald U, Sjoden PO. Development of the preterm infant breastfeeding behavior scale (PIBBS): a study of nurse-mother agreement. J Hum Lact 1996; 12(3):207-19.

143. Kavanaugh K, Mead L, Meier P, Mangurten HH. Getting enough: mothers' concerns about breastfeeding a preterm infant after discharge. J Obstet Gynecol Neonatal Nurs 1995; 24(1):23-32.

144. Meier PP, Engstrom JL, Fleming BA, Streeter PL, Lawrence PB. Estimating milk intake of hospitalized preterm infants who breastfeed. J Hum Lact 1996; 12(1):21-6.

145. Meier PP, Engstrom JL, Crichton CL, Clark DR, Williams MM, Mangurten HH. A new scale for in-home test-weighing for mothers of preterm and high risk infants. J Hum Lact 1994; 10(3):163-8.

146. Scanlon K, Alexander M, Serdula M, et al. Assessment of infant feeding: the validity of measuring milk intake. Nutrition Reviews 2002; 60(8):235-51.

147. Meier P, Lysakowski T, Engstrom JL et al. The accuracy of test weighing for preterm infants. J Pediatr Gastroenterol Nutr 1990; 10:62-5.

148. Hurst NM, Meier PP, Engstrom JL, Myatt A. Mothers performing in-home measurement of milk intake during breastfeeding of their preterm infants: maternal reactions and feeding outcomes. J Hum Lact 2004; 20(2):178-87.

149. Arthur PG, Hartmann PE, Smith M. Measurement of the milk intake of breast-fed infants. J Pediatr Gastroenterol Nutr 1987; 6(5):758-63.

150. Woolridge M. The 'anatomy' of infant suckling. Midwifery 1986; 2:164.

151. Howard C. Randomized clinical trial of pacifier use and bottle-feeding or cupfeeding and their effect on breastfeeding. Pediatrics 2003; 111:511-8.

152. Howard C, deBlieck E, ten Hoopen C, Howard F, Lanphear B, Lawrence R. Physiologic stability of infants during cup- and bottle-feeding. Pediatrics 1999; 104(5 Part 2):1204-7.

153. Kramer M, Chalmers B, Hodnett E, et al. Promotion of breastfeeding intervention trial (PROBIT): a cluster-randomized trial in the republic of Belarus. JAMA 2001; 285(4):1-15.

154. Lang S, Lawrence C, Orme R. Cup-feeding:an alternative method of infant feeding. Arch Dis Child 1994; 71(4):365-9.

155. Schubiger G, Schwarz U, Tonz O. UNICEF/WHO baby-friendly hospital initiative: does the use of bottles and pacifiers in the neonatal nursery prevent successful breastfeeding? Neonatal Study Group. Eur J Pediatr 1997; 156(11):874-7.

156. Malhotra N, Vishwambaran L, Sundaram K, Narayanan I. A controlled trial of alternative methods of oral feeding in neonates. Early Hum Dev 1999; 54(1):29-38.

157. Mizuno K, Kani K. Sipping/lapping is a safe alternative feeding method to suckling for preterm infants. Acta Paediatr 2005; 94:574-80.

158. Collins CT, Ryan P, Crowther CA, McPhee AJ, Paterson S, Hiller JE. Effect of bottles, cups, and dummies on breast feeding in preterm infants: a randomised controlled trial. BMJ 2004; 329(7459):193-8.

159. Rocha NM, Martinez FE, Jorge SM. Cup or bottle for preterm infants: effects on oxygen saturation, weight gain, and breastfeeding. J Hum Lact 2002; 18(2):132-8.

160. Dowling D, Meier P, DiFiore J, Blatz M, Martin R. Cup-feeding for preterm infants: mechanics and safety. J Hum Lact 2002; 18(1):13-20.

161. Aloysius A, Hickson M. Evaluation of paladai cup feeding in breast-fed preterm infants compared with bottle feeding. Early Hum Dev 2007; 83(9):619-21.

162. Oddy WH, Glenn K. Implementing the baby friendly hospital initiative: the role of finger feeding. Breastfeed Rev 2003; 11(1):5-10.

163. Clum D, Primomo J. Use of a silicone nipple shield with premature infants. J Hum Lact 1996; 12(4):287-90.

164. Meier PP, Brown LP, Hurst NM, et al. Nipple shields for preterm infants: effect on milk transfer and duration of breastfeeding. J Hum Lact 2000; 16(2):106-14; quiz 29-31.

165. Hurst N. Assessing and facilitating milk transfer during breastfeeding for the premature infant. Newborn and Infant Nursing Reviews 2005; 5(1):19-26.

166. The baby-friendly hospital initiative. 1989. Available at: http://www. unicef.org/programme/breastfeeding/baby.htm#10. Accessed September 2, 2006.

167. Spatz DL. Ten steps for promoting and protecting breastfeeding for vulnerable infants. J Perinat Neonatal Nurs 2004; 18(4):385-96.

Chapter 9:
BREASTFEEDING THE LATE PRETERM INFANT

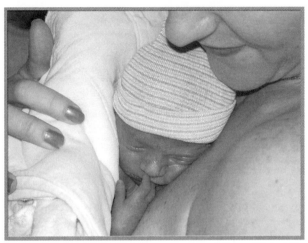

Photo courtesy of Nancy Wight MD

Introduction/Epidemiology

In the United States, the rate of preterm birth (< 37 weeks gestation) has increased more than 30% since the early 1980s,[1] with much of the recent increase in preterm births due to late preterm infants (34-36 completed weeks). From 1990 to 2004, the percentage of all births that were late preterm increased 22%, from 7.3% to 8.9%.[2] Preterm infants of 34-36 weeks comprise almost 75% of all preterm singleton births[1] (Figure 1).

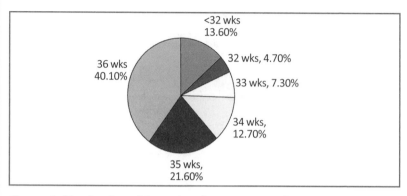

Figure 1: Distribution of Gestational Age, US, 2002(N= 394,996 preterm singletons) Source: Davidoff et al., 2006.[1] Reprinted with permission from Elsevier.

In addition, deliveries from 37-39 weeks gestation have increased 11% from 1993-2003 in the USA, shifting the peak of deliveries from 40 to 39 weeks in only 13 years[3] (Figure 2). Some of the reasons for the increase in late preterm births are: increased fetal surveillance and intervention, problems with gestational age estimations, multiple gestation with assisted reproductive technologies, maternal health and demographics (e.g., advanced maternal age), maternal autonomy regarding delivery timing, legal risks, and the perception that late preterm infants are at no greater risk of serious morbidity and mortality than full term (37-41 week) infants.[4] Unfortunately, both morbidity and mortality rates are significantly increased in late preterm infants.[2,5]

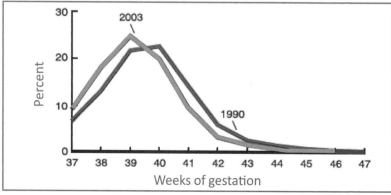

Figure 2: Gestational Age at Delivery, US, 1990-2003[3]

The currently accepted definition of preterm is birth at less than 37 completed weeks.[6] Until recently, "near term" was the nomenclature for infants born from 34-37 weeks.[7, 8] In 2005, the National Institute of Child Health and Human Development (NICHD) consensus panel recommended the use of "late preterm" to describe infants born at 34 0/7 to 36 6/7 completed weeks gestation,[9, 10] in order to appropriately communicate that these infants are still premature. Born only a few weeks early, and often only slightly smaller than a full-term infant, "near-term," "borderline premature," or, the now preferred term, "late preterm" infants are all too frequently treated as full-term, although they are at significantly greater risk for health and developmental problems[4,11,12] and complications of feeding.[8,13] Lacking the last few weeks of in-utero growth and development, these infants may demonstrate a more subtle immaturity requiring a trained eye and proactive management to prevent subsequent problems. Although technically at full term, 37-39 week infants may have similar immaturities and problems.

All problems of the term infant are magnified in the late preterm infant, with higher risks for hypothermia, hypoglycemia, jaundice, and kernicterus,[14] excessive weight loss and dehydration, fever secondary to dehydration, slow weight gain, failure to thrive, prolonged artificial milk supplementation, hospital readmission, and breastfeeding failure.[12, 15-23] Late preterm infants are likely to stay longer in the hospital, thereby incurring additional cost.[12] One study of all California singleton live births who survived to one year of age found that infants born at 34 to 36 weeks gestation were three to nine times more likely to require mechanical ventilation than infants born at 38 weeks gestation,[24] increasing hospital costs dramatically. In addition, late preterm infants are four times more likely than term infants to have at least one medical condition diagnosed, and 3.5 times more likely to have two or more conditions diagnosed.[12]

Several case-control studies have identified late preterm birth as a significant risk factor for readmission,[17, 25-27] and other studies that compared readmission rates noted that late preterm infants are much more likely to be readmitted than are full term infants.[18, 21-23] Readmission to the hospital is expensive, averaging $1163 per day, with an average stay of 3.2 days.[28] The risk of rehospitalization appears to increase as gestational age decreases,[21,22] with the relatively healthy late preterm infant who remains with mother in the mother-infant unit at particular risk of readmission.[22]

The long-term health consequences of being born at late preterm are not yet known.[29] Late preterm infants are born before their nervous systems have fully developed.[30] Small clinical reports suggest a higher risk of cerebral palsy, speech problems, neurodevelopmental handicaps, and behavioral abnormalities.[4,29]

There is a huge variability in breastfeeding ability in this group, with many infants and mothers having significant problems initiating and maintaining breastfeeding.[8,13] Exclusively breastfed infants less than 39 weeks are significantly more likely to be readmitted for jaundice and dehydration.[22,25,31] Late preterm infants who are breastfed have a two-fold risk of neonatal morbidity, while there was no association among infants who were not breastfed.[18] Breastfed late preterm infants are more likely to have feeding problems and are at greater risk for hospital readmission or observation stay related to inadequate weight gain, jaundice, or feeding difficulties.[32] These infants may have special needs and close follow-up is essential to prevent unnecessary morbidity and the loss of a successful breastfeeding relationship.[8,13,33,34] Both late preterm infants and their mothers bring risk factors to establishing successful lactation.[13]

Characteristics and Morbidities of the Late Preterm Infant

The late preterm infant presents with significant variability in physical appearance and a wide range of normal weights (Table 1), with an even greater range if we consider small for gestational age (SGA) and large for gestational age (LGA) infants. Neither size nor gestational age can reliably predict maturity of all organ systems.[9]

Table 1: Range of Normal Weights for Infants 34-38 Week's Gestation

Gestational Age	Metric (g)		
	10th %tile	50th %tile	90th %tile
34 weeks	1500	2100	2800
35 weeks	1700	2300	3000
36 weeks	1900	2600	3200
37 weeks	2100	2800	3400
38 weeks	2300	2950	3550

Cardiorespiratory

Late preterm infants appear to have more respiratory instability with poorer ability to clear normal lung fluid,[21,35] especially if delivered by elective repeat cesarean section without labor.[35,36] They may have an increased incidence of apnea[12,37] and little cardiac and respiratory reserve.[4,12,21] Because of a relatively large head and overall decreased tone, late preterm infants may experience respiratory instability in some breastfeeding positions or even in a car seat.

Neurodevelopment

Late preterm infants have developmentally immature central nervous systems, with brains approximately two-thirds the size of a term infant's brain[30] (Figure 3).

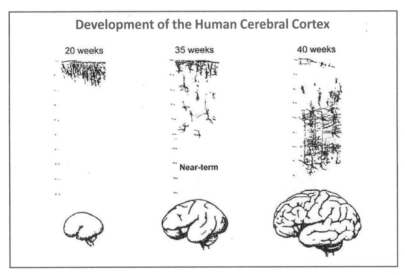

Figure 3: Development of the Human Cerebral Cortex.
Source: Kinney, 2006.[30] Figure reprinted with permission from Elsevier.

They sleep more and have immature state regulation,[38] changing state rapidly (hyper-alert to deep sleep without intervening stages). Despite lower overall tone (causing poor latch and suckling), they are easily over stimulated and may "shut down" before adequate intake is achieved. The suck/swallow/breathe (S/S/B) pattern may be uncoordinated or more immature in late preterm infants, resulting in poor latch-on and inadequate milk transfer,[38,39] although preterm and late preterm infants may not need a fully mature S/S/B pattern to breastfeed successfully.[40]

Thermoregulation

An infant's response to cold exposure after birth is related to gestational age and is affected by physical size, the amount of brown and white fat, and the maturity of the hypothalamus.[4] Although most preterm infants are capable of maintaining normal body temperature in an open crib by 1500 grams,[41] late preterm infants are still at risk for hypothermia in the delivery room (wet) and on the post-partum floor (drafts, air-conditioning). Hypothermia, sleepiness, and poor suck may be misinterpreted as sepsis, leading to unnecessary separation from the mother and treatment.[34] Brown fat has the unique ability to generate heat, but is less abundant in preterm infants. Late preterm infants are usually smaller than term infants and are likely to lose heat more readily because they have a larger surface area to weight ratio.

Energy Metabolism

The younger the gestational age, the less energy reserve, as less glycogen and brown fat stores are available to protect against hypoglycemia.[42,43] After birth, these reserves are used in combination with the gradually increasing volume of colostrum to ensure metabolic homeostasis.[44] This transition may not occur smoothly in late preterm infants because of possible increased metabolic expenditures, poor breastfeeding skills, lack of access to the breast, or delay in onset of "milk coming in" (lactogenesis II) in their mothers.[8]

The ketone body compensatory mechanisms for hypoglycemia may also be less effective.[45] However, Hawdon et al. studied 46 healthy babies of 34 to 36 weeks gestation who were randomized to exclusive breastfeeding or formula supplements, which were decreased in amount over 72 hours. The unsupplemented group had significantly more hypoglycemia than the supplemented group, but also had higher ketone bodies. Despite the transient hypoglycemia and ketone response, they were asymptomatic. They concluded that formula supplements given to healthy breastfed borderline preterm infants inhibited postnatal adaptation by blunting the normal ketogenic response.[46]

Glucose concentration is inversely correlated with time between feedings,[45] supporting the importance of frequent feeding. Continuous mother-infant contact in the postnatal period will facilitate frequent, on-request nursing episodes and provide adequate metabolic fuels for cerebral function.[47]

Hematologic Stability

Late preterm infants' reduced ability to conjugate and excrete bilirubin may result in more need for phototherapy and supplemental feedings.[14,48,49] Early unconjugated hyperbilirubinemia in breastfed infants is a common marker for poor breastfeeding and inadequate intake of milk[14,16,48] and is known as *breastfeeding jaundice*, or more accurately as *breast non-feeding jaundice*. It is the infant clinical equivalent of "starvation jaundice," which is characterized by infrequent stools and increased enterohepatic circulation of bilirubin.[48] Reduced breastfeeding frequency and supplementation with water or glucose water have been associated with increased serum bilirubin concentrations in the first five days of life.[48,50,51] Clinical jaundice is usually accompanied by slow weight gain or dehydration, demonstrating limited milk intake during the first few days of life as the primary etiology of the jaundice.[14,48]

Preterm infants fed maternal or banked human milk tend to have higher peak bilirubin concentrations and more prolonged jaundice than infants fed artificial preterm formulas.[52] Bilirubin encephalopathy (kernicterus) appears to be returning, with late preterm infants at increased risk because of ineffective breastfeeding.[25,53] Optimal breastfeeding management does not eliminate neonatal jaundice in late preterm breastfed infants. Some degree of hyperbilirubinemia may be protective as bilirubin is a potent anti-oxidant. Clinical evaluation of breastfeeding, together with weighing and physical examination, will identify infants with breastfeeding problems leading to inadequate intake and exaggeration of jaundice needing intervention.[48]

Immunologic

Maternal infections may induce preterm labor or premature rupture of the membranes. Late preterm infants are more frequently screened and treated for sepsis because they exhibit symptoms of possible infection, including respiratory distress, apnea, tachycardia, poor perfusion, hypoglycemia, poor feeding, lethargy, hypotonia, irritability, and temperature instability.[33]

Immunologic competence develops over years.[54] Late preterm infants are at higher risk for infection because of an immature immune system, possible exposure to antibiotics which change gut flora, delayed or insufficient feedings, and separation from the mother.[55,56]

Gastrointestinal/Feeding Maturity and Growth

Late preterm infants have immature gastrointestinal function and feeding difficulties that put them at special risk for slow growth and failure to thrive. Healthy term infants should lose a maximum of 6-8% of birth weight by day three to four after delivery, then start to gain 20-30 grams per day, reaching birth weight by seven to ten days of life.[44,57] The late preterm infant is vulnerable to slow or poor growth because of inadequate intake during exclusive feeding at the breast. Supplementation is often necessary.

Small or late preterm infants seldom nurse as well as do larger, full-term infants, as they may have trouble grasping the breast and extracting the milk.[58] They may appear to nurse well with colostrum alone, but after lactogenesis II, they usually cannot extract enough milk to maintain a mother's milk supply.[16] There is considerable information regarding breast- and bottle-feeding of preterm infants at various gestational ages, suggesting that sucking efficiency and milk consumption increases through term postconceptional age.[58-63]

Negative pressure during pauses in sucking appears to prevent an infant from slipping off the breast.[58] Lau et al.[58] described five stages of sucking maturity (bottle-feeding) based on the relative contributions of expression and suction to milk removal, with the less mature pattern relying more on expression. The most mature pattern, Stage 5, was not reached until a mean gestational age of 36 weeks, but with a wide range of 34 to 44 weeks. Weak suction, characterized by earlier stages of sucking maturity, may explain why preterm and late preterm infants often cannot maintain an effective latch.[13]

Two additional studies suggest that late preterm infants may have difficulty extracting milk from the breast and need considerable time at home transitioning to exclusive breastfeeding.[64,65] With adequate maternal milk supply, an average discharge age of 36 weeks, and assessment of milk intake at breast by test-weighing, there was a slow transition from 30% of daily intake taken at breast during the first week at home to 52% taken at breast during week four.[64,66] The transition to exclusive breastfeeding was at approximately 42 weeks corrected age, six weeks after discharge. Another study which included late preterm infants (mean gestational age 33.7 weeks, range 30-35 weeks) found that most infants were discharged home primarily bottle-feeding breastmilk with a gradual transition to direct feeding at the breast over four weeks or longer.[65] The key message of this study was that success in achieving full direct breastfeeding was dependent on the adequacy of the milk supply, with mothers requiring supplements other than expressed breastmilk having less success with the transition to exclusive feeding at the breast (Figure 4).

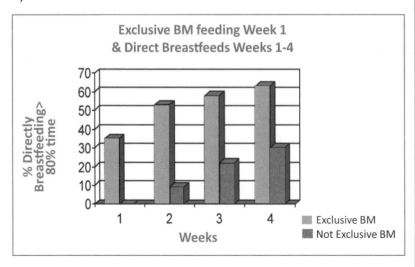

Figure 4: Posthospitalization Breastfeeding Patterns of Moderately Preterm Infants. Source: Wooldridge & Hall, 2003.[65] Reprinted with permission from Lippincott, Williams and Wilkins.

Poor growth may be due to infant reasons, such as limited energy and ability to obtain the milk; mother problems, such as insufficient milk production; or a combination of mother-infant factors, such as inappropriate feeding routines leading to inadequate milk supply (common)[67] (Figure 5).

Separation

Because of all of the developmental issues noted above, late preterm infants may need to be separated from their mothers for observation and procedures (intravenous fluids, phototherapy, lumbar puncture, bladder catheterization, etc.), limiting the mother's opportunity to observe early feeding cues and practice positioning and latch. Such procedures may leave the infant exhausted and unable to feed. Current studies suggest that being held and breastfed can minimize the pain of heel sticks and other procedures.[68]

Maternal Issues

Mothers who deliver at 34–38 weeks often have problems that affect establishing the maternal milk supply and putting the infant

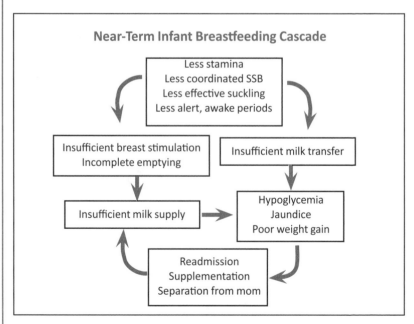

Figure 5: Near-Term Infant Breastfeeding Cascade
Source: Wight, 2003.[8] Figure reprinted with permission from Slack Inc.

to breast. The cause of prematurity, such as infection, pregnancy-induced hypertension, or multiples, may prevent the mother from putting the infant to breast immediately, or the mode of delivery may affect her ability to hold or position her infant. Medications, such as anesthesia, analgesia, antibiotics, and anti-hypertensive medications, may be given as reasons (either accurately or inaccurately) not to breastfeed. Mothers may need monitoring or special care themselves post-partum, resulting in mother-baby separation and missed infant awake periods. Sometimes simple maternal exhaustion from a difficult labor and delivery or too many well-meaning visitors creates barriers to continuous rooming in and frequent breastfeeding.[8]

Due to maternal illness, such as diabetes, cesarean section, or simple stress, mothers may experience delayed lactogenesis II (the onset of full milk production).[69-73] The concentration of four markers of lactogenesis II (lactose, citrate, sodium, and total protein) in milk from preterm mothers (31 to 35 weeks) at day five postpartum had much greater variation around the mean than was observed in term breastfeeding mothers.[70] In addition, ineffective milk removal over several days will down-regulate milk production.[73]

Recommendations for Care of the Breastfeeding Late Preterm Infant and His Mother

There are two basic principles involved in breastfeeding the late preterm infant:

- feed the baby,
- establish and maintain the mother's milk supply.

Establishing breastfeeding of the late preterm infant will take extra effort by both the mother and the physician, but is well worth it. Late preterm infants will have a better chance of exclusive breastfeeding in hospitals that adhere to the WHO/UNICEF Baby-Friendly Hospital Initiative "Ten Steps." [74,75]

Breastfeeding-Friendly Birth and Immediate Post-Partum Care

At delivery, all infants should be quickly dried, assessed, and if stable, placed immediately in uninterrupted skin-to-skin contact with their mother until the first breastfeed is accomplished. Such contact provides the infant optimal physiologic stability, warmth, and opportunities for the first feeding.[76-78] In addition, kangaroo care improves oxygen saturation and gas exchange, decreases crying, enhances the enteromammary immune system, improves breastmilk production, and lengthens the times of exclusive and total breastfeeding post discharge.[79] Unnecessary and aggressive suctioning, excessive handling, and immediate procedures can cause thermal and metabolic stress for the late preterm infant. Delaying the administration of vitamin K, eye prophylaxis, and hepatitis B vaccine minimizes crying (which depletes metabolic reserves and disrupts early feeding behavior) and enhances early parent-infant interaction.[44] To encourage infant self-attachment to the breast, all extraneous distractions should be removed: the lights should be dim, noise kept to a minimum, and all visitors except for the father of the baby or significant other escorted from the room.[8]

After the initial few hours of skin-to-skin contact, the infant should have a complete physical exam, including a gestational age assessment and necessary procedures performed in the mother's room. Routinely removing the infant to an observation nursery or NICU for a specified period (4, 6, 12, 24 hours) interferes with frequent breastfeeding and prevents the mother from observing and responding to early feeding cues. However, if adequate nursing supervision is not available, the safety of the infant must be the primary concern, and admission to a transition or observation nursery until respiratory, metabolic, and temperature stability are assured may be warranted. Glucose screening should be limited to symptomatic infants, low birth weight infants (< 2500 g), and those with other risk factors.[47] Unstable infants (respiratory distress, apnea, cyanosis, symptomatic hypoglycemia, cold despite kangaroo care) should be moved immediately to a special care nursery for observation and treatment.[8]

Establishing Breastfeeding and Mother's Milk Supply

Mothers of late preterm infants should be instructed to pump after every feeding attempt, or approximately every three hours. Using a combination of frequent hand expression (> five times per day for the first three days) in addition to pumping has been shown to increase production more effectively than reliance on electric pumping alone.[80-82] An instructional video on the technique can be found at http://newborns.stanford.edu/Breastfeeding/HandExpression.html. The goal is eight to twelve feedings or expressions per 24 hours, including through the night. If the mother is too ill or exhausted to attempt breastfeeding every time, she should be encouraged to breastfeed when her infant is most alert and awake, and just pump when the infant is sleepy or difficult to arouse.[13] Frequency of pumping appears more crucial than early initiation, but starting pumping at less than 12-24 hours postpartum is recommended.[83] A full milk supply should be initiated within the first week, as with any term infant.[84]

As late preterm infants tend to be sleepier than full-term infants, they may need to be awakened every two to four hours for feeding attempts for several days. Keeping mothers and babies together as much as possible will facilitate response to early feeding cues and parental confidence in their ability to care for their borderline premature infant. The infant should be kept warm using kangaroo care or an isolette if necessary. Professional, experienced, lactation support can maximize feeding efficiency through positioning, jaw support, breast massage, etc. and spot potential problems, such as sore nipples from poor latch.[85,86] Breastfeeding positions, such as the football hold, that provide head support may help the infant feed more effectively.[84,87]

Lactation consultants can also instruct the mother (and the physician!) in the use of breastfeeding accessories, such as the thin silicone nipple shield and nursing supplementer. Nipple shields appear to function by compensating for the late preterm infant's weak suction pressures, preventing "slipping off," and have been demonstrated to significantly increase milk transfer in preterm infants.[88,89] Used in this context, they are not associated with shorter breastfeeding duration.[90] A detailed description of proper fit and infant latch with the thin silicone nipple shield is available.[13] In addition, the simple technique of hand expressing colostrum into a spoon and feeding this to the infant after each breastfeeding increases both breast stimulation and infant intake.

Assessment and Monitoring

A lactation consultant or other breastfeeding knowledgeable professional should evaluate the dyad within 24 hours of delivery and daily. Just "hanging out" at the breast does not equal effective feeding. Pre- and post-breastfeeding weights, if done correctly on an electronic scale, can generate valuable information when planning supplementation.[91] The infant's stool output, weight loss/gain, and jaundice should be closely monitored. The mother must be monitored for timing of lactogenesis II and ongoing milk supply, as well as general health and emotional well-being. Anticipatory guidance should be provided regarding nipple tenderness, breast engorgement, signs of effective milk transfer, and normal weight patterns.[8]

Supplementation

Most infants are well hydrated via the placenta at birth. Small colostrum feedings are physiologic: appropriate for the size of the newborn infant's stomach, sufficient to prevent hypoglycemia in healthy term infants, and easy to manage as the infant learns to coordinate sucking, swallowing, and breathing.[8] Many late preterm infants, however, will require at least some supplementation. Volume of supplement should be approximately 5-10 mL per feeding on day one, 10-20 mL/feeding on day two, and 20-30 cc per feeding on subsequent days, depending on the infant's size and metabolic needs. Supplement can be gradually decreased based on scale measured pre-post breastfeeding intakes, maternal perception of pre-post feeding breast fullness, or demonstrated continued weight gain as supplement is withdrawn.[8]

Expressed mothers' own milk is the first choice for supplementation followed, in order, by pasteurized donor human milk, elemental formulas, standard formula, soy formula, and glucose water.[92] Adding glucose water to drops of colostrum may be sufficient as a supplement for one to three feedings; however, it is inadequate nutrition for repeated feedings. Elemental formulas are preferred over standard formulas as they decrease bilirubin faster, taste terrible so infants prefer the breast, are expensive so parents are less likely to continue them unnecessarily, reduce exposure to whole cow's milk proteins (which is associated with increased risk of allergy in susceptible infants), and convey the message to parents that the supplementation is *medical therapy* and *temporary.*[8]

When supplemental feedings are needed, many techniques may be used: a supplemental nursing device at the breast, cup-feeding, spoon or dropper-feeding, finger-feeding, or bottle-feeding. There is little evidence regarding the efficacy or long-term effect on breastfeeding of most alternative feeding methods.[8] Cup feeding has been shown to be safe for term and preterm infants and may help to preserve breastfeeding duration among those infants that require multiple supplemental feedings.[92,93] Mothers' preferences for feeding method should be respected whenever possible.

The practice of breastfeeding, supplementing with previously pumped milk or artificial milks, then pumping to remove residual milk has been called "**triple feeding.**" The infant gets the supplement he needs, but is not relied upon to maintain the mother's milk supply. Late preterm infants often do not have the stamina to thoroughly drain their mother's breasts, and milk production will decrease due to milk stasis.[94]

Discharge Planning

As many late preterm infants need to remain in the hospital longer than their mothers, efforts should be made to keep mother and baby together as much as possible. Most late preterm infants are not discharged exclusively feeding at the breast and are vulnerable to inadequate intake until they are approximately term to slightly postterm corrected age.[84,87] A multidisciplinary post-discharge feeding plan should be developed *before* discharge and approved by all involved: parents, lactation consultant, current and follow-up physician. Equipment needs, such as an electric breast pump with a "double-pump" kit (to enable pumping both breasts at the same time), home scale, nipple shields, milk storage bottles, etc., should be arranged.[8] Test-weights at home, using an appropriate, commercially-available scale may be helpful in determining the amount of supplementation needed, can be performed accurately by mothers,[95] and do not increase maternal stress or anxiety.[96]

A follow-up visit with the physician is recommended 24-48 hours after discharge, then weekly until the infant is fully, exclusively breastfeeding, or is at least 40 weeks corrected age.[34] Close follow-up by a lactation consultant is also advisable. Referral to, or continuation of, a support group or peer counseling program can be very effective in getting mom and baby over the "rough spots." Extended family should be included in anticipatory guidance sessions and discharge planning to give the mother added, knowledgeable support.[8] Mothers of late preterm infants are often surprised that their infant, who appears so healthy and "mature," takes so long and so much effort to feed.

Discharge criteria include: temperature stability in an open crib, bilirubin stable or decreasing (below phototherapy levels), weight stable or increasing, evidence of some milk transfer, mother's milk supply becoming established, anticipatory guidance provided to mother, and a home feeding and follow-up plan as above. A pumping and feeding log kept by the mother will help the physician and lactation consultant catch problems and apply corrective solutions sooner.[97]

Administrative Issues

To provide consistency, written hospital policies and procedures should be evidence-based and delineate a pathway for care for late preterm infants, as well as procedures for alternate feeding methods, supplementation, etc.[33,34] Nurses caring for late preterm infants should be trained in how to assist with breastfeeding, and not abdicate this responsibility solely to the lactation consultant. Where differences in approach or recommendations occur (and they will!), care must be taken to educate the other caregiver without undermining the mother's trust.[8] Following a defined care and feeding plan may minimize inconsistencies[8,33] (Figure 6). Consistent, frequent communication can prevent many problems and the loss of breastfeeding.

Sample crib card for LPI care plan

My name is _____

Help me stay warm by • Keeping my hat on at all tmes
         • Holding me skin-to-skin OR
         • Swaddling me in several dry blankets
         • Checking my temperature before each feeding

My feeding plan ❏ Breastfeed me every 2 to 3 hrs. for_____min on each breast.
       I need at least 8 to 10 feedings in 24 hours!
       ❏ My mom pumps after I eat.
       Pump both breasts at the same time for _____ min
       ❏ Also give me breast milk and/or _____
       _____ mL every _____ hours
       By: ❏ tube at breast ❏ tube with finger
       ❏ No pacifiers please!
       ❏ My mother prefers to bottle feed me_____
       Feed me _____ mL _____ hours

Completed by _____ Date _____

Figure 6: Sample crib card for Late Preterm Infant Care Plan.[33] (Image courtesy of Lisa Stellwagen MD, UCSD Medical Center, San Diego.)

CONCLUSIONS

Human milk is the preferred feeding for all infants, including premature and sick newborns, with rare exceptions.[98] Late preterm infants may look very much like full term infants, but act more like the premature infants they are. An individual mother's breastfeeding intentions and support structure should be assessed before delivery and a plan developed based on what will work for both the baby *and* the mother. Close follow-up should be maintained until it is clear the infant is gaining well and the mother is confident and comfortable. The extra effort expended by both the mother and the health care team will be rewarded in longer duration of exclusive and total breastfeeding, a healthier mother and infant, and clear economic savings. Whether breastfeeding is achieved for a week, a month, a year, or longer, **any** amount of breastmilk is better than none!

RESOURCES

There are many resources available outlining guidelines for the overall care, as well as breastfeeding support, for the late preterm infant. The Academy of Breastfeeding Medicine protocol,[34] the Association of Women's Health, Obstetric and Neonatal Nurses Near Term Initiative,[7] and the California Perinatal Quality Care Collaborative[99] each add important information and recommendations to support this very special group of infants.

KEY CONCEPTS

- Human milk is the optimum feeding for late preterm infants.

- Late preterm infants may look like term infants, but physiologically and developmentally they are preterm infants.

- Establishing and maintaining a full milk supply is essential in transitioning the late preterm infant to the breast.

- Supplementation will usually be necessary for late preterm infants, with mother's own expressed milk preferred.

- Mother and infant should be kept together as much as possible.

- Anticipatory guidance and close follow-up are the keys to establishing full breastfeeding in late preterm infants.

- Any human milk is better than none.

REFERENCES

1. Davidoff MJ, Dias T, Damus K, et al. Changes in the gestational age distribution among U.S. singleton births: impact on rates of late preterm birth, 1992 to 2002. Semin Perinatol 2006; 30(1):8-15.

2. Tomashek KM, Shapiro-Mendoza CK, Davidoff MJ, Petrini JR. Differences in mortality between late-preterm and term singleton infants in the United States, 1995-2002. J Pediatr 2007; 151:450-6.

3. Martin J, Hamilton BE, Sutton, PD, Ventura, SJ, Menacker, F, Munson, ML. Births: final data for 2003. Atlanta: Centers for Disease Control and Prevention; September 8, 2005. Report No.: Volume 54, Number 2.

4. Engle WA, Tomashek KM, Wallman C. "Late-preterm" infants: a population at risk. Pediatrics 2007; 120(6):1390-401.

5. Clark RH, The Near-Term Respiratory Failure Research Group. The epidemiology of respiratory failure in neonates born at an estimated gestational age of 34 weeks or more. J Perinatol 2005; 25:251-7.

6. American Academy of Pediatrics and the American College of Obstetricians and Gynecologists Appendix E: Standard terminology for reporting of reproductive health statistics in the United States. Guidelines for perinatal care. 5th Ed. Elk Grove Village, IL: American Academy of Pediatrics; 2002.

7. Medoff-Cooper B, Bakewell-Sachs S, Buus-Frank ME, Santa-Donato A, Near-Term Advisory Panel. The AWHONN near-term infant initiative: a conceptual framework for optimizing health for near-term infants. J Obstet Gynecol Neonatal Nurs 2005; 34:666-71.

8. Wight NE. Breastfeeding the borderline (near-term) preterm infant. Pediatric Annals 2003; 32(5):329-36.

9. Raju TN, Higgins RD, Stark AR, Leveno KJ. Optimizing care and outcome for late-preterm (near-term) infants: a summary of the workshop sponsored by the National Institute of Child Health and Human Development. Pediatrics 2006; 118(3):1207-14.

10. Engle WA. A recommendation for the definition of "late preterm" (near-term) and the birth weight-gestational age classification system. Semin Perinatol 2006; 30(1):2-7.

11. Institute of Medicine. Preterm birth: causes, consequences, and prevention. Washington, DC: Institute of Medicine; 2006.

12. Wang M, Dorer D, Flemming M, Catlin E. Clinical outcomes of near-term infants. Pediatrics 2004; 114(2):372-6.

13. Meier PP, Furman LM, Degenhardt M. Increased lactation risk for late preterm infants and mothers: evidence and management strategies to protect breastfeeding. J Midwifery and Women's Health 2007; 52(6):579-87.

14. Bhutani VK, Johnson L. Kernicterus in late preterm infants cared for as term healthy infants. Semin Perinatol 2006; 30(2):89-97.

15. Edmonson M, Stoddard J, Owens L. Hospital readmission with feeding related problems after early postpartum discharge of normal newborns. JAMA 1997; 278:299-303.

16. Neifert M. Prevention of breastfeeding tragedies. Pediatr Clin NA 2001; 48(2):273-97.

17. Soskolne E, Schumacher R, Fyock C, et al. The effect of early discharge and other factors on readmission rates of newborns. Arch Pediatr Adolesc Med 1996; 150:373-9.

18. Tomashek KM, Shapiro-Mendoza CK, Weiss J, et al. Early discharge among late preterm and term newborns and risk of neonatal morbidity. Semin Perinatol 2006; 30(2):61-8.

19. Moritz ML, Manole MD, Bogen DL, Ayus JC. Breastfeeding-associated hypernatremia: are we missing the diagnosis? Pediatrics 2005; 116(3): e343-7.

20. Tarcan A, Tiker F, Vatandas NS, Haberal A, Gurakan B. Weight loss and hypernatremia in breast-fed babies: frequency in neonates with non-hemolytic jaundice. J Paediatr Child Health 2005; 41(9-10):484-7.

21. Escobar GJ, Clark RH, Greene JD. Short-term outcomes of infants born at 35 and 36 weeks gestation: we need to ask more questions. Semin Perinatol 2006; 30(1):28-33.

22. Escobar GJ, Greene JD, Hulac P, et al. Rehospitalisation after birth hospitalisation: patterns among infants of all gestations. Arch Dis Child 2005; 90(2):125-31.

23. Oddie SJ, Hammal D, Richmond S, Parker L. Early discharge and readmission to hospital in the first month of life in the Northern Region of the UK during 1998: a case cohort study. Arch Dis Child 2005; 90(2):119-24.

24. Gilbert WM, Nesbitt TS, Danielsen B. The cost of prematurity: quantification by gestational age and birth weight. Obstet Gynecol 2003; 102(3):488-92.

25. Maisels M, Kring E. Length of stay, jaundice and hospital readmission. Pediatrics 1998; 101:995-8.

26. Maisels MJ, Newman TB. Jaundice in full-term and near-term babies who leave the hospital within 36 hours. The pediatrician's nemesis. Clin Perinatol 1998; 25(2):295-302.

27. Grupp-Phelan J, Taylor JA, Liu LL, Davis RL. Early newborn hospital discharge and readmission for mild and severe jaundice. Arch Pediatr Adolesc Med 1999; 153(12):1283-8.

28. Paul IM, Phillips TA, Widome MD, Hollenbeak CS. Cost-effectiveness of postnatal home nursing visits for prevention of hospital care for jaundice and dehydration. Pediatrics 2004; 114(4):1015-22.

29. Adams-Chapman I. Neurodevelopmental outcome of the late preterm infant. Clin Perinatol 2006; 33(4):947-64; abstract xi.

30. Kinney HC. The near-term (late preterm) human brain and risk for periventricular leukomalacia: a review. Semin Perinatol 2006; 30(2):81-8.

31. Hall RT, Simon S, Smith MT. Readmission of breastfed infants in the first 2 weeks of life. J Perinatol 2000; 20(7):432-7.

32. Shapiro-Mendoza CK, Tomashek KM, Kotelchuck M, Barfield W, Weiss J, Evans S. Risk factors for neonatal morbidity and mortality among "healthy," late preterm newborns. Semin Perinatol 2006; 30(2):54-60.

33. Hubbard E, Stellwagen L, Wolf A. The late preterm infant: a little baby with big needs. Contemporary Pediatrics 2007; 24(11):51-9.

34. Academy of Breastfeeding Medicine. ABM Protocol # 10: Breastfeeding the near-term infant (35-37 weeks gestation). In: http://wwwbfmedorg/ace-files/protocol/near_termpdf; 2004.

35. Jain L, Eaton DC. Physiology of fetal lung fluid clearance and the effect of labor. Semin Perinatol 2006; 30(1):34-43.

36. van den Berg A, van Elburg, RM, van Geijn, HP, Fetter, WP, . Neonatal respiratory morbidity following elective caesarean section in term infants. A 5-year retrospective study and a review of the literature. Eur J Obstet Gynecol Reprod Biol 2001 Sept; 98(1):9-13.

37. Hunt CE. Ontogeny of autonomic regulation in late preterm infants born at 34-37 weeks postmenstrual age. Semin Perinatol 2006; 30(2):73-6.

38. Wolf L, Glass R. Feeding and swallowing disorders in infancy: Assessment and management. Tucson: Therapy Skill Builders; 1992.

39. Neu J. Gastrointestinal maturation and feeding. Semin Perinatol 2006; 30(2):77-80.

40. Lau C, Sheena HR, Shulman RJ, Schanler RJ. Oral feeding in low birth weight infants. J Pediatr 1997; 130(4):561-9.

41. Medoff-Cooper B. Transition of the preterm infant to an open crib. J Obstet Gynecol Neonatal Nurs 1994 May; 23(4):329-35.

42. Garg M, Devaskar SU. Glucose metabolism in the late preterm infant. Clin Perinatol 2006; 33(4):853-70.

43. Laptook A, Jackson GL. Cold stress and hypoglycemia in the late preterm («near-term») infant: impact on nursery of admission. Semin Perinatol 2006; 30(1):24-7.

44. Black L. Incorporating breastfeeding care into daily newborn rounds and pediatric office practice. Pediatr Clin NA 2001; 48(2):299-319.

45. Hawdon J, Ward Platt, MP, Aynsley-Green, A. Patterns of metabolic adaptation for preterm and term neonates in the first postnatal week. Arch Dis Child 1992; 67:357-65.

46. Hawdon J, Williams A, Lawrence Sea. Formula supplements given to healthy breastfed preterm babies inhibit postnatal metabolic adaptation: results of a randomized controlled trial. Arch Dis Child 2000; 82(Suppl 1):A30, Abstract # G102.

47. Eidelman A. Hypoglycemia and the breastfed neonate. Ped Clin NA 2001; 48(2):377-87.

48. Gartner L, Herschel M. Jaundice and breastfeeding. Pediatr Clin NA 2001; 49(2):389-99.

49. Maisels MJ, Kring E. Transcutaneous bilirubin levels in the first 96 hours in a normal newborn population of > or = 35 weeks' gestation. Pediatrics 2006; 117(4):1169-73.

50. DeCarvalho M, Klaus M. Frequency of breastfeeding and serum bilirubin concentration. Am J Dis Child 1982; 136:747-8.

51. Yamauchi Y, Yamanouchi I. Breast-feeding frequency during the first 24 hours after birth in full-term neonates. Pediatrics 1990; 86(2):171-5.

52. Lucas A, Baker B. Breast milk jaundice in premature infants. Arch Dis Child 1986; 61:1063-7.

53. Centers for Disease Control and Prevention. Kernicterus in full-term infants -- United States, 1994-1998. Morbidity & Mortality Weekly Report June 15, 2001; 50(23):491-4.

54. Hanson LA. Immunobiology of human milk: how breastfeeding protects babies. Amarillo: Pharmasoft Publishing; 2004.

55. Goldman A, Cheda S, Keeney S, Schmalstieg F, Schanler R. Immunologic protection of the preterm newborn by human milk. Sem Perinatol 1994; 18(6):495-501.

56. Clapp DW. Developmental regulation of the immune system. Semin Perinatol 2006; 30(2):69-72.

57. MacDonald P, Ross S, Grant L, Yound D. Neonatal weight loss in breast and formula fed infants. Arch Dis Child Fetal Neonatal Ed 2003; 88(6): F472-6.

58. Lau C, Alagugurusamy R, Schanler RJ, Smith EO, Shulman RJ. Characterization of the developmental stages of sucking in preterm infants during bottle feeding. Acta Paediatr 2000; 89(7):846-52.

59. Gewolb IH, Vice FL. Maturational changes in the rhythms, patterning, and coordination of respiration and swallow during feeding in preterm and term infants. Dev Med Child Neurol 2006; 48(7):589-94.

60. Gewolb IH, Vice FL, Schwietzer-Kenney EL, Taciak VL, Bosma JF. Developmental patterns of rhythmic suck and swallow in preterm infants. Dev Med Child Neurol 2001; 43(1):22-7.

61. Lau C, Smith EO, Schanler RJ. Coordination of suck-swallow and swallow respiration in preterm infants. Acta Paediatr 2003; 92(6):721-7.

62. Medoff-Cooper B, McGrath JM, Bilker W. Nutritive sucking and neurobehavioral development in preterm infants from 34 weeks PCA to term. MCN Am J Matern Child Nurs 2000; 25(2):64-70.

63. Medoff-Cooper B, McGrath JM, Shults J. Feeding patterns of full-term and preterm infants at forty weeks postconceptional age. J Dev Behav Pediatr 2002; 23(4):231-6.

64. Hurst N, Meier P, Engstrom J. Milk volume consumed at breast during the first month post-discharge (PDC) for preterm infants (PT): implications for management of breastfeeding and infant growth. Pediatr Res 2000; 47:197A.

65. Wooldridge J, Hall W. Posthospitalization breastfeeding patterns of moderately preterm infants. J Perinat Neonat Nurs 2003; 17(1):50-64.

66. Hurst NM, Meier PP, Engstrom JL. Mother's performing in-home measurement of milk intake during breastfeeding for their preterm infants: effects on breastfeeding outcomes at 1, 2, and 4 weeks post-NICU discharge. Pediatr Res 1999; 45:287A.

67. Morton J. The role of the pediatrician in extended breastfeeding of the preterm infant. Pediatric Annals 2003; 32(5):308-16.

68. Gray L, Miller L, Phillip B, Blass E. Breastfeeding is analgesic in healthy newborns. Pediatrics 2002; 109:590-3.

69. Chen DC, Nommsen-Rivers L, Dewey KG, Lonnerdal B. Stress during labor and delivery and early lactation performance. Am J Clin Nutr 1998; 68(2):335-44.

70. Cregan MD, De Mello TR, Kershaw D, McDougall K, Hartmann PE. Initiation of lactation in women after preterm delivery. Acta Obstet Gynecol Scand 2002; 81(9):870-7.

71. Hartmann P, Cregan M. Lactogenesis and the effects of insulin-dependent diabetes mellitus and prematurity. J Nutr 2001; 131(11):3016-20S.

72. Hartmann PE, Cregan MD, Ramsay DT, Simmer K, Kent JC. Physiology of lactation in preterm mothers: initiation and maintenance. Pediatr Ann 2003; 32(5):351-5.

73. Neville M, Morton J, Umemura S. Lactogenesis. Pediatric Clinics of North America 2001; 48(1):35-52.

74. DiGirolamo AM, Grummer-Strawn LM, Fein S. Maternity care practices: implications for breastfeeding. Birth 2001; 28(2):94-100.

75. World Health Organization. Evidence for the ten steps to successful breastfeeding, WHO/CHD/98.9. Geneva: World Health Organization; 1998. Report No.: WHO/CHD/98.9.

76. Academy of Breastfeeding Medicine. Clinical Protocol # 5: Peripartum breastfeeding management for the healthy mother and infant at term, www.bfmed.org. 2002.

77. Christensson K, Siles C, Moreno L, Belaustequi A, de la Fuente P, Lagercrantz H, et al. Temperature, metabolic adaptation and crying in healthy full-term newborns cared for skin-to-skin or in a cot. Acta Paediatrica 1992; 81(6-7):488-93.

78. Durand R, Hodges S, LaRock S, et al. The effect of skin-to-skin breastfeeding in the immediate recovery period on newborn thermo regulation and blood glucose values. Neonatal Intensive Care 1997; Mar-Apr:23-9.

79. Kirsten G, Bergman N, Hann F. Kangaroo mother care in the nursery. Pediatr Clin NA 2001; 48(2):443-52.

80. Jones E, Dimmock PW, Spencer SA. A randomised controlled trial to compare methods of milk expression after preterm delivery. Arch Dis Child Fetal Neonatal Ed 2001; 85(2):F91-5.

81. Morton JA, Hall JY, Thairu L, et al. Breast massage maximizes milk volumes of pump-dependent mothers, Abstract. In: Society for Pediatric Research; 2007; Toronto Canada; 2007.

82. Morton JA, Hall JY, Thairu L, et al. Early hand expression affects breastmilk production in pump-dependent mothers of preterm infants, Abstract # 7720.9. In: Pediatric Academic Societies; 2007; May 5-8, Toronto, Canada; 2007.

83. Hill PD, Aldag JC, Chatterton RT. Initiation and frequency of pumping and milk production in mothers of non-nursing preterm infants. J Hum Lact 2001; 17(1):9-13.

84. Meier P. Supporting lactation in mothers with very low birth weight infants. Pediatric Annals 2003; 32(5):317-25.

85. Gonzalez KA, Meinzen-Derr J, Burke BL, et al. Evaluation of a lactation support service in a children's hospital neonatal intensive care unit. J Hum Lact 2003; 19(3):286-92.

86. Sisk PM, Lovelady CA, Dillard RG, Gruber KJ. Lactation counseling for mothers of very low birth weight infants: effect on maternal anxiety and infant intake of human milk. Pediatrics 2006; 117(1):e67-75.

87. Meier PP. Breastfeeding in the special care nursery. Prematures and infants with medical problems. Pediatr Clin North Am 2001; 48(2):425-42.

88. Meier P, Brown L, Hurst N, et al. Nipple shields for preterm infants: effect on milk transfer and duration of breastfeeding. J Hum Lact 2000; 16:106-13.

89. Chertok IR, Schneider J, Blackburn S. A pilot study of maternal and term infant outcomes associated with ultrathin nipple shield use. J Obstet Gynecol Neonatal Nurs 2006; 35(2):265-72.

90. Meier PP, Brown LP, Hurst NM, et al. Nipple shields for preterm infants: effect on milk transfer and duration of breastfeeding. J Hum Lact 2000; 16(2):106-14; quiz 29-31.

91. Meier P, Lysakowski T, Engstrom JL, et al. The accuracy of test weighing for preterm infants. J Pediatr Gastroenterol Nutr 1990; 10:62-5.

92. Academy of Breastfeeding Medicine. Clinical protocol #3: Hospital guidelines for the use of supplementary feedings in the healthy term breastfed neonate. 2001, www.bfmed.org, revised 2008.

93. Wight NE. Management of common breastfeeding issues. Pediatric Clinics of North America 2001; 48(2):321-44.

94. California Perinatal Quality Care Collaborative PQIP. Toolkit: Nutritional support of the VLBW infant, part 2. In: California Perinatal Quality Care Collaborative, Perinatal Quality Improvement Panel, www.cpqcc.org; 2005.

95. Meier PP, Engstrom JL, Crichton CL, Clark DR, Williams MM, Mangurten HH. A new scale for in-home test-weighing for mothers of preterm and high risk infants. J Hum Lact 1994; 10(3):163-8.

96. Hurst NM, Meier PP, Engstrom JL, Myatt A. Mothers performing in-home measurement of milk intake during breastfeeding of their preterm infants: maternal reactions and feeding outcomes. J Hum Lact 2004; 20(2):178-87.

97. California Perinatal Quality Care Collaborative PQIP. Toolkit: Nutritional support of the VLBW infant, part 1. In: California Perinatal Quality Care Collaborative, Perinatal Quality Improvement Panel, www.cpqcc.org; 2004.

98. American Academy of Pediatrics, Section on Breastfeeding. Policy Statement: Breastfeeding and the use of human milk. Pediatrics 2005; 115(2):496-506.

99. California Perinatal Quality Care Collaborative PQIP. Toolkit: Care and management of the late preterm infant. 2007. www.cpqcc.org.

Chapter 10:
BREASTFEEDING THE NICU GRADUATE

"It would be ideal to prevent postnatal malnutrition in preterm infants, but so far that has proved difficult. Catch up growth may have many benefits, and may lead to improved development, as well as reduce the stigma of small stature. Its long-term metabolic consequences, for good or bad, are currently unclear." [1]

Clinical experience and research confirm that although many preterm infants receive breastmilk at some time in their NICU course, many fewer are receiving breastmilk or breastfeeding at discharge, and even less are receiving any breastmilk or breastfeeding at 2, 4, 6, and 12 months after discharge home. [2-7]

In the U.S., the average corrected age of preterm infants at discharge is approximately 35-36 weeks and the weight is 1800-2500 grams, but infants vary enormously in age, weight, medical condition, and nutritional needs. In many parts of the world, preterm infants are discharged much heavier and older than in the U.S. and have, therefore, had much more opportunity to mature and learn to breastfeed. Also, in many countries, mothers have had the opportunity to remain in the hospital or close by, thereby facilitating breastfeeding. [8]

In a country like Sweden where breastfeeding is part of the culture, mothers have guaranteed parental leave of 480 days and access to child health care is cost-free, so prematurity, birth weight, and neonatal disorders appear to have no effect on breastfeeding duration. [9] However, in the U.S., socioeconomic status, maternal education, and unemployment are significantly associated with earlier weaning. In another Swedish study, [7] the duration of breastfeeding among preterm infants was significantly shorter than in infants born at term, but still significantly higher than even term infants in the U.S. (Table 1). In this study, exclusive breastfeeding was defined as feeding at the breast only! Partial breastfeeding was breastfeeding plus additional expressed breastmilk, formula, or other foods.

Table 1: Breastfeeding at Discharge from the Neonatal Unit and at 2, 4, and 6 Months Corrected Age

	<28 wks (n=27)	28-31 wks (n=82)	32-36 wks (n=301)	≥ 37 wks (n=517)
Breastfeeding at discharge (%)				
Exclusively	38*	34*	56	63
Partly	38	50	40	35
Not breastfed	24*	16*	4	2
Breastfeeding at 2 months CA (%)				
Exclusively	44*	44*	66*+	83+
Partly	19	28*	24*	11
Not breastfed	37*	28*	10*	6
Breastfeeding at 4 months CA (%)				
Exclusively	26*	34*	51*	70
Partly	30	21	28*	19
Not breastfed	44*	45*	21*	11
Breastfeeding at 6 months CA (%)				
Exclusively	4*+	6*+	17+	24+
Partly	37	41	48	54
Not breastfed	59*	52*	35*	22
Exclusive breastfeeding is feeding only at breast. Partly breastfeeding is breastfeeding plus expressed breastmilk or other liquids or solids. *p<0.05, versus infants born at term +p<0.05, versus exclusive breastfeeding at discharge				

Source: Akerstrom et al., 2007.[7] Reprinted with permission from Blackwell Publishing.

The multiple benefits of breastmilk and breastfeeding should not terminate at hospital discharge. Adequate support should be arranged to allow each mother to reach her breastfeeding goal, while ensuring appropriate growth and nutrition for the infant. Exclusive breastfeeding without supplementation at hospital discharge is *not* the primary goal for most ex-very low birth weight infants. In addition, many preterm infants are discharged home significantly malnourished, falling from appropriate for gestational age at birth to small for gestational age at discharge.[10, 11]

Post-Discharge Nutrition

At the time of discharge, when infants are allowed ad libitum intake, the intake volume varies widely and varies with caloric density.[12-14] Infants tend to consume higher volumes of lower caloric formulas.[12-14] In theory, human milk is inadequate to support the requirements for the very low birth weight (VLBW) infant during the first six to twelve months after discharge.[15] Whether discharged at or before term, most VLBW infants have continued higher needs for protein than that for term infants[15,16] (Table 2). The general recommendation is for exclusively breastfed preterm infants to receive supplementation or fortification post-discharge, although there are many important questions remaining to be studied.[11]

Table 2: Macronutrients Supplied by Commonly Used Formulas for Preterm Infants at the Time of Discharge, Assuming Intake of 200 mL/kg/day

	Target	Human Milk	Similac Advance w/Fe 20 cal/oz	Enfamil Lipil w/ Fe 20 cal/oz	Similac Neosure Advance 22 cal/oz	Enfamil Enfacare Lipil 22 cal/oz
Calories/kg	120-130	138	136	136	150	148
Protein g/kg	2.5-3.5	2.0	2.8	2.8	4.2	4.2
Fat g/kg	6.0-8.0	7.8	7.2	7.2	8.2	7.8
CHO g/kg	10-14	13.2	14.6	14.6	15.4	15.8
Vitamin A IU/kg	1000	780	406	406	686	666
Vitamin D IU	200-400	4	80	80	104	118
Vitamin E IU/kg	6-12	2.0	4.0	2.6	5.4	6.0
Ca mg/kg	150-175	50	106	106	156	178
P mg/kg	90-105	26	56	72	92	98
Fe mg/kg	2-4	0.2	2.4	2.4	2.6	2.6

Source: Greer, 2007.[15] Reprinted with permission from Elsevier.

Fortification of human milk has been demonstrated to have short-term growth advantages for preterm infants born less than approximately 34 weeks gestation or 1800 grams birth weight, when given both during and after initial hospitalization.[1, 18-21] Very low birth weight infants grow faster and, in most studies, have higher bone mineral content up to one year of age if provided with additional nutrients (especially protein, calcium, and phosphorus).[21-25] In one study, when mothers' own milk was fed at 200 mL/kg/day from one week of age to 36 weeks corrected age in preterm infants less than 32 weeks at birth, neither phosphate supplementation alone, human milk multi-nutrient fortifier, or preterm formula had any effect on bone mineral content at term.[26]

In the first randomized controlled trial (pilot study) conducted to evaluate the impact of adding energy and multiple nutrients to human milk-fed low birth weight infants after discharge, O'Connor et at.[27] randomly assigned human milk-fed (≥80% feeding/day) low birth weight (750-1800 g) infants (n=39) at hospital discharge to either a control or an intervention group. The control group was discharged from the hospital on unfortified human milk and the intervention group had approximately one half of their human milk intake fortified each day with a powdered multinutrient human milk fortifier (Similac Human Milk Fortifier, Abbot Nutrition; 4 packets per 100 mL expressed breastmilk) for 12 weeks after discharge. Mothers in both study groups were provided free of charge iron/vitamin drops, a double breast-expression electric pump (Purely Yours, Ameda), and extensive lactation support. Mothers in the intervention group also received the human milk fortifier free of charge.

Of 143 infants who were known to be primarily human milk fed, approximately one third did not meet eligibility criteria and one third refused to participate. Of the remaining 39 infants, there were 34 with sufficient data at 12 weeks after discharge for an intention to treat analysis. The average weight at discharge was 2598 ± 535 g (control) and 2785 ± 465 (intervention) with an average discharge gestational age of 38 weeks. Twenty-five percent of the infants were small for gestational age (SGA), so all statistical analyses were rerun excluding the SGA infants, with no significant differences in findings. Growth parameters, enteral intake, and duration of breastfeeding were assessed. Infants in the intervention group were longer during the study period (12 weeks from discharge), and those born at 1250 grams or less had larger head circumferences than infants in the control group. Interestingly, two-thirds of the women in both groups had the galactogogue domperidone prescribed.[27]

The mean volume of feedings (mL/kg/d) from any source (human milk+formula+other) was greater in the control group than in the intervention group at the 4-, 8-, and 12-week home visits (p=0.02), confirming the tendency to self-regulate intake based on energy density.[12-14] In addition, they saw no differences between groups with respect to the number of infants who were being human milk-fed, the total volume of human milk provided each day, or the percentage of daily feedings provided as human milk. At 12 weeks after discharge, 71 ± 38% (control) and 88 ± 15.4% (intervention) of daily feedings were provided as human milk, a percentage much higher than usually reported,[3, 28-30] presumably because of the high proportion of predominant milk feeding at discharge and the significant amount of lactation support received post-discharge.[27]

Exclusively breastfed former preterm infants tend to "catch-up" if given sufficient time (two to eight years).[31-33] The optimal growth rate (reference target) has not yet been established for post-discharge preterm infants.[15,34] It is unclear whether the rapid catch-up growth seen with supplementation is of benefit or harm for long term overall health, growth and neurodevelopment, cardiovascular health, or insulin resistance.[1,18,35,36] There is, however, an association of slower weight gain and delayed head circumference growth with adverse neurodevelopmental outcome.[37] Despite this, one study demonstrated a positive association between duration of human milk feeding and the Bayley Mental Index at 12 months corrected age (CA), after controlling for confounding variables of home environment and maternal intelligence.[21] In addition, infants with chronic lung disease fed 50% or more human milk until term CA had a mean Bayley Motor Index about 11 points higher at 12 months CA compared with infants predominantly formula-fed until term.

All infants less than 34 weeks or less than 1800 grams at birth, and other larger infants with nutritional risk factors (chronic lung disease, short gut, neurologic impairment, etc.), should have a complete nutritional assessment prior to discharge which includes both growth parameters (weight, length, head circumference) and biochemical measurements (phosphorus, alkaline phosphatase, urea nitrogen, transthyretin/prealbumin).[1, 18, 38] Although recommended by several authors, routine measurements of serum alkaline phosphatase and serum phosphate in one study of preterm infants less than 32 weeks were not predictive of bone mineralization at term.[39] If the infant is taking ≥ 160-180 cc/kg/day or more and growth parameters are normal (Table 3) or improving on human milk alone for a week or more prior to discharge, human milk alone should be adequate post-discharge.

Table 3: Post-Discharge Nutritional Monitoring

Nutritional Assessment	Action Values
Growth	
Weight gain	< 20-25 gm/day
Linear growth	< 0.5-1 cm/wk
Head circumference	< 0.5 cm/wk
Biochemical Assessment	
Phosphorus	< 4.5 mg/dL
Alkaline phosphatase	> 450 IU/L
BUN	< 5 mg/mL
Pre-albumin/transthyretin	< 10 mg/dL

Source: Modified from Hall, 2000; 2001.

If supplementation is deemed necessary, breastfeeding can be supported by having the mother directly breastfeed, then substitute from one to four feedings (as calculated for nutritional needs) per 24 hours of preterm or post-discharge enhanced formula to reach growth and biochemical goals.[38] Alternately, powdered follow-up formula can be added to expressed breastmilk as a fortifier. Human milk fortifier and powdered preterm formula are not usually recommended post-discharge because the nutrient content is far too great for the infant at the time of discharge, and it is expensive and difficult to prepare correctly.[38, 40] Hindmilk (the fat-rich milk at the end of a breastfeed) may supply extra calories, but provides no extra protein or minerals,[41] and recent evidence suggests no improvement in growth.[42]

Multivitamins, dosed to deliver at least 1500 IU/day of vitamin A, 20-70 mg/day of vitamin C, and 400 IU/day of vitamin D should be added at discharge. B vitamins are also necessary for the former preterm infant receiving unfortified human milk. A multivitamin preparation dosed at 1 mL/day will usually supply all of the above. If formula constitutes more than 50% of an infant's daily intake, the dose should be 0.5 mL per day. Multivitamin administration should be continued for at least three to six months, although the optimum length of use has yet to be determined.[1, 18]

At discharge, elemental iron should be continued/added at 2 mg/kg/day. If formula constitutes 50% or more of the diet, the dose should be reduced to 1 mg/kg/day.[18,19] When the multivitamin with iron preparation is stopped, the infant should be started on oral vitamin D drops or ACD vitamins to provide at least 200 IU per day until such time as the child is drinking sufficient milk to provide that amount of vitamin D.[43]

A repeat biochemical assessment has been recommended at one week and one month post-discharge.[18,19,38] Repeat biochemical assessments may be appropriate through at least one year corrected age. Follow-up should be arranged with the dietitian as needed to adjust calorie, protein, and other nutrient intake.[40]

Discharge Planning

Discharge planning should be initiated upon admission to the NICU with an assessment of the mother's breastfeeding goals and preferences.[44,45] Prenatal intention to breastfeed is one of the strongest predictors of initiation and duration of breastfeeding.[46-49] Due to the physiology of breastfeeding, milk expression should begin soon after the infant's birth.[50] A full milk supply at discharge is one of the best predictors of successful breastfeeding post-discharge.[3,51]

Mothers are more likely to eventually succeed in transitioning their infants when they are exclusively breastmilk fed by discharge.[51] The duration of human milk feedings is significantly longer for those who transition to breastfeeding versus those who only receive expressed milk. In one study,[4] the breastfeeding rates at four months of age for these two groups was 72% versus less than 10%. Healthier infants with shorter hospital stays and singletons versus multiples were more likely to be breastmilk fed for an extended duration.[4,6,52]

In the week prior to discharge, an individualized nutritional plan should be prepared in coordination with the neonatologist, lactation consultant, dietitian, and family. If possible, the plan should be reviewed with the post-discharge primary physician at the time of discharge and an in-hospital growth chart, as well as a discharge summary sent home with the patient. Post-discharge nutrition is a newly understood concern and many physicians may not be aware of the need for special diets and frequent visits to monitor growth and biochemical status.[38,40] The plan should be based on the skills of the infant, the mother's milk production, the infant's nutritional needs, and the mother's parenting skills and support, and should include provisions for making the transition to full breastfeeding.[44,45]

Many parents of VLBW infants expect (incorrectly) that the infant will be able to breastfeed exclusively at discharge and thrive. If a rooming-in suite is available and parents are amenable, a one to two night stay before discharge can point out problems and maximize learning.[40,44] At present, however, there are no randomized controlled trials that address whether rooming-in prior to discharge is associated with higher exclusive or any breastfeeding rates, or better long term outcomes for VLBW infants.[40]

Transition to Full Breastfeeding at Home

Prior to discharge, the majority of infants receive supplementary feeds (a feeding in place of a breastfeeding session and/or a feeding given in conjunction with a breastfeeding session). It remains unclear how the type of delivery system of these feeds, i.e., tube, cup, or bottle, affects the long term likelihood of breastfeeding. Studies, which report an advantage with one method over another, have not controlled for milk production, and therefore may self-select mothers with copious production, already more likely to succeed.[53,54] More specifically, in mothers with milk production less than approximately 500cc/day, the infant will have more difficulty accessing his entire feed at the breast, in contrast to the efficient, high flow rate of other systems, such as the bottle.[55,56] Keeping milk production ahead of infant requirement allows the infant a faster rate of flow and, therefore, an advantage in effective milk transfer.

Continue pumping: Mothers should continue to pump to maintain milk supply for at least one to two months post-discharge. A common mistake is to advise the pump-dependent mother to stop pumping and just breastfeed. As the hospital-grade electric pump is typically more effective in milk removal than the infant, and the infant is more successful in milk transfer when the flow rate is high,[57] "triple feeding" (breastfeeding, supplementation, then pumping) may be an acceptable initial and temporary option. When the volume of supplementation decreases, the mother can alternate between limited breastfeeds followed by supplementation, and limited breastfeeds followed by pumping. Initially, as small infants fall asleep at the breast due to fatigue rather than satiety, time limits of 20-30 minutes are advised. Once unlimited demand breastfeeding is undertaken, the frequency of feeding typically increases, while the pumping frequency can be tapered, dropping a session every two to three days.[44,45,51,55,58]

Maximize skin-to-skin care: Kangaroo care should be continued after discharge home. The multiple benefits of skin-to-skin care, even in limited sessions, include improved milk production and faster transitioning to direct breastfeeding.[59,60] In a center where 93% of infants are breastmilk-fed at discharge and 80% have established full breastfeeding at a mean post menstrual age of 36.0 weeks (33.4-40.0 weeks), the time spent holding and feeding the infant was highly correlated with developing competency at the breast.[6, 61]

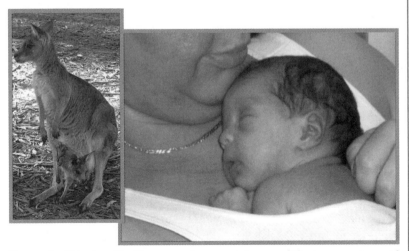

Figure 1: Skin-to-skin (kangaroo) care at home. (Photos courtesy of Nancy Wight MD)

Provide mothers with tools to assess milk intake: Clinical estimates of milk intake are unreliable.[62,63] Test weighing pre- and post-breastfeeding enables mothers of preterm infants to quantify milk intake without increasing their stress level or jeopardizing the success of breastfeeding.[62-64] Scales may be rented for post-discharge use. Daily weight gains, averaging 15-30 g/day, may relax the need for frequent clinic visits. Although preterm birth may not limit milk production capacity, preterm infants are vulnerable to under consumption until term corrected age or beyond,[65] so close monitoring is critical. Other strategies involve giving mothers a 24-hour minimum intake goal.[40]

Provide realistic time guidelines and frequent follow-up: A recent study provides anticipatory guidance. During the first week home for a group of preterm infants (corrected age of 35-36 weeks), the mean milk intake at breast was approximately one-third of the total daily milk intake, with the remaining two-thirds coming from expressed milk by bottle. By the end of week four at home, two-thirds of the total daily milk intake was at breast and one-third was from the bottle.[66]

Routine primary care follow-up should be arranged as needed, usually two to five days post discharge. The method of supplementation initiated in the hospital and agreed upon by mother, physician, nurse, and lactation consultant should be continued at home. Lactation follow-up should be scheduled for two to three days post-discharge, and thereafter as needed until full direct breastfeeding is achieved, or the mother ceases breastfeeding.[44,45] Dietitian follow-up is recommended post-discharge for both infant assessment and maternal nutrition counseling.[40]

Breastfeeding educational and promotional efforts, as well as support groups, have been shown to improve breastfeeding rates in the hospital and at discharge.[67-70] "Graduate" mothers should be encouraged to continue to attend these support groups, as they can both give and receive support and information. The mother should also be referred to other community nutritional and breastfeeding support resources, such as Women, Infants, and Children Supplemental Nutrition Program (WIC), La Leche League International, and other services locally available.[44,45,58]

Although an optimal outcome may be for preterm infants to transition to at-breast feedings prior to or shortly after hospital discharge, earlier discharges and limited home health care follow-up may compromise this outcome. In addition, various reasons for mothers' inability to feed their infants at breast (low milk supply, lack of maternal confidence, etc.) or resistance to feeding at the breast (lack of commitment to breastfeeding prior to the preterm birth, embarrassment of feeding in public) may prevent full at-breast feeding.[71] The choice to breastfeed or provide breastmilk is different for the mother of a preterm infant.[72]

CONCLUSION

There is much we don't know about the optimal growth rates and nutrition for the premature infant after discharge. Mothers should be encouraged to spend as much time as possible with their infants in the NICU, and they should be supported in their efforts to establish and maintain a full milk supply. Kangaroo care, non-nutritive breastfeeding, and earlier direct breastfeeding in the NICU, along with a full milk supply will help mothers continue to provide "liquid gold" for their growing infants long after discharge from the NICU.

KEY CONCEPTS

- The optimal growth rate (reference target) has not yet been established for post-discharge preterm infants.

- VLBW infants grow faster and have higher bone mineral content up to one year if provided with additional nutrients (especially protein, calcium, and phosphorus).

- Exclusively breastfed former preterm infants tend to "catch-up" if given sufficient time (two to eight years).

- It is unclear whether "catch-up" growth is good or bad.

- As all infants do not require fortification post-discharge, select the population for enriched diets.

- Breastfeeding should be encouraged for preterm infants post-discharge.

- Monitor growth and nutritional status in post-discharge preterm infants.

- Preterm infants are vulnerable to under consumption until term or more corrected age.

- Adequacy of milk supply is a key factor in successful transition to full direct breastfeeding.

- Mothers should continue to pump to maintain milk supply for at least one month post-discharge.

- "Discharge planning" starts at or before admission to the NICU.

- Prepare a post-discharge nutritional plan with input from the mother, dietician, lactation consultant, neonatologist, and follow-up primary care physician.

- Kangaroo care should be continued at home.

REFERENCES:

1. Griffin IJ. Postdischarge nutrition for high risk neonates. Clin Perinatol 2002; 29(2):327-44.

2. Killersreiter B, Grimmer I, Buhrer C, Dudenhausen JW, Obladen M. Early cessation of breast milk feeding in very low birthweight infants. Early Hum Dev 2001; 60(3):193-205.

3. Furman L, Minich N, Hack M. Correlates of lactation in mothers of very low birth weight infants. Pediatrics 2002; 109(4):e57 www.pediatrics.org/cgi/content/full/109/4/e57.

4. Smith MM, Durkin M, Hinton VJ, Bellinger D, Kuhn L. Initiation of breastfeeding among mothers of very low birth weight infants. Pediatrics 2003; 111(6 Pt 1):1337-42.

5. Hedberg Nyqvist K, Ewald U. Infant and maternal factors in the development of breastfeeding behaviour and breastfeeding outcome in preterm infants. Acta Paediatr 1999; 88(11):1194-203.

6. Flacking R, Nyqvist KH, Ewald U, Wallin L. Long-term duration of breastfeeding in Swedish low birth weight infants. J Hum Lact 2003; 19(2):157-65.

7. Akerstrom S, Asplund I, Norman M. Successful breastfeeding after discharge of preterm and sick newborn infants. Acta Paediatr 2007; 96(10):1450-4.

8. Galtry J. The impact on breastfeeding of labour market policy and practice in Ireland, Sweden, and the USA. Soc Sci Med 2003; 57(1):167-77.

9. Flacking R, Wallin L, Ewald U. Perinatal and socioeconomic determinants of breastfeeding duration in very preterm infants. Acta Paediatr 2007; 96(8):1126-30.

10. Cazacu A, Fraley J, Schanler R. We are inadequately nourishing healthy low birth weight infants. Pediatric Research 2001; 49:343A.

11. Dusick AM, Poindexter BB, Ehrenkranz RA, Lemons JA. Growth failure in the preterm infant: can we catch up? Semin Perinatol 2003; 27(4):302-10.

12. Carver JD, Wu PY, Hall RT, et al. Growth of preterm infants fed nutrient-enriched or term formula after hospital discharge. Pediatrics 2001; 107(4):683-9.

13. Cooke RJ, McCormick K, Griffin IJ, et al. Feeding preterm infants after hospital discharge: effect of diet on body composition. Pediatr Res 1999; 46(4):461-4.

14. Fomon SJ, Filmer LJ, Jr., Thomas LN, Anderson TA, Nelson SE. Influence of formula concentration on caloric intake and growth of normal infants. Acta Paediatr Scand 1975; 64(2):172-81.

15. Greer FR. Post-discharge nutrition: what does the evidence support? Semin Perinatol 2007; 31(2):89-95.

16. Carlson SJ, Ziegler EE. Nutrient intakes and growth of very low birth weight infants. J Perinatol 1998; 18(4):252-8.

17. Tsang RC, Lucas A, Uauy R, et al. (eds). Nutrition of the preterm infant: scientific basis and practical guidelines (Ed 2). Cincinnati, OH: Digital Educational Publishing, Inc.; 2005.

18. Hall RT. Nutritional follow-up of the breastfeeding premature infant after hospital discharge. Pediatr Clin North Am 2001; 48(2):453-60.

19. Schanler R. Post-discharge nutrition for the preterm infant. Acta Paediatrica 2005; 94(Suppl 449):68-73.

20. Carver JD. Nutrition for preterm infants after hospital discharge. Adv Pediatr 2005; 52:23-47.

21. O'Connor DL, Jacobs J, Hall R, et al. Growth and development of premature infants fed predominantly human milk, predominantly premature infant formula, or a combination of human milk and premature formula. J Pediatr Gastroenterol Nutr 2003; 37(4):437-46.

22. Friel J, Andrews W, Matthew J, et al. Improved growth of very low birthweight infants. Nutr Res 1993; 13:611-20.

23. Lucas A, Bishop N, King F, Cole T. Randomized trial of nutrition for preterm infants after discharge. Arch Dis Child 1992; 67: 324-7.

24. Wheeler RE, Hall RT. Feeding of premature infant formula after hospital discharge of infants weighing less than 1800 grams at birth. J Perinatol 1996; 16(2 Pt 1):111-6.

25. Worrell L, Thorp J, Tucker Rea. The effects of the introduction of a high-nutrient transitional formula on growth and development of very-low-birth-weight infants. J Perinatol 2002; 22:112-9.

26. Faerk J, Petersen S, Peitersen B, Michaelsen KF. Diet and bone mineral content at term in premature infants. Pediatr Res 2000; 47(1):148-56.

27. O'Connor DL, Khan S, Weishuhn K, et al. Growth and nutrient intakes of human milk-fed preterm infants provided with extra energy and nutrients after hospital discharge. Pediatrics 2008; 121(4):766-76.

28. Callen J, Pinelli J. A review of the literature examining the benefits and challenges, incidence and duration, and barriers to breastfeeding in preterm infants. Adv Neonatal Care 2005; 5(2):72-88; quiz 90-92.

29. Kaufman KJ, Hall LA. Influences of the social network on choice and duration of breast-feeding in mothers of preterm infants. Res Nurs Health 1989; 12(3):149-59.

30. Pinelli J, Atkinson SA, Saigal S. Randomized trial of breastfeeding support in very low-birth-weight infants. Arch Pediatr Adolesc Med 2001; 155(5):548-53.

31. Backstrom M, Maki R, Kuusela A, et al. The long-term effect of early mineral, vit D, and breast milk intake on bone mineral status in 9-to 11-year-old children born prematurely. J Pediatr Gastroenterol Nutr 1999; 29:575-82.

32. Morley R, Lucas A. Randomized diet in the neonatal period and growth performance until 7.5-8 yr of age in preterm children. Am J Clin Nutr 2000; 71(3):822-8.

33. Schanler R, Burns P, Abrams S, Garza C. Bone mineralization outcomes in human milk-fed preterm infants. Pediatr Res 1992; 31(6):583-6.

34. Schanler RJ. Post-discharge nutrition for the preterm infant. Acta Paediatr Suppl 2005; 94(449):68-73.

35. Regan F, Cutfield W, Jefferies C, Robinson E, Hofman P. The impact of early nutrition in premature infants on later childhood insulin sensitivity and growth. Pediatrics 2006; 118(5):1943-9.

36. Singhal A, Lucas A. Early origins of cardiovascular disease: is there a unifying hypothesis? Lancet 2004; 363(9421):1642-5.

37. Ehrenkranz RA, Dusick AM, Vohr BR, Wright LL, Wrage LA, Poole WK. Growth in the neonatal intensive care unit influences neurodevelopmental and growth outcomes of extremely low birth weight infants. Pediatrics 2006; 117(4):1253-61.

38. Academy of Breastfeeding Medicine. Clinical Protocol #12: Transitioning the breastfeeding/breastmilk-fed premature infant from the neonatal intensive care unit to home. www.bfmed.org. 2004.

39. Faerk J, Peitersen B, Petersen S, Michaelsen KF. Bone mineralization in premature infants cannot be predicted from serum alkaline phosphatase or serum phosphate. Arch Dis Child Fetal Neonatal Ed 2002; 87(2):F133-6.

40. California Perinatal Quality Care Collaborative PQIP. Toolkit: Nutritional support of the VLBW infant, part 2. In: California Perinatal Quality Care Collaborative, Perinatal Quality Improvement Panel, www.cpqcc.org; 2005.

41. Valentine C, Hurst N, Schanler R. Hindmilk improves weight gain in low-birth-weight infants fed human milk. J Pediatr Gastroenterol Nutr 1994; 18(4):474-7.

42. Dayanikli P, et al. Hindmilk feeding in very low birth weight infants. Abstr # 2526 & #2194. In: Pediatric Academic Societies; 2004; San Francisco; 2004.

43. American Academy of Pediatrics, Section on Breastfeeding and Committee on Nutrition. Clinical Report: Prevention of rickets and vitamin d deficiency: new guidelines for vitamin D intake. Pediatrics 2003; 111(4):908-10.

44. Morton J. The role of the pediatrician in extended breastfeeding of the preterm infant. Pediatric Annals 2003; 32(5):308-16.

45. Morton JA. Strategies to support extended breastfeeding of the premature infant. Adv Neonatal Care 2002; 2(5):267-82.

46. Coreil J, Murphy J. Maternal commitment, lactation practices, and breastfeeding duration. JOGNN 1988; July/August:273-8.

47. de Oliveira MI, Camacho LA, Tedstone AE. Extending breastfeeding duration through primary care: a systematic review of prenatal and postnatal interventions. J Hum Lact 2001; 17(4):326-43.

48. Dennis CL. Breastfeeding initiation and duration: a 1990-2000 literature review. J Obstet Gynecol Neonatal Nurs 2002; 31(1):12-32.

49. Donath SM, Amir LH. Relationship between prenatal infant feeding intention and initiation and duration of breastfeeding: a cohort study. Acta Paediatr 2003; 92(3):352-6.

50. California Perinatal Quality Care Collaborative PQIP. Toolkit: Nutritional support of the VLBW infant, part 1. In: California Perinatal Quality Care Collaborative, Perinatal Quality Improvement Panel, www.cpqcc.org; 2004.

51. Wooldridge J, Hall W. Posthospitalization breastfeeding patterns of moderately preterm infants. J Perinat Neonat Nurs 2003 2003; 17(1):50-64.

52. Geraghty SR, Pinney SM, Sethuraman G, Roy-Chaudhury A, Kalkwarf HJ. Breast milk feeding rates of mothers of multiples compared to mothers of singletons. Ambul Pediatr 2004; 4(3):226-31.

53. Collins CT, Ryan P, Crowther CA, McPhee AJ, Paterson S, Hiller JE. Effect of bottles, cups, and dummies on breast feeding in preterm infants: a randomised controlled trial. BMJ 2004; 329(7459):193-8.

54. Kliethermes PA, Cross ML, Lanese MG, Johnson KM, Simon SD. Transitioning preterm infants with nasogastric tube supplementation: increased likelihood of breastfeeding. J Obstet Gynecol Neonatal Nurs 1999; 28(3):264-73.

55. Blaymore Bier JA, Ferguson AE, Morales Y, Liebling JA, Oh W, Vohr BR. Breastfeeding infants who were extremely low birth weight. Pediatrics 1997; 100(6):E3.

56. Furman L, Minich N. Efficiency of breastfeeding as compared to bottle-feeding in very low birth weight (VLBW, <1.5 kg) infants. J Perinatol 2004; 24(11):706-13.

57. Schrank W, Al-Sayed LE, Beahm PH, Thach BT. Feeding responses to free-flow formula in term and preterm infants. J Pediatr 1998; 132(3 Pt 1):426-30.

58. Wight NE. Breastfeeding the borderline (near-term) preterm infant. Pediatric Annals 2003; 32(5):329-36.

59. Bier JA, Ferguson AE, Morales Y, et al. Comparison of skin-to-skin contact with standard contact in low-birth-weight infants who are breast-fed. Arch Pediatr Adolesc Med 1996; 150(12):1265-9.

60. Hurst NM, Valentine CJ, Renfro L, Burns P, Ferlic L. Skin-to-skin holding in the neonatal intensive care unit influences maternal milk volume. J Perinatol 1997; 17(3):213-7.

61. Nyqvist KH, Sjoden PO, Ewald U. The development of preterm infants' breastfeeding behavior. Early Hum Dev 1999; 55(3):247-64.

62. Meier PP, Engstrom JL, Crichton CL, Clark DR, Williams MM, Mangurten HH. A new scale for in-home test-weighing for mothers of preterm and high risk infants. J Hum Lact 1994; 10(3):163-8.

63. Scanlon K, Alexander M, Serdula M, et al. Assessment of infant feeding: the validity of measuring milk intake. Nutrition Reviews 2002; 60(8):235-51.

64. Hurst NM, Meier PP, Engstrom JL, Myatt A. Mothers performing in-home measurement of milk intake during breastfeeding of their preterm infants: maternal reactions and feeding outcomes. J Hum Lact 2004; 20(2):178-87.

65. Meier P. Supporting lactation in mothers with very low birth weight infants. Pediatric Annals 2003; 32(5):317-25.

66. Hurst N, Meier P, Engstrom J. Milk volume consumed at breast during the first month post-discharge (PDC) for preterm infants (PT): implications for management of breastfeeding and infant growth. Pediatr Res 2000; 47:197A.

67. Meier PP, Engstrom JL, Mingolelli SS, Miracle DJ, Kiesling S. The Rush Mothers' Milk Club: breastfeeding interventions for mothers with very-low-birth-weight infants. J Obstet Gynecol Neonatal Nurs 2004; 33(2):164-74.

68. Merewood A, Chamberlain LB, Cook JT, Philipp BL, Malone K, Bauchner H. The effect of peer counselors on breastfeeding rates in the neonatal intensive care unit: results of a randomized controlled trial. Arch Pediatr Adolesc Med 2006; 160(7):681-5.

69. Sisk PM, Lovelady CA, Dillard RG. Effect of education and lactation support on maternal decision to provide human milk for very-low-birth-weight infants. Adv Exp Med Biol 2004; 554:307-11.

70. Sisk PM, Lovelady CA, Dillard RG, Gruber KJ. Lactation counseling for mothers of very low birth weight infants: effect on maternal anxiety and infant intake of human milk. Pediatrics 2006; 117(1):e67-75.

71. Buckley K, Charles G. Benefits and challenges of transitioning preterm infants to at-breast feedings. International Breastfeeding Journal; 2006: doi:10.1186/746-4358-1-13.

72. Miracle DJ, Meier PP, Bennett PA. Mothers' decisions to change from formula to mothers' milk for very-low-birth-weight infants. J Obstet Gynecol Neonatal Nurs 2004; 33(6):692-703.

Chapter 11:
THE BREASTFEEDING SUPPORTIVE NICU

Mothers of very low birth weight (VLBW) infants are less likely to breastfeed than mothers of healthy, term infants.[1-7] While an average of 69-71% of term infants in the U.S. does any breastfeeding in the hospital before discharge,[8,9] the average rate of preterm infants receiving *any* breastmilk at hospital discharge is approximately 50%.[3,4] This is especially concerning because the evidence suggests that human milk may especially benefit premature and high-risk infants.[10] Other countries seem to have more success with breastfeeding in the NICU and at discharge.[11-13] As seen in prior chapters, breastfeeding preterm infants present multiple challenges because of physiology (of both mother and infant), psychology, and environment. In this chapter, we consider the physical and social environment of the preterm infant and his mother, and suggest ways in which both initiation and duration of breastfeeding may be enhanced.

BARRIERS/CHALLENGES TO BREASTFEEDING IN THE NICU

Physical Environment

It is fairly easy to see that the physical environment of the NICU may be a significant impediment to successful breastfeeding. It is noisy, brightly lit, and intimidating, without much privacy, and with a perceived high stress level.[3] Often the infant cannot be handled or held for some time because of physiologic instability and a multitude of tubes and wires (Figure 1). In addition, many times the infant has been transported from a distant delivery hospital or the mother is too ill herself to visit the NICU.

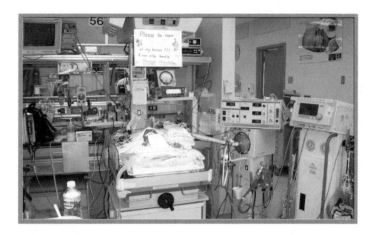

Figure 1: NICU Environment (Photo courtesy of Nancy Wight MD)

Infant Factors

The small size and perceived fragility of the infant, the infant's physical appearance, and medical complications are barriers to breastfeeding.[3,14] A preterm infant has a disproportionately large head when compared to the average term infant, and specific congenital malformations, poor perfusion, or just a lack of response to the parents' voice or touch may compromise bonding and breastfeeding. The small size of the infant's mouth when compared to the mother's nipple, combined with poor oro-motor skills and suck-swallow-breathing dyscoordination, are often frightening to the mother (Figure 2).

Maternal Factors

Family members and health care professionals sometimes discourage mothers of premature infants from initiating lactation, as they think that providing milk will be an added stress.[15] Mothers may be advised, usually in error,[16] that their medications preclude the use of their milk. Similarly, mothers may be inappropriately advised that their high-risk conditions may interfere with adequate volumes or composition of milk. Mothers of VLBW infants often feel a loss of control of their lives and a loss of their role as a mother. The infant is in the hands of strangers and she is the outsider.[17] Several studies indicate that providing milk for their infants helps mothers cope with

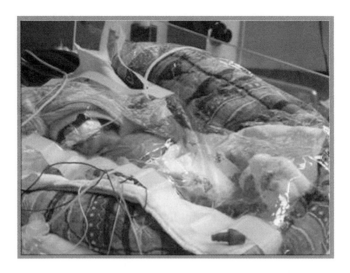

Figure 2: The Preterm Infant (Photo courtesy of Nancy Wight MD)

---

the emotional stresses surrounding the NICU experience and gives them a tangible claim on their infants.[18,19]

Mothers who deliver preterm are at increased risk for delayed lactogenesis and stress mediated lactation problems that can affect milk volume adversely. The prevention, diagnosis, and treatment of low milk volume needs to be given a high priority with evidence-based strategies and appropriate investment of NICU resources.[20] Mothers often report a decline in milk supply in response to stress, such as when their infant has a complication or when the mother returns to work. Maternal exhaustion, either due to peripartum events, or later, due to return to work or home duties, is also a barrier to establishing breastfeeding.[3] Mothers who have had prolonged antenatal inpatient stays before delivery may feel guilty for being away from home, spouse, and children. Maternal anxiety over her ill infant and misinformation about breastfeeding in general, and breastfeeding a preterm infant specifically, are significant barriers to making the decision to provide breastmilk, establishing and maintaining a milk supply, and eventually direct breastfeeding.

A recent qualitative analysis of barriers to breastfeeding for preterm infants in the hospital and post discharge noted six key barriers and a time-dependent pattern of the barriers.[14] The barriers were:

- Maternal perception of infant's physically compromised status
- Poor breastfeeding technique (inability to latch and transfer milk)
- Mother's emotional compromise
- Low milk volume
- Nipple and breast problems
- Complementary feeding (bottle feeding before breastfeeding)[3]

Breast and nipple problems predominated during the NICU stay with low milk supply being the biggest barrier at the time of discharge, and poor technique and a perceived compromised infant predominating post discharge. Reasons for weaning included: infant fighting at the breast, weak suck, infant refusing the breast, inadequate milk supply, fussy and hungry infant, difficulty latching, and mother concerned about the infant not getting enough milk.[4]

Social Environment

The infant's father, grandparents, and other family members or friends may also have significant influence over the mother, providing either enormous support or significant barriers to establishing breastfeeding. Although most studies of fathers' influence on breastfeeding have been done with fathers of term infants, after controlling for potentially confounding demographic and biomedical factors, the father's reported preference for breastfeeding was found to be the most important factor influencing a woman's decision to breastfeed (OR=10.18)[21] or bottle feed.[22] Where breastfeeding is the social norm (e.g., Sweden), a greater percentage of mothers of preterm infants provide breastmilk at infant discharge, but a shorter duration of breastfeeding is still seen over full-term controls.[11]

Financial Factors

Financial barriers also contribute: availability and cost of breast pump rental or purchase, cost of other supplies to support breast pumping or feeding, availability and cost of travel to and from the hospital, availability and cost of storing pumped milk, and the housing cost of remaining close by the infant for an extended period of time, if free facilities are not available at the hospital or near by.

Healthcare System

Unfortunately, one of the biggest barriers to successful breastfeeding is the healthcare system and well-meaning health care providers. Inconsistent advice, lack of knowledge or misinformation, personal experience, poor attitude, lack of time, and hospital policies have all been noted to create barriers to successful breastfeeding for mothers of NICU infants. With the Office on Women's Health, Department of Health and Human Services, Centers for Disease Control, American Academy of Pediatrics, American Academy of Family Physicians, American College of Obstetricians and Gynecologists, National Medical Association, American Dietetic Association, National Association of Neonatal Nurses, International Childbirth Education Association, Association of Women's Health, Obstetric and Neonatal Nurses, National Association of Pediatric Nurse Practitioners, National Perinatal Association, and many other organizations actively promoting and supporting breastfeeding, our families are becoming more knowledgeable about breastfeeding issues. Inconsistent, inaccurate information and lack of support by health care professionals have been cited as reasons for breastfeeding failure among many groups of mothers.[23-27]

Many healthcare providers have not had the education and training to support breastfeeding families.[28-36] Education alone will not change professional behavior.[37] Existing studies also suggest that nursing knowledge or attitudes can influence mothers' breastfeeding decisions in the NICU.[18, 38-41] Significant increases in knowledge are possible with nursing education, but attitudes are more difficult to change.[42]

Despite adjustment for other significant variables, the site of care significantly influences breastmilk use at the time of discharge.[43] High breastmilk use sites tend to have physicians who openly express support for breastmilk use, nurses who facilitate breastmilk use and help maximize breastmilk supply, and maternity nurses who convey the need for and expectation of breastmilk production while guiding mothers through the process. Low breastmilk use sites have physicians who have no position or are silent on breastmilk use, have nurses who do not facilitate breastmilk use or help maintain maternal milk supply, and maternity nurses who avoid breastmilk issues and provide no guidance regarding breastmilk production. In short, high breastmilk use sites do not present obstacles to breastmilk use, and low use sites allow such obstacles.[44]

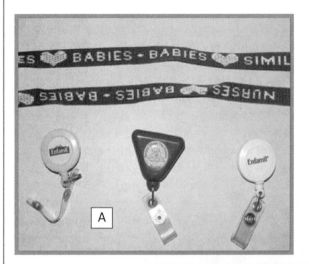

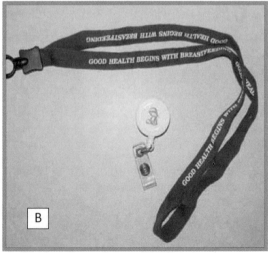

Figure 3: Marketing formula (A-top) vs. marketing health (B-bottom)

Obstetricians, pediatricians, family practitioners and hospital staff may unintentionally undermine breastfeeding by providing formula company access to patients via commercial literature and formula marketing strategies, such as baby clubs, gift bags, and free formula.[45-49] Patient education materials and "gifts" are attractive and perceived as "free." In reality, formula prices include the costs of those materials and gifts. Medical staff wearing lanyards and badge-holders, or using pens, pads, and coffee mugs with formula company logos implies (hopefully unintended) endorsement (Figure 3). Because marketing clearly influences physician choices,[50] the AMA, ACOG, AAP, and other professional societies have developed ethical guidelines that recognize and advise how to mitigate the influence of pharmaceutical company marketing messages and gifts.[50-53] A full review of this issue is available at www.nofreelunch.org. The AAP's policy statement "Breastfeeding and the Use of Human Milk" encourages physicians to "work actively toward eliminating hospital policies and practices that discourage breast feeding (e.g., promotion of infant formula in hospitals including infant formula discharge packs and formula discount coupons....").[54]

Perinatal Support for Breastfeeding

The decision to breastfeed is usually made early in the pregnancy if not before.[55-57] Provider encouragement significantly increases breastfeeding initiation among women of all social and ethnic backgrounds.[58-63] Obstetric and family practice physicians, nurses, and other staff are especially well placed to begin education, risk screening, and anticipatory guidance regarding lactation.[64, 65] Counseling allows patients to become familiar with the fact that breastfeeding is best from a medical perspective.[66] Prenatal intention to breastfeed is one of the strongest predictors of initiation and duration of breastfeeding.[67-70]

"An obstetrician's advice is critical to the mother's decision-making. It takes very little time and effort. It's your gift to the mother, and it's her gift to her baby."

John T. Queenan, MD, Deputy Editor
OBSTETRICS & GYNECOLOGY
July 2003; 102(1):3-4

Antepartum hospital stays are opportunities for dispelling myths (e.g., "I can't breastfeed because I have a premature infant.") and for providing anticipatory guidance regarding procedures to ensure a full milk supply and safe storage and use of pumped milk. After controlling for mother's prenatal breastfeeding intentions, father's feeding preference, and demographic and psychosocial variables, a recent study by the CDC concluded that the mother's perceptions of her prenatal physician's and hospital staff's attitudes on infant feeding was a strong predictor variable of later breastfeeding. Adjusted analyses indicated that patient perceived "no preference" regarding infant feeding by hospital staff was a significant risk factor for failure to breastfeed after six weeks.[71]

Despite considerable evidence to the contrary, breastfeeding is still perceived by some as a lifestyle choice, not a healthcare issue. Health care providers are afraid to "push" breastfeeding for fear of making mothers feel "guilty" if they do not breastfeed.[60, 72, 73] As breastfeeding is even more important for preterm/NICU patients than for term infants, physicians and other healthcare providers have a responsibility to provide accurate evidence-based information of the consequences of a mother's decision, just as we do with other recommendations and parental decisions in the NICU. "Withholding such information would be considered unethical if it involved respiratory care or a surgical procedure. Providing parents with research-based options for infant feeding should be handled in a manner consistent with NICU policies for other decisions about infant management."[74]

The physician(s) in charge of the mother's care should reinforce the importance of breastmilk by inquiring about the mother's pumping or breastfeeding progress during routine post-partum care. The first visit in the NICU with the neonatologist, NNP, PA, or pediatrician should include discussion of the value and benefits of human milk for the NICU infant (with documentation in the medical record). Care should be taken to separate the decision to provide a few days or weeks of pumped breastmilk from the commitment to long-term, exclusive breastfeeding.[75] Physicians should find opportunities to praise mothers' efforts to provide this "liquid gold" for their NICU infant. Preprinted or standing admission orders should include a lactation consultation for all NICU infants. Physician advocacy for

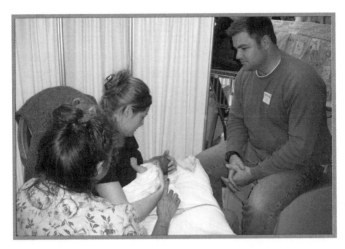

Figure 4: Lactation consultant assisting parents (Photo courtesy of Nancy Wight MD)

---

breastfeeding can have tremendous impact.[58-62, 76] If the doctor tells the mother that her milk is best for the baby's health, the mother will probably attempt to provide it. *Any* breastmilk is better than none, especially for the VLBW infant.[77]

Although all healthcare professionals who care for mothers and infants should have a general knowledge of lactation physiology and breastfeeding management, supporting the mother of a NICU infant often requires special knowledge, skill, and experience. Several models of support have been developed[6,78,79] (Figure 4).

International Board Certified Lactation Consultants (IBCLC) are one method to assist in increasing breastfeeding rates in the NICU through staff and mother education, clinical consultation, and support.[63,78,80-85] Lactation counseling by health care professionals for mothers of VLBW infants has been shown to increase the incidence of lactation initiation and breastmilk feeding without increasing maternal stress and anxiety.[86] In this study, the most common reasons for stopping milk expression were low milk supply, returning to work or school, and inability to pump as needed. A recent study comparing NICU breastfeeding rates found breastfeeding rates at hospital discharge to be 50% in hospitals with lactation consultants and 37% in those hospitals without lactation consultants.[84]

In some units, well-trained NICU RNs and peer counselors may have the knowledge and experience to counsel and manage complicated NICU breastfeeding issues.[15,75] NICU peer counselors have been shown to significantly increase the odds of breastfeeding at 2, 4, 8, and 12 weeks after birth.[87] Postnatal peer counseling was also found to increase both exclusive and any breastfeeding of term LBW infants at six months.[88]

An IBCLC or lactation resource person should be part of the NICU multidisciplinary care team, participating in multidisciplinary and teaching rounds, providing consultations and systematic follow-up, creating and evaluating patient literature, providing education and support for other NICU staff, participating in a breastfeeding support committee or program and research, as appropriate.[17] Given the ever-changing methods of hospital reimbursement for NICU patients, if lactation consultants (LC) are used, they should "bill" (i.e., keep records of services performed) even if their services are not directly reimbursed at present. It has been our experience that where LCs are used extensively, there is a tendency for NICU nursing staff to abdicate most lactation responsibilities to the LCs, rather than participate appropriately in maternal education and support.

Policies & Procedures

In addition to a basic breastfeeding policy for birthing hospitals, the NICU should have its own NICU breastmilk/breastfeeding policy or policies to cover, at a minimum:

- basic principles,

- collection, storage and handling of a mother's own milk for her infant, and

- misadministration of one mother's milk to another mother's infant.

NICUs using fresh and/or heat-treated donor human milk should also have policies and procedures covering this area.[17, 89]

Ancillary policies could also include trophic feeding and other uses for small amounts of colostrum (e.g., mouth care), kangaroo care, alternative feeding methods, co-bedding twins, continuous visitation and pre-discharge rooming-in, outpatient follow-up, and

Table 1: Comprehensive Lactation Program
Patient Education
Prenatal
Perinatal
Postnatal
Consultation
Prenatal outpatient/inpatient
Perinatal inpatient
Postnatal outpatient clinic
Postnatal home health
Durable Medical Equipment
Breast pump rental
Breast pump sales
Supplies
Pump kits
Mother supplies (pads, shield, shells)
Infant supplies (SNS, feeders)
Donor Human Milk
Heat-treated donor human milk
Fresh donor human milk
Support
Support groups
Telephone hot lines or warm lines
Peer counselors
Other
Coordination of care
Staff support and education
Advocacy/public education
Program evaluation/CQI

vendors/gifts. As noted above, a simple formula-logo lanyard can have unintended consequences when worn by a health care employee. All policies should clearly specify who is responsible for each component of lactation support.

Costs & Benefits of Lactation Support in the NICU

Providing lactation support in the NICU is not without cost. Lactation consultants, staff education, pump kits and other supplies, non-commercial patient education materials, breastmilk storage bottles and caps, and dedicated space and equipment for pumping are expenses to the NICU. However, when both the general cost savings from breastfeeding[90,91] and the specific cost savings to the NICU through reduced NEC, late-onset sepsis, shorter hospital stays, and less use of hospital resources, such as total parenteral nutrition (TPN),[92-94] are considered, the investment gives dramatic returns.

Of course, the most important benefit of lactation support in the NICU is the decreased morbidity and mortality and improved long-term outcomes associated with the provision of human milk for preterm and ill newborns (see Chapter 4). In addition, animal data and a few recent human studies suggest that the neuroendocrinology of the lactating mother may down-regulate the magnitude of the maternal postpartum stress response.[95]

Breastfeeding Continuous Quality Improvement (CQI)

Multicenter studies have found that mean infant growth varies significantly among NICUs.[96-98] In one study, variations in nutritional intake had the largest impact on explaining growth differences among sites.[99] Use of breastmilk and breastfeeding is also extremely variable across sites.[43] As few evidence-based standards of care are available for complex nutritional practices, such differences are understandable, but not desirable.[17]

Recent studies have demonstrated the effectiveness of quality improvement measures directed towards the nutrition of NICU infants. Consistent and comprehensive monitoring of growth, nutritional status, and nutritional outcome measures were part of the approach that led to markedly improved and more cost-effective nutrition outcomes for VLBW infants.[82] In this study, a focus on using human milk as best practice increased the use of breastmilk as the first feeding from 47% to 62%. By evaluating and sharing the nutritional practices of several best performing NICUs, Bloom demonstrated improvement in nutritional outcomes of over 75% of NICUs where process improvements were implemented.[96] By preparing for and achieving BFHI certification for the delivery service, Merewood et al. reported improved breastfeeding initiation rates in the NICU from 35% to 74%.[83] Having a coordinated, multi-faceted breastfeeding support program has been demonstrated to improve breastfeeding initiation and continuation rates, even in populations least likely to breastfeed[100, 101] (Table 1).

Common program components are:

- a room for milk expression with hospital-grade breast pumps provided,

- active education and support by a lactation consultant,

- education for nursing and other staff on breastfeeding,

- a pamphlet for the mother and her support person(s) on breastfeeding given at the time of infant admission to the NICU,

- use of a galactogogues when milk supply decreased, and

- weekly meetings for the mothers.[101]

The "measure to improve" paradigm has proven as effective in breastfeeding CQI efforts as in other areas of medical quality improvement.[102] There are many possible measures of breastfeeding exposure (primarily duration and exclusivity) and outcomes, for example: first feeding as human milk; some breastmilk during NICU stay or at discharge; exclusive breastmilk at discharge, 3 months, 6 months, etc. post discharge; some breastfeeding in the NICU or at discharge; exclusive breastfeeding at discharge, 3 months, 6 months, etc. post discharge; some breastfeeding at 3, 6, 9, 12, 24 months, etc; and percentage of total NICU enteral intake. Long term outcomes of exposure to human milk can also be measured (e.g., incidence of NEC, ROP, LOS), but require more planning, time, and resources. The California Perinatal Quality Care Collaborative (CPQCC) has established a methodology which includes assessment, toolkits, workshops, and webcasts, with close attention to human milk and breastfeeding as a method of improving nutrition for VLBW infants.[17, 89] The Vermont-Oxford Network (VON) has also established nutrition in the NICU as a priority in its *Tools for Improvement Series*, 2005.

An initial step towards assessing and improving the nutrition of premature infants is determining who is going to be held responsible for evaluating and tracking breastfeeding and overall nutritional outcomes. Potential participants include nutritionists, physicians/ nurse practitioners, nursing staff, discharge planners, pharmacy staff, developmental specialists, and occupational therapists (who may have expertise in oral feeding practices). There are data documenting the benefit of including a nutritionist and having a team approach to this clinical challenge.[82,98,103,104]

The use of human milk and breastfeeding in preterm, vulnerable infants requires staff educated on the science of human milk, the physiology of milk production, and the best practices to facilitate transition to direct breastfeeding. **"Providing this care and support to families in the ICN requires time, positive attitudes, and encouragement by all members of the healthcare team. In order to improve outcomes of vulnerable infants, the provision of human milk must be viewed not as a choice but a necessity of care."[105]**

KEY CONCEPTS

- There are many barriers to establishing breastfeeding in the NICU, the main one being the healthcare system itself.

- Physicians (especially prenatally) and other health care providers have significant influence on a mother's decision to provide her milk for her preterm or ill infant.

- Based on the current research regarding the value of human milk for preterm infants, parents should be provided with accurate information on which to base an informed choice regarding providing a mother's own milk for her infant.

- Mothers should not be pressured to commit to breastfeeding for any length of time, only encouraged to provide breastmilk for as long as they can. The choice to breastfeed can come later.

- Mothers providing breastmilk for their preterm infants should be praised for their efforts, regardless of the length of time or amount of milk produced.

- There are many possible models for lactation support.

- NICU policies and procedures are necessary to ensure the safety and quality of the milk provided the preterm infant.

- Breastfeeding statistics and outcomes can be improved using available continuous quality improvement models.

REFERENCES

1. Bell RP, McGrath JM. Implementing a research-based kangaroo care program in the NICU. Nurs Clin North Am 1996;31(2):387-403.

2. Ehrenkranz R, Ackerman B, Mezger J, Bracken M. Breastfeeding premature infants: incidence and success. Pediatric Research 1985;19:199A (abstract # 530).

3. Furman L, Minich NM, Hack M. Breastfeeding of very low birth weight infants. J Hum Lact 1998;14(1):29-34.

4. Hill PD, Ledbetter RJ, Kavanaugh KL. Breastfeeding patterns of low-birth-weight infants after hospital discharge. J Obstet Gynecol Neonatal Nurs 1997;26(2):189-97.

5. Lefebvre F, Ducharme M. Incidence and duration of lactation and lactational performance among mothers of low-birth-weight and term infants. Canadian Medical Association Journal 1989;140(10):1159-64.

6. Meier PP, Engstrom JL, Mangurten HH, Estrada E, Zimmerman B, Kopparthi R. Breastfeeding support services in the neonatal intensive-care unit. J Obstet Gynecol Neonatal Nurs 1993;22(4):338-47.

7. Merewood A, Brooks D, Bauchner H, MacAuley L, Mehta S. Maternal birthplace and breastfeeding initiation among term and preterm infants: a statewide assessment for Massachusetts. Pediatrics 2006;118(4):e1048-54.

8. Li R, Darling N, Maurice E, Barler L, Grummer-Strawn L. Breastfeeding rates in the United States by characteristics of the child, mother, or family: the 2002 National Immunization Survey. Pediatrics 2005;115(1): e31-7.

9. Ryan A, Wenjun Z, Acosta A. Breastfeeding continues to increase into the new millenium. Pediatrics 2002;110:1103-9.

10. Schanler RJ. The use of human milk for premature infants. Pediatr Clin North Am 2001;48(1):207-19.

11. Flacking R, Nyqvist KH, Ewald U, Wallin L. Long-term duration of breastfeeding in Swedish low birth weight infants. J Hum Lact 2003;19(2):157-65.

12. Nyqvist K. Breastfeeding Support in Neonatal Care: An example of the integration of international evidence and experience. Newborn & Infant Nursing Reviews 2005;5(1):34-48.

13. Reinert do Nascimento M, Issler H. Breastfeeding the premature infant: experience of a baby-friendly hospital in Brazil. J Hum Lact 2005;21(1):47-52.

14. Callen J, Pinelli J, Atkinson S, Saigal S. Qualitative analysis of barriers to breastfeeding in very-low-birthweight infants in the hospital and postdischarge. Adv Neonatal Care 2005;5(2):93-103.

15. Meier PP. Breastfeeding in the special care nursery. Prematures and infants with medical problems. Pediatr Clin North Am 2001;48(2):425-42.

16. Hale TW. Medications in breastfeeding mothers of preterm infants. Pediatr Ann 2003;32(5):337-47.

17. California Perinatal Quality Care Collaborative PQIP. Toolkit: nutritional support of the VLBW infant, part 1. In: California Perinatal Quality Care Collaborative, Perinatal Quality Improvement Panel, www.cpqcc.org; 2004.

18. Kavanaugh K, Meier P, Zimmermann B, Mead L. The rewards outweigh the efforts: breastfeeding outcomes for mothers of preterm infants. J Hum Lact 1997;13(1):15-21.

19. Spanier-MIngolelli SR, Meier PP, Bradford LS. "Making the difference for my baby": a powerful breastfeeding motivator for mothers of preterm and high risk infants (abstract). Pediatr Res 1998;43:269.

20. Meier PP, Engstrom JL. Evidence-based practices to promote exclusive feeding of human milk in very low-birthweight infants. NeoReviews 2007;8(11):e467-77.

21. Scott JA, Binns CW, Aroni RA. The influence of reported paternal attitudes on the decision to breast-feed. J Paediatr Child Health 1997;33(4):305-7.

22. Arora S, McJunkin C, Wehrer J, Kuhn P. Major factors influencing breastfeeding rates: mother's perception of father's attitude and milk supply. Pediatrics 2000;106(5):E67.

23. Ellis DJ, Hewat RJ. Do nurses help or hinder mothers who breastfeed? J Adv Nurs 1983;8(4):281-8.

24. Humenick SS, Hill PD, Spiegelberg PL. Breastfeeding and health professional encouragement. J Hum Lact 1998;14(4):305-10.

25. Raisler J. Promoting breast-feeding among vulnerable women. J Nurse Midwifery 1993;38(1-4):1-4.

26. Winikoff B, Laukaran VH, Myers D, Stone R. Dynamics of infant feeding: mothers, professionals, and the institutional context in a large urban hospital. Pediatrics 1986;77(3):357-65.

27. Winikoff B, Myers D, Laukaran VH, Stone R. Overcoming obstacles to breast-feeding in a large municipal hospital: applications of lessons learned. Pediatrics 1987;80(3):423-33.

28. Freed GL, Clark SJ, Cefalo RC, Sorenson JR. Breast-feeding education of obstetrics-gynecology residents and practitioners. Am J Obstet Gynecol 1995;173(5):1607-13.

29. Freed GL, Clark SJ, Curtis P, Sorenson JR. Breast-feeding education and practice in family medicine. J Fam Pract 1995;40(3):263-9.

30. Freed GL, Clark SJ, Harris BG, Lowdermilk DL. Methods and outcomes of breastfeeding instruction for nursing students. J Hum Lact 1996;12(2):105-10.

31. Freed GL, Clark SJ, Lohr JA, Sorenson JR. Pediatrician involvement in breast-feeding promotion: a national study of residents and practitioners. Pediatrics 1995;96(3 Pt 1):490-4.

32. Freed GL, Clark SJ, Sorenson J, Lohr JA, Cefalo R, Curtis P. National assessment of physicians' breast-feeding knowledge, attitudes, training, and experience. Jama 1995;273(6):472-6.

33. Freed GL, Jones TM, Fraley JK. Attitudes and education of pediatric house staff concerning breast-feeding. South Med J 1992;85(5):483-5.

34. U.S. Department of Health and Human Services. HHS blueprint for action on breastfeeding. Office on Women's Health, U.S. Dept. of Health and Human services, Washington, D.C., (www.4woman.gov/breastfeeding/index.htm).; 2000.

35. US Department of Health & Human Services. Report of the Surgeon General's workshop on breastfeeding & human lactation. DHHS Publication No. HRS-D-MC 84-2. US Department of Health & Human Services, Health Resources and Services Administration, Rockville, MD; 1984.

36. US Department of Health & Human Services. Follow-up report: the Surgeon General's workshop on breastfeeding & human lactation. DHHS Publication No. HRS-D-MC 85-2. Health Resources and Services Administration, US Department of Health & Human Services, Rockville, MD; 1985.

37. Oxman AD, Thomson MA, Davis DA, Haynes RB. No magic bullets: a systematic review of 102 trials of interventions to improve professional practice. CMAJ 1995;153(10):1423-31.

38. Bernaix LW. Nurses' attitudes, subjective norms, and behavioral intentions toward support of breastfeeding mothers. J Hum Lact 2000;16(3):201-9.

39. Jaeger MC, Lawson M, Filteau S. The impact of prematurity and neonatal illness on the decision to breast-feed. J Adv Nurs 1997;25(4):729-37.

40. Kavanaugh K, Mead L, Meier P, Mangurten HH. Getting enough: mothers' concerns about breastfeeding a preterm infant after discharge. J Obstet Gynecol Neonatal Nurs 1995;24(1):23-32.

41. Wheeler JL, Johnson M, Collie L, Sutherland D, Chapman C. Promoting breastfeeding in the neonatal intensive care unit. Breastfeed Rev 1999;7(2):15-8.

42. Siddell E, Marinelli K, Froman R, Burke G. Evaluation of an educational intervention on breastfeeding for NICU nurses. J Hum Lact 2003;19(3):293-302.

43. Powers N, Bloom B, Peabody J, Clark R. Site of care influences breastmilk feedings at NICU discharge. J Perinatol 2003;23:10-3.

44. Powers N, Gwyn L, Bloom B, et al. Process differences related to breastmilk use at NICU discharge. ABM News and Views, Conference Abstract P11, 8(3):25 2002.

45. Donnelly A, Snowden H, Renfrew M, Woolridge M. Commercial hospital discharge packs for breastfeeding women. Cochrane Database of Systematic Reviews http://wwwcochraneorg/cochrane/revabstr/AB002075htm 2003.

46. Howard C, Howard F, Weitzman M. Infant formula distribution and advertising in pregnancy: a hospital survey. Birth 1994;21(1):14-9.

47. Howard C, Howard F, Weitzman M, Lawrence RA. Commentaries: antenatal formula advertising: another potential threat to breast-feeding. Pediatrics 1994;94(1):102-4.

48. Howard C, Schaffer S, Lawrence R. Attitudes, practices, and recommendations by obstetricians about infant feeding. Birth 1997;24(4):240-6.

49. Dusdieker LB, Dungy CI, Losch ME. Prenatal office practices regarding infant feeding choices. Clin Pediatr (Phila) 2006;45(9):841-5.

50. Wazana A. Physicians and the pharmaceutical industry: is a gift ever just a gift? JAMA 2000;283(3):373-80.

51. American College of Physicians, American Society of Internal Medicine. Position paper: physician-industry relations. Part 1: individual physicians. Ann Intern Med 2002;136:396-402.

52. American College of Physicians, American Society of Internal Medicine. Position paper: physician-industry relations. Part 2: organizational issues. Ann Intern Med 2002;36:403-6.

53. Lexchin J. Interactions between physicians and the pharmaceutical industry: what does the literature say? CMAJ 1993;149:1401-7.

54. American Academy of Pediatrics, Section on Breastfeeding. Policy statement: breastfeeding and the use of human milk. Pediatrics 2005;115(2):496-506.

55. Ekwo E, Dusdieker L, Booth B. Factors influencing initiation of breast-feeding. Am J Dis Child 1983;137:375-7.

56. Hill P. Maternal attitudes and infant feeding among low-income mothers. J Hum Lact 1988;4(1):7-11.

57. Noble L, Hand I, Haynes D, McVeigh T, Kim M, Yoon JJ. Factors influencing initiation of breast-feeding among urban women. Am J Perinatol 2003;20(8):477-83.

58. Lu M, Lange L, Slusser W, Hamilton J, Halfon N. Provider encouragement of breast-feeding: evidence from a national survey. Obstet Gynecol 2001;97(2):290-5.

59. Meier P, Engstrom J, Spanier-Mingolelli S, et al. Dose of own mothers' milk provided by low-income and non-low income mothers of very low birthweight infants (abstract). Pediatric Research 2000;47:292A.

60. Miracle DJ, Meier PP, Bennett PA. Mothers' decisions to change from formula to mothers' milk for very-low-birth-weight infants. J Obstet Gynecol Neonatal Nurs 2004;33(6):692-703.

61. Sikorski J, Renfrew M, Pindoria S, Wade A. Support for breastfeeding mothers. Cochrane Database Systematic Reviews 1, http://www.cochrane.org/cochrane/revabstr/AB001141.htm. 2003.

62. Sikorski J, Renfrew M, Pindoria S, Wade A. Support for breastfeeding mothers: a systematic review Paediatric and Perinatal Epidemiology 2003;17:407-17.

63. Junior WS, Martinez FE. Effect of intervention on the rates of breastfeeding of very low birth weight newborns. J Pediatr (Rio J) 2007;83(6):541-6.

64. American Academy of Family Physicians. Breastfeeding (Position Paper), http://www.aafp.org/online/en/home/policy/policies/b/breastfeedingpositionpaper.html 2002.

65. American College of Obstetrician-Gynecologists. Breastfeeding: maternal and infant aspects. Educational Bulletin # 258, July; 2000.

66. Berens P. Prenatal, intrapartum, and postpartum support of the lactating mother. Pediatr Clin NA 2001;48(2):365-75.

67. Coreil J, Murphy J. Maternal committment, lactation practices, and breastfeeding duration. JOGNN 1988;July/August:273-8.

68. de Oliveira MI, Camacho LA, Tedstone AE. Extending breastfeeding duration through primary care: a systematic review of prenatal and postnatal interventions. J Hum Lact 2001;17(4):326-43.

69. Dennis CL. Breastfeeding initiation and duration: a 1990-2000 literature review. J Obstet Gynecol Neonatal Nurs 2002;31(1):12-32.

70. Donath SM, Amir LH. Relationship between prenatal infant feeding intention and initiation and duration of breastfeeding: a cohort study. Acta Paediatr 2003;92(3):352-6.

71. DiGirolamo AM, Grummer-Strawn LM, Fein S. Maternity care practices: implications for breastfeeding. Birth 2001;28(2):94-100.

72. Wight NE. Management of common breastfeeding issues. Pediatric Clinics of North America 2001;48(2):321-44.

73. Rodriguez NA, Miracle DJ, Meier PP. Sharing the science on human milk feedings with mothers of very-low-birth-weight infants. J Obstet Gynecol Neonatal Nurs 2005;34(1):109-19.

74. Hurst N, Meier P. Chapter 13: Breastfeeding the preterm infant. In: Riordan J (ed). Breastfeeding and human lactation. 3rd Ed. Boston: Jones and Bartlett; 2005:367-408.

75. Meier P. Supporting lactation in mothers with very low birth weight infants. Pediatric Annals 2003;32(5):317-25.

76. Taveras EM, Capra AM, Braveman PA, Jensvold NG, Escobar GJ, Lieu TA. Clinician support and psychosocial risk factors associated with breastfeeding discontinuation. Pediatrics 2003;112(1 Pt 1):108-15.

77. Furman L, Taylor G, Minich N, Hack M. The effect of maternal milk on neonatal morbidity of very low-birth-weight infants. Arch Pediatr Adolesc Med 2003;157(1):66-7.

78. Hurst NM, Myatt A, Schanler RJ. Growth and development of a hospital-based lactation program and mother's own milk bank. J Obstet Gynecol Neonatal Nurs 1998;27(5):503-10.

79. Jones E. Strategies to promote preterm breastfeeding. Mod Midwife 1995;5(3):8-11.

80. Baker BJ, Rasmussen TW. Organizing and documenting lactation support of NICU families. J Obstet Gynecol Neonatal Nurs 1997;26(5):515-21.

81. Gonzalez KA, Meinzen-Derr J, Burke BL, et al. Evaluation of a lactation support service in a children's hospital neonatal intensive care unit. J Hum Lact 2003;19(3):286-92.

82. Kuzma-O'Reilly B, Duenas ML, Greecher C, et al. Evaluation, development, and implementation of potentially better practices in neonatal intensive care nutrition. Pediatrics 2003;111(4 Pt 2):e461-70.

83. Merewood A, Philipp BL, Chawla N, Cimo S. The baby-friendly hospital initiative increases breastfeeding rates in a US neonatal intensive care unit. J Hum Lact 2003;19(2):166-71.

84. Castrucci B, Hoover K, Lim S, Maus K. A Comparison of breastfeeding rates in an urban birth cohort among women delivering infants at hospitals that employ and do not employ lactation consultants. J Public Health Management Practice 2006;12(6):578-85.

85. Dweck N, Augustine M, Pandya D, Valdes-Greene R, Visintainer P, Brumberg HL. NICU lactation consultant increases percentage of outborn versus inborn babies receiving human milk. J Perinatol 2008;28(2):136-40.

86. Sisk PM, Lovelady CA, Dillard RG, Gruber KJ. Lactation counseling for mothers of very low birth weight infants: effect on maternal anxiety and infant intake of human milk. Pediatrics 2006;117(1):e67-75.

87. Merewood A, Chamberlain LB, Cook JT, Philipp BL, Malone K, Bauchner H. The effect of peer counselors on breastfeeding rates in the neonatal intensive care unit: results of a randomized controlled trial. Arch Pediatr Adolesc Med 2006;160(7):681-5.

88. Agrasda G, Gustafsson J, Kylberg E, Ewald U. Postnatal peer counselling on exclusive breastfeeding of low-birthweight infants: a randomized, controlled trial. Acta Paediatrica 2005;94:1109-15.

89. California Perinatal Quality Care Collaborative PQIP. Toolkit: nutritional support of the VLBW infant, part 2. In: California Perinatal Quality Care Collaborative, Perinatal Quality Improvement Panel, www.cpqcc.org; 2005.

90. Ball TM, Wright AL. Health care costs of formula-feeding in the first year of life. Pediatrics 1999;103(4 Part 2):870-6.

91. Weimer J. The economic benefits of breastfeeding: a review and analysis. Food and Rural Economics Division, Economic Research Service, US Dept. of Agriculture. Food Assistance and Nutrition Research Report No. 13, 1800 M Street, NW, Washington, DC 20036-5831 www.ers.usda.gov/publications/fanrr13/; 2001.

92. Schanler RJ, Lau C, Hurst NM, Smith EO. Randomized trial of donor human milk versus preterm formula as substitutes for mothers' own milk in the feeding of extremely premature infants. Pediatrics 2005;116(2):400-6.

93. Schanler RJ, Shulman RJ, Lau C. Feeding strategies for premature infants: beneficial outcomes of feeding fortified human milk vs preterm formula. Pediatr 1999;103:1150-7.

94. Wight NE. Commentary: donor human milk for preterm infants. J Perinatol 2001;21:249-54.

95. Groer M, Davis M, Hemphill J. Postpartum stress: current concepts and the possible protective role of breastfeeding. J Obstet Gynecol Neonatal Nurs 2002;31(4):411-7.

96. Bloom BT, Mulligan J, Arnold C, et al. Improving growth of very low birth weight infants in the first 28 days. Pediatrics 2003;112(1 Pt 1):8-14.

97. Clark RH, Wagner CL, Merritt RJ, et al. Nutrition in the neonatal intensive care unit: how do we reduce the incidence of extrauterine growth restriction? J Perinatol 2003;23: 337-44.

98. Rubin L, Richardson D, Bodarek F, McCormick M. Growth in hospital of VLBW infants. Identification of patient characteristics and inter-NICU differences. Pediatric Research 1997;41:Abstract 239A.

99. Olsen IE, Richardson DK, Schmid CH, Ausman LM, Dwyer JT. Intersite differences in weight growth velocity of extremely premature infants. Pediatrics 2002;110(6):1125-32.

100. Meier PP, Engstrom JL, Mingolelli SS, Miracle DJ, Kiesling S. The Rush Mothers' Milk Club: breastfeeding interventions for mothers with very-low-birth-weight infants. J Obstet Gynecol Neonatal Nurs 2004;33(2):164-74.

101.Dall'Oglio I, Salvatori G, Bonci E, Nantini B, D'Agostino G, Dotta A. Breastfeeding promotion in neonatal intensive care unit: impact of a new program toward a BFHI for high-risk infants. Acta Paediatr 2007;96(11):1626-31.

102.Galvin R, McGlynn E. Using performance measurement to drive improvement: a road map for change. Med Care 2003 Jan;41(1 Suppl):I 48-60.

103.Olsen I, Richardson D, Schmid C, SAusman L, Dwyer J. Dietitian involvement in the neonatal intensive care unit: more is better. J Am Diet Assoc 2005;105(8):1224-123.

104.Valentine C, Schanler R. Neonatal nutritionist intervention improves nutrition support and promotes cost containment in the management of LBW infants. J Parenter Enteral Nutr 1993(Suppl 46):466.

105.Spatz DL. State of the science: use of human milk and breast-feeding for vulnerable infants. J Perinat Neonatal Nurs 2006;20(1):51-5.

Appendices

POLICIES & PROCEDURES

Collection, Storage and Handling of Breastmilk for Hospitalized Infants
Use of Heat Processed, Donor Human Milk
Use of Fresh Donor Human Milk in the NICU
Breastmilk Misadministration Policy
Alternate Feeding Methods for Breastfeeding NICU Infants
Test-Weighing
Non-nutritive ("Dry") Breastfeeding in the NICU
Kangaroo Care: Skin to Skin Contact in the NICU

MISCELLANEOUS

Insurance Letter: Explanation of Medical Need for Breast Pump
Insurance Letter: Explanation of Medical Need for Donor Human Milk
Mother's Discharge Checklist
Staff Attitude/Knowledge Survey
Resources

POLICY & PROCEDURE: COLLECTION, STORAGE & HANDLING OF BREASTMILK FOR HOSPITALIZED INFANTS

I. Purpose

To provide guidelines for the collection, storage, and handling of breastmilk to optimize nutritional and immunological protection while minimizing the chance of contamination or error.

II. Definitions

Fresh Milk: milk at room temperature at approximately 25° C (77° F) or refrigerated at 1-4°C (35-40º F)

Frozen Milk: milk held at approximately -20°±2°C (-4°±4°F) or -70°C (-36° F)

Thawed Milk: milk that has been previously frozen

Heat Processed Milk: fresh-raw and/or fresh-frozen milk that has been heat-treated as per milk banking guidelines

Donor Milk: breastmilk that is voluntarily given by women other than the biological mother of the baby

III. Text

A. OSHA has determined that health care providers handling breastmilk are not required to wear gloves.

B. HBsAg positive and Hepatitis C positive mother's milk will be stored in a small refrigerator in a designated area of the NICU, labeled and separated from other mother's milk.

C. In general, use the first two weeks of milk in chronological order first, then proceed to fresh breastmilk.

D. Breastmilk will be stored as follows:

Method	Term Infant	Preterm Infant	Heat-processed Banked Donor Breast Milk	Fresh Donor Breast Milk
Room Temperature	10 hours	4 hours *	4 hours	4 hours
Refrigerator (fresh expressed or transferred from freezer to refrigerator)	Up to 5 days	48 hours	48 hours	48 hours
Completely thawed & placed in refrigerator	48 hours	24 hours	48 hours	24 hours
Freezer Compartment (1 door refrigerator)	2 weeks	Not recommended	Not recommended	Not recommended
Freezer Compartment (2 door refrigerator) *not in door	Up to 4 months	3 months	3 months	3 months
Deep Freezer	Up to 12 months	6 months	6 months	6 months

* Refrigerate as soon as possible, holding at room temperature no longer than 4 hours.

E. Fresh expressed refrigerated milk that will not be used may be frozen within 48 hours for the preterm infant and within five days for the term infant.

F. Store fortified human milk in the refrigerator and use within 24 hours.

G. At all times, all containers (syringes, volufeeds, etc.) will be labeled with patient identification label, including infant's name and medical record number.

H. Syringes for feedings will be changed every 4 hours.

IV. Procedure	Responsibility
A. Collection	RN/LC

1. Provide instruction to MOB/Donor on "Pumping, Storing & Transporting Breastmilk for Hospitalized Infants" with attached handout.

2. Direct parent to in house pumps and/or to rental of electric pump at the Lactation Center or appropriate community rental center.

   Responsibility: RN/LVN/LC

3. Obtain accessory kit from unit supply cart.

4. Provide individualized labels with the infant's name and medical record number, containers (no plastic bags) and bottle caps.

5. Instruct MOB/Donor to write the date, time of expression, and any illnesses or medications used on the label.

6. Breast pumps will be wiped down with a hospital approved germicide as follows:

   a. Prior to and after each use in the NICU
   b. Prior to each new patient use in areas other than NICU
   c. If a spill occurs

   Responsibility: Parent; RN/LVN/MA/LC; RN/LVN/MA/LC

B. Handling

   Responsibility: RN/LVN

1. Thaw breastmilk in refrigerator or in warm water at the bedside. Do not place breastmilk in boiling water or microwave.

2. To prevent the water from contaminating the breastmilk:

   a. For Volufeed, maintain the level of the warm water below the bottle cap.
   b. For Syringe, after removing from warm water, wipe syringe dry prior to uncapping.

3. Transferring Breastmilk

   a. In the Nutrition Room   RN/LVN/LC

     i. Transferring breastmilk from the original container to a secondary feeding container, two licensed personnel (i.e., RN, LVN, RCP, OT, physician or NNP) will double check the patient labels on both containers for accuracy.

     ii. The labeled secondary container will be double checked with the patient ID band by two licensed personnel (i.e., RN, LVN, RCP, OT, physician or NNP) at the bedside prior to feeding.

   b. At the bedside

   Prior to transfer of breastmilk to any other feeding container (i.e., syringe, volufeed, etc.) and before administration, infant's name and medical record number will be double checked between original container label and infant band by two licensed personnel (i.e., RN, LVN, RCP, OT, physician or NNP)

4. Warm breastmilk in container of warm water at bedside. Styrofoam cups are an appropriate container that can be used to warm breastmilk at the bedside.

5. For breastmilk delivered via syringe pump:

   a. Position the syringe pump with the tip upright 45 – 90 degrees (avoid horizontal positioning of pump as the lipids will rise to the top, and fortifier will settle at the bottom).

6. Following the infant feeding, discard any unused, warmed breastmilk.

C. Documentation

1. Label breastmilk (refrigeration, freezing, thawing, etc.) as per TEXT guidelines as appropriate. Document date and times on breastmilk containers.	RN/LVN
2. Document parent education on Parent Education Screen or appropriate form.	
3. Verification of double checking breastmilk by two licensed personnel (i.e., RN, LVN, RCP, OT, physician, NNP).	RN/LC
a. Nurse administering breastmilk will initial the flow sheet in the appropriate column verifying the infant's name and medical record number between the original container and infant band.	RN/LVN
b. Second licensed personnel will initial confirming that she/he has verified the infant's name and medical record number between the original container and infant band.	
4. Type of feeding, amount, any additives, residuals	
D. If infant receives wrong breastmilk:	
1. Notify charge nurse and MD/NNP of both source and recipient infants.	RN/LVN
2. Notify source and recipient parents or legal guardian.	Charge Nurse
3. Review appropriate chart for maternal history and order appropriate lab-work on source parent's blood which includes:	MD/NNP
a. HIV	
b. Hepatitis C Antibody	
c. Hepatitis B surface antigen	
d. Syphilis (RPR or VDRL Serology)	
e. Culture source parent's Breastmilk a provided (e.g., fresh, refrigerated or frozen), for CMV.	

4. Obtain source informed consent for HIV Test and authorization for disclosure of the results if results are not already available.

5. Notify primary physician of recipient to provide follow-up care as needed.

6. Complete and obtain signature on Consent for the HIV Test Form and Authorization for Disclosure of the Results of the HIV Test Form if needed. Utilize the following guidelines to fill out the forms:

RN

Consent for the HIV Test Form:

   a. Name of patient: (source parent)

   b. Date, time and signature: (of source parent)

   c. Witness:

Authorization For Disclosure of the Results of the HIV Test Form:

   a. Name of patient: (source parent)

   b. I hereby authorize: (the physician or health-care entity or clinic which currently has the results of the test, ie., source parent physician or Sharp HealthCare hospital)

   c. To furnish to: (recipient infant's physician)

   d. Use limitations and/or duration limitations, if any, copy request initials, date, time, and signature

   e. Witness

7. Process any ordered lab tests with Universal Requisition form and include on the form:

RN/LVN

   a. Name of patient: (source parent)

   b. Ordering physician:

c. Send test results in sealed envelope marked "Breastmilk Workup" to ordering physician via unit Charge Nurse

d. Charge to Infection Control Shared Service account

8. Hand deliver test results in sealed envelope marked "Breastmilk Workup" with ordering physician's name to unit Charge Nurse.

9. Relay sealed envelope marked "Breastmilk Workup" to ordering/covering physician or epidemiologist.

   Lab Personnel

10. If source parent refuses to give consent for the HIV Test and/or to authorize release of the test result to the recipient's physician, do not proceed with the test or with disclosure. Notify the physician(s) for both source and recipient patient to encourage counseling of both.

    Unit Charge Nurse

    RN

V. References

American Academy of Pediatrics & American College of Obstetricians and Gynecologists (2002). *Guideline for perinatal care. (5ᵗʰ Ed).* Elk Grove Village, IL & Washington AC: Author.

American Academy of Pediatrics Policy Statement (2005). Breastfeeding and the use of human milk. *Pediatrics, 115* (2), 496-506.

CPQCC Nutritional support of the VLBW infant: Part II Appendix I. a (n.d.) *Policy and procedure: Collection, storage, and handling of breastmilk.* Retrieved May 1, 2005 from http://www.cpqcc.org/Documents/ NutritionToolkit/NutriDoc2/Appendix%20I.a.pdf.

Howard CR, Howard FM. (2004). Management of breastfeeding when the mother is ill. *Clinical Obstetrics and Gynecology. 47*(3) 683-695.

Human Milk Banking Association of North America, Inc. (2006). Best practice for expressing, storing and handling human milk in hospitals, daycares, and homes. 2ⁿᵈ Ed. Raleigh, NC www.hmbana.org.

Meier PP. (1997). Professional guide to breastfeeding premature infants. Ross Products Division, Abbott Laboratories.

Pardou A, et al. (1994). Human milk banking: Influence of storage process and of bacterial contamination on some milk constituents. *Biol Neonate* 65; 302 – 309.

Spicer K. (2001). What every nurse needs to know about breast pumping: instructing and supporting mothers of premature infants in the NICU. *Neonatal Network 20* (4) 35-40.

Hamosh M, Ellis LA, Pollock DR, Henderson TR, Hamosh P. (1996). Breastfeeding and the working mother: effect of time and temperature of short-term storage proteolysis, lipolysis, and bacterial growth in milk. *Pediatrics* Apr; 97(4): 492-8.

Ogundele MA. (2000). Techniquest for the storage of human breast milk: implications for the anti-microbial functions and safety of stored milk. *EUR J Pediatr* 159: 793-797.

Lawrence RA, Lawrence RM. (2005). *Breastfeeding: a guide for the medical profession.* (6th ed). Philadelphia, Elsevier Mosby. 1019.

VI. Cross References

VII. Attachment

Parent Information Sheet: "Pumping, Storing and Transporting Breastmilk for Hospitalized Infants"

VIII. Approvals

IX. Replaces

PARENT INFORMATION SHEET
PUMPING, STORING AND TRANSPORTING
BREASTMILK FOR HOSPITALIZED INFANTS

Your infant has been admitted to the NICU (Neonatal Intensive Care Unit). You may have been planning on or thinking about breastfeeding and wonder if it is still possible. It is!

Breastfeeding and providing breastmilk for your newborn is one of the most important things you can do for your baby. Even if you had not planned to breastfeed or to breastfeed for only a few weeks, breastmilk will give your baby the very best start in life.

Breastmilk provides the best nutrition for your baby. Factors in breastmilk prevent infections and help shorten your baby's time in the hospital. Milk from mothers who deliver prematurely differs from milk of mothers who deliver at term and is specially designed for the baby's needs. Even a few drops of the first milk you produce, called colostrum, contains important infection-fighting cells. It is often yellow in color and we call it "Liquid Gold." We use every drop!

Establishing Your Milk Supply

The best way to establish a good milk supply is to pump as often as you would nurse a newborn baby.

1. Begin pumping as soon as possible after delivery, within 6-12 hours if possible. The hospital will provide a pump for use during your stay.

2. Pump every 2-3 hours during the day and every 3-4 hours through the night. For example, if you pump before bed at 11pm, pump once during the night and again at 6 or 7am. The goal is to pump 8-10 times in a 24 hour day.

3. Initially, pump each breast for 15-20 minutes each, or 15-20 minutes total if you are double pumping. After your full milk supply "comes in," pump for 1-2 minutes after you see only drops.

4. Breast massage and warm compresses to the breasts for several minutes before pumping will help to express more milk.

5. Relax while you are pumping. Think of your baby and visualize him or her nursing at your breast.

6. In the first two weeks, and/or if your milk supply is down, pumping during the night is essential.

More Helpful Tips on Establishing a Good Milk Supply

1. Plan to rent a hospital grade electric breast pump at least until your due date plus one month.

2. When visiting your baby, you may use one of the electric breast pumps available in the NICU. Be sure and bring your kit to the hospital with you. Wipe down the pump with a germicidal wipe prior to and after use.

3. Allow 20-30 minutes of quiet time for pumping.

4. The most common causes of low milk supply are fatigue and infrequent milk expression (the more you pump, the greater your milk supply).

5. It may help you to relax and your milk to flow if you keep a picture of your baby nearby during pumping, or pump at the baby's bedside, or after holding your baby.

6. Whether your baby is premature or term, you should produce a full milk supply of at least 20 ounces per 24 hours by 5-7 days post-partum.

7. Eat a balanced diet and drink to satisfy thirst. You don't need to drink milk to make milk.

8. Please review all medications you are taking with your baby's nurse, physician, or Lactation Consultant.

Collecting and Storing Your Breastmilk

1. Remember to wash your hands before handling your breast pump and storage containers. If using a pump in the NICU, wipe down the pump with germicidal wiper prior to and after use.

2. Wash your pump parts (the parts that touch your breast and milk) with hot soapy water after each use. Don't wash the tubing. If you notice moisture in the tube, run the

pump with tubing attached for 1 to 2 minutes or until dry. Daily sanitizing may be done at home by washing pumps kit parts in the top rack of a dishwasher or by boiling parts, except tubing, for 10 minutes.

3. Obtain containers, caps and labels from your baby's nurse.

4. Write the date and time the milk was collected on the baby label and place it on each container of milk.

5. The containers will hold 2-3 ounces of milk. Milk from each pumping should be put in its own container.

6. After pumping milk into the container, place a cap on it and put it in the freezer. Place the milk in the refrigerator if you plan to use it within 48 hours. Breastmilk cannot be refrozen if thawed.

7. Breastmilk may be stored in the hospital as follows:

Method	Term Infant	Hospitalized & Preterm Infant
Room Temperature	10 hours	4 hours
Refrigerator	Up to 3 to 5 days	48 hours
Freezer Compartment (1-door refrigerator)	2 weeks	Not recommended
Freezer (2-door refrigerator – not in the door)	Up to 4 months	3 months
Deep Freezer	Up to 12 months	6 months

Transporting Your Breastmilk

1. When bringing your milk to the hospital, it must be kept frozen (if frozen) and cold (if refrigerated). Put it on ice in a cooler.

2. Refrigerated and frozen breastmilk may separate as the cream layer forms on top. This is normal.

3. Breastmilk may be other colors such as yellow, white, or greenish. These are normal variations based on your diet.

POLICY & PROCEDURE: USE OF HEAT PROCESSED, BANKED DONOR HUMAN MILK

I. PURPOSE

To provide clinical guidelines for the use of heat processed, banked donor breastmilk.

II. DEFINITIONS

CLC – Certified Lactation Consultant

NNP – Neonatal Nurse Practitioner

Donor Milk - Breastmilk that is voluntarily given by women, other than the birth mother of the baby.

Donor Human Milk Bank - A donor human milk bank is a service established for the purpose of collecting, screening, processing, storing, and distributing donated human milk to meet the specific needs of individuals, for whom, human milk is prescribed by physician.

Fresh - Raw milk - Milk stored continuously at approximately 4 degrees C for use not longer than 72 hours following expression.

Fresh – Frozen milk – Fresh – raw milk that has been frozen and kept at approximately –20 degrees C for not longer than 12 months from date of collection.

Heat Processed milk – Fresh-raw and/or fresh-frozen milk that has been heat-treated as per milk banking guidelines.

HMBANA – Human Milk Banking Association of North America.

Pooled milk – Milk from more than one donor.

Preterm milk – Milk pumped within the first month post partum by a mother who delivered at or before 37 weeks gestation.

III. Text

A. Heat treated frozen donor milk will be used from a Donor Human Milk Bank that is licensed by the State of California.

B. Heat treated donor milk may be used for multiple infants.

IV. PROCEDURE	RESPONSIBILITY
A. Notify parent(s)/legal representative of recipient infant of the need for and use of heat processed banked donor breastmilk with an opportunity to ask questions and refuse the use of donor breastmilk.	MD/NNP
B. Write order/prescription including: 1. Infant diagnosis 2. Explanation of medical necessity for donor milk 3. Amount needed 4. Anticipated length of time donor milk will be needed	MD/NNP
C. Give parent(s)/legal representative Heat Processed, Banked Donor Breastmilk Information Sheet when they are available.	MD/NNP/CLC/RN
D. Place signed original in recipient infant's medical record. Copy to parents/legal representative if they wish.	RN/CLC
E. Notify Lactation of need for heat processed, banked donor breastmilk.	RN/LVN/Clerk
F. Transfer 1 week supply of heat processed banked donor breastmilk from depot freezer to NICU freezer and label each bottle with recipient infant's stamped label.	CLC
G. Store and handle donor breastmilk per Policy & Procedure : Collection, Storage and Handling of Mother's Breastmilk for Hospitalized Infants.	RN/LVN

V. REFERENCES

Human Milk Banking Association of North America, Inc. (1999). Recommendations for collection storage, and handling of a mother's milk for her own infant in the hospital setting. West Hartford, CT: HMBANA.

Meier PP. (1997). Professional guide to breastfeeding premature infants. Ross Products Division, Abbott Laboratories.

Pardou A, et al. (1994). Human milk banking: Influence of storage process and of bacterial contamination on some milk constituents. Biol Neonate; 65; 302 – 309.

Pierce KY, Tully MR. (1992). Mother's own milk: Guidelines for storage and handling. Journal of Human Lactation; 8 (3); 159 – 160.

VI. CROSS REFERENCES

VII. ATTACHMENT

Heat Processed, Banked Donor Breastmilk Information Sheet

VIII. APPROVALS

IX. REPLACES

X. HISTORY

HEAT PROCESSED, BANKED DONOR
BREASTMILK INFORMATION SHEET

You may request or your infant's physician may recommend and prescribe, heat-processed, banked breastmilk for your ill or preterm infant.

The health benefits of using heat-processed breastmilk for your baby may include:

- Infection-fighting factors
- Active growth and developmental hormones
- Ideal nutrition
- Better digestion

I understand that the milk donor must fit certain criteria. She must be:

- A healthy lactating woman
- Screened for certain diseases/illnesses
- Tested to be free from:
  - *HIV – 1, 2
  - *Hepatitis C antibody
  - *Hepatitis B surface antigen
  - *Tuberculosis (PPD)
  - *Syphilis (RPR or VDRL)
  - *HTLV – 1, 2

- Free from the following activities which might put her at risk for transmitting blood-born diseases:
  - *Unauthorized injection of drugs or medications
  - *Body/ear piercing at home in the last year
  - *Tatoo in the last year
  - *Since 1977, she should not have:
    - +Been a sex worker
    - +Been born in or received blood products while in Cameroon, Central African Republic, Chad, Congo, Equatorial Guinea, Gabon, Niger or Nigeria
    - +Had sexual contact with anyone born in or who lived in the above countries

Heat-processed, donor breastmilk is collected and processed by a human milk bank that is a member of the Human Milk Banking Association of North America and licensed by the state of California. It is important that you discuss with your baby's doctor any questions that you may have about the use of heat-processed, banked donor breastmilk.

VERIFICATION OF RECEIPT OF THIS INFORMATION SHEET

My signature below indicates I have received this information form and have had the opportunity to have my questions answered.

_____   __/__/__   ___:___AM/PM
SIGNATURE   DATE   TIME

_____
RELATIONSHIP TO PATIENT

POLICY & PROCEDURE: USE OF FRESH DONOR HUMAN MILK IN THE NICU

I. Purpose

To provide clinical guidelines for the use of fresh donor breastmilk.

II. Definitions

CLC – Certified Lactation Consultant

NNP – Neonatal Nurse Practitioner

Donor Milk - Breastmilk that is voluntarily given by women other than the birth mother of the baby.

Donor Human Milk Bank - A donor human milk bank is a service established for the purpose of collecting, screening, processing, storing, and distributing donated human milk to meet the specific needs of individuals for whom human milk is prescribed by a physician.

Fresh - Raw milk - Milk stored continuously at approximately 4 degrees C for use not longer than **72 hours** following expression.

Fresh – Frozen milk – Fresh – raw milk that has been frozen and kept at approximately –20 degrees C for no longer than **12 months** from date of collection.

Heat Processed milk – Fresh-raw and/or fresh-frozen milk that has been heat-treated as per milk banking guidelines.

HMBANA – Human Milk Banking Association of North America.

Pooled milk – Milk from more than one donor.

Preterm milk – Milk pumped within the first month post partum by a mother who delivered at or before 37 weeks gestation.

III. Text

A. Donors will meet "Criteria for Donor selection" (as per HMBANA Guidelines):

1. Negative medical history

2. No history of communicable disease

3. A normal diet history

4. No life style exclusionary factors

5. Confirmed negative serology

   a. HIV-1, 2

   b. HTLV –1,2

   c. Hepatitis C antibody

   d. Hepatitis B surface antigen

   e. Tuberculosis (PPD), if indicated

   f. Syphilis (RPR or VDRL)

   g. CMV – if fresh donor is CMV positive, milk may be used after frozen as described below

B. Screening test results will be within six months prior to the first donation and must be repeated every six months while milk is being donated.

C. Fresh donor breastmilk will be used only for the specific baby for whom it has been requested/ordered. It will **not** be used for any other baby.

D. The donor and/or the parents of the baby receiving the fresh donor milk will be financially responsible for any lab tests or processing costs incurred.

IV. Procedure	Responsibility
A. Write MD/NNP order to begin Fresh Donor Breastmilk Evaluation.	MD/NNP
B. Give recipient parent(s)/legal representative Fresh Donor Breastmilk Information Sheet (Attachment A1)	MD/NNP/CLC/RN
C. Placed signed original in recipient infant's medical record. Copy to parents/ legal representative.	RN/CLC

D. Obtain recipient informed consent for Fresh Donor Breastmilk.	MD/NNP
E. Have parents/legal representative whose baby is receiving the donor milk sign "Authorization for and Consent to Surgery or Special Diagnostic or TherapeuticProcedure" form. Place signed original in recipient infant's medical record. Copy to parents/legal representative.	RN/LVN
F. Have potential milk donor complete, sign, and file confidentially: 1. Fresh Donor Breastmilk Information Sheet (Attachment A2) 2. Mother and Infant Medical History (Attachment B) 3. Breastmilk Donor Agreement (Attachment C) 4. Information Request and Medical Release from Donor's HealthCare Provider (Attachment D) 5. Information Request and Medical Release from Donor's Infants' HealthCare Provider (Attachment E)	CLC
G. Obtain donor informed consent for HIV test and Authorization forDisclosure if test results are not already available.	MD/NNP
H. If results are not already available and MD/NNP has obtained informed consent, complete and obtain signature on Consent for the HIV Test Form and Authorization for Disclosure of the Results of the HIV Test *Consent for the HIV Test:* 1. Name of patient: (potential milk donor) 2. Date, time, and signature: (potential milk donor) 3. Witness:	RN/CLC

Authorization for Disclosure of the Results of the HIV Test: 1. Name of patient: (Potential milk donor) 2. I hereby authorize: (the physician or healthcare entity or clinic, which currently has the results of the test, i.e., potential milk donor physician or Sharp hospital) 3. To furnish to: (recipient infant's physician) 4. Limitations of use and/or duration limitations, if any, copy request initials, date, time and signature 5. Witness	
I. If required laboratory tests have been done within the past 6 months, Medical Director of Lactation Services receives results (Attachment D)	Medical Director of Lactation Services
J. If laboratory tests required, write prescription for required lab tests.	MD
1. Request donor to register as an outpatient in admitting.	RN/LVN/CLC
2. Send donor to Lab with requisition form and include on the form: a. ordered lab tests b. name of patient: (donor) c. ordering physician d. send test results in sealed envelope marked "Breastmilk Workup" to ordering physician via unit charge nurse. 3. Hand deliver test results in sealed envelope marked "Breastmilk Lab Workup" with ordering physician's name to unit charge nurse	Lab Personnel

4. Relay sealed envelope marked "Breastmilk Workup" to ordering/ covering physician or Medical Director of Lactation Services.	Unit Charge Nurse
K. Review donor mother and infant medical history and lab results to determine eligibility.	Medical Director of Lactation Services
L. Write MD/NNP order for use of specific donor milk.	MD/NNP
M. Store and handle donor breastmilk per Policy & Procedure Breastmilk: Collection, Storage, and Handling of Mother's Breastmilk for Hospitalized Infants.	RN/LVN

V. References

Human Milk Banking Association of North America, Inc. (1999). *Recommendations for collection storage, and handling of a mother's milk for her own infant in the hospital setting.* West Hartford, CT: HMBANA.

Meier PP. (1997). *Professional guide to breastfeeding premature infants.* Ross Products Division, Abbott Laboratories.

Pardou A, et al. (1994). Human milk banking: Influence of storage process and of bacterial contamination on some milk constituents. *Biol Neonate*; 65; 302 – 309.

Pierce KY, Tully MR. (1992). Mother's own milk: Guidelines for storage and handling. *Journal of Human Lactation*; 8 (3); 159 – 160.

VI. Cross References

Collection, Storage & Handling of Mother's Breastmilk for Hospitalized Infants

VII. Attachments (Click on attachment name to access)

Attachment A1 – Fresh Donor Breastmilk Information Sheet for Recipient Parent

Attachment A2 – Fresh Donor Breastmilk Information Sheet for Potential Fresh Breastmilk Donor

Attachment B – Mother & Infant Medical History

Attachment C – Breastmilk Donor Agreement

Attachment D – Information Request and Medical Release from Donor's HealthCare Provider

Attachment E – Information Request and Medical Release from Infants' HealthCare Provider

VIII. Approvals

IX. Replaces: None

X. History

Attachment A1

FRESH DONOR BREASTMILK INFORMATION SHEET
FOR RECIPIENT PARENT

Fresh Donor Breastmilk may be recommended/prescribed for ill or preterm infants.

The health benefits of using breastmilk for an infant may include:

- Active infection-fighting cells
- Other infection-fighting factors
- Active growth and developmental hormones
- Ideal nutrition
- Better digestion

I understand that the milk donor must fit certain criteria. She must be:

- A healthy lactating woman
- Screened for certain diseases/illnesses/medications
- Tested to be free from:
  - *HIV – 1, 2
  - *Hepatitis C antibody
  - *Hepatitis B surface antigen
  - *Tuberculosis (PPD)
  - *Syphilis (RPR or VDRL)
  - *HTLV – 1, 2

- Free from the following activities which might put her at risk for transmitting blood-borne diseases:
  - *Unauthorized injection of drugs or medications
  - *Body/ear piercing at home in the last year
  - *Tatoo in the last year
  - *Since 1977, she should not have:
    - +Been a sex worker
    - +Been born in or received blood products while in Cameroon, Central African Republic, Chad, Congo, Equatorial Guinea, Gabon,

Niger or Nigeria

+Had sexual contact with anyone born in or who lived in the above countries

Fresh breastmilk is a living biological fluid, and as such carries with it the risk of infection, despite careful screening.

When fresh milk from closely related donors is given to extremely premature or immuno-compromised infants, there is a theoretical risk of graft-vs-host disease, although this has never been reported. To reduce this theoretical risk, fresh milk may be frozen or irradiated.

It is important that you discuss with a doctor any questions that you may have about the use of fresh donor breastmilk.

VERIFICATION OF RECEIPT OF THIS INFORMATION SHEET

My signature below indicates I have received this information form and have had the opportunity to have my questions answered.

_____   ___/___/___   ___:___AM/PM
SIGNATURE   DATE   TIME

_____
RELATIONSHIP TO PATIENT

FRESH DONOR BREASTMILK INFORMATION SHEET FOR POTENTIAL FRESH BREASTMILK DONOR

Fresh Donor Breastmilk may be recommended/prescribed for ill or preterm infants.

The health benefits of using breastmilk for an infant may include:
- Active infection-fighting cells
- Other infection-fighting factors
- Active growth and developmental hormones
- Ideal nutrition
- Better digestion

I understand that the milk donor must fit certain criteria. She must be:
- A healthy lactating woman
- Screened for certain diseases/illnesses/medications
- Tested to be free from:
    - HIV – 1, 2
    - Hepatitis C antibody
    - Hepatitis B surface antigen
    - Tuberculosis (PPD)
    - Syphilis (RPR or VDRL)
    - HTLV – 1, 2

- Free from the following activities which might put her at risk for transmitting blood-borne diseases:
    - Unauthorized injection of drugs or medications
    - Body/ear piercing at home in the last year
    - Tatoo in the last year
    - Since 1977, she should not have:
        - Been a sex worker
        - Been born in or received blood products while in Cameroon, Central African Republic, Chad, Congo, Equatorial Guinea, Gabon, Niger or Nigeria
        - Had sexual contact with anyone born in or who lived in the above countries

Fresh breastmilk is a living biological fluid, and as such carries with it the risk of infection, despite careful screening.

When fresh milk from closely related donors is given to extremely premature or immuno-compromised infants, there is a theoretical risk of graft-vs-host disease, although this has never been reported. To reduce this theoretical risk, fresh milk may be frozen or irradiated.

It is important that you discuss with a doctor any questions that you may have about the use of fresh donor breastmilk.

VERIFICATION OF RECEIPT OF THIS INFORMATION SHEET

My signature below indicates I have received this information form and have had the opportunity to have my questions answered.

_____ _____/___/___ ___:____AM/PM
SIGNATURE DATE TIME

_____
RELATIONSHIP TO PATIENT

Attachment B

Recipient Infant Name:

MR #

D.O.B.

MOTHER & INFANT MEDICAL HISTORY
FOR POTENTIAL FRESH BREASTMILK DONORS

Please use the bottom of this form to explain in detail any "yes" answers. Answering yes to a question does not necessarily prevent you from becoming a donor. If you answer yes to any of these questions, provide details below.

Have you ever had:	YES	NO
1. A positive test for hepatitis?	___	___
2. A history of hepatitis or yellow jaundice?	___	___
3. Liver problems?	___	___
4. Hepatitis B immune globulin in the last 12 months?	___	___
5. Exposure to hepatitis or HIV in the past 12 months?	___	___
6. Ears, body part pierced, acupuncture, or tattoos, in the past 12 months?	___	___
7. Heart disease or high blood pressure?	___	___
8. Tuberculosis, exposure to TB or a positive TB test or X-ray?	___	___
9. Insulin dependent diabetes?	___	___
10. Sexually transmitted disease (syphilis, gonorrhea, chlamydia)?	___	___
11. Genital or oral herpes?	___	___
12. Cold sores? If yes, how often?	___	___
13. Skin disease or skin lesions?	___	___
14. Rubella or polio vaccinations or inoculations in the last 4 weeks?	___	___
15. Accidental needle sticks in the last 12 months?	___	___
16. Unexplained swollen lymph glands?	___	___
17. Unexplained weight loss, fever, or night sweats?	___	___
18. White sores or lesions in your mouth?	___	___
19. History of yeast infections (systemic, vaginal, oral)?	___	___

Have you ever had: Yes   No

20. Persistent diarrhea? ___ ___
21. Received blood, blood products, or had surgery in the past 12 months? ___ ___
22. Ever received human pituitary growth hormone? ___ ___
23. An organ or tissue transplant? ___ ___
24. History of cancer or unexplained lumps? ___ ___
25. Serious illness in the past year? ___ ___
26. Intimate contact with someone who has injected drugs or used injected drugs yourself? ___ ___
27. Intimate contact with someone who is at risk for HIV, HTLV or hepatitis exposure (including anyone with hemophilia)? ___ ___
28. Intimate contact with anyone who has Creutzfeldt-Jakob Disease? ___ ___
29. Have you ever been told not to donate blood or milk? ___ ___
30. Did your baby have an in utero (before birth) blood transfusion? ___ ___
31. Are you under a doctor's care for anything? ___ ___
32. Do you have a silicone breast implant? ___ ___

Detailed information: _____

_____

_____

_____

1. How many children do you have?

   Names: Ages:

   _____   _____

   _____   _____

   _____   _____

   _____   _____

2. During this last pregnancy, delivery, and post-   YES   NO
   delivery time period, have you had any complications,
   such as infection, excessive bleeding or high blood   ___   ___
   pressure? If yes, please explain:

   _____

   _____

3. Have you expressed and stored milk before?   ___   ___
   If yes, when and how much? _____
   If you use a breast pump, what kind is it? _____

4. Have you ever had breast infections with this baby? ___   ___
   If yes, please describe and give dates:

   _____

   _____

5. Are you on a special diet? (such as: low salt, low
   dairy products, vegetarian, diabetic, weight loss, etc.?) ___ ___
   If yes, please explain:

   _____

   _____

BABY'S HEALTH HISTORY

1. Has your baby ever had a yeast infection (thrush or
   diaper rash)?   ___   ___

2. Has your baby been exposed to any communicable
   disease, such as chicken pox, mumps, etc.?   ___   ___

3. Does your baby have repeated infections, such as
   colds, ear infections, diaper rash or skin infections? ___ ___

4. Is your baby gaining weight and growing well?   ___   ___

5. Is your baby totally breastfed?   ___   ___

_____   __/__/__   __:__ am/pm
Donor's Signature   Date   Time

Attachment C

BREASTMILK DONOR AGREEMENT

1. I have voluntarily chosen to donate my breastmilk to_____
                                                        (Infants name)
   I understand that I will not be paid for the milk I donate.
2. I will make every effort to see that my milk is donated
   according to the instructions provided. I understand that it is
   my responsibility to notify the infant's physician:
   a. In the case of illness in myself, my baby, or a
      member of my household;
   b. When I need to take any medications;
   c. When family obligations prevent continuing
      donations;
   d. When I have any questions about being a donor;
   e. When I have been exposed to a contagious illness
      or disease.
3. I am also aware that once my milk has been donated, it
   becomes the property of _____.
                                      (Infant's name)
4. I understand that I am encouraged to discontinue donating milk
   anytime my participation interferes with my own family's needs.
5. I understand that all donor information is confidential and will
   be released only to the physicians caring for the infant who will
   receive my milk, unless I authorize further release in writing.
6. I understand and have answered all the questions about my
   and my infant's medical history truthfully and to the best of
   my ability. I do not consider myself to be a person at risk for
   spreading HIV.
7. I agree to be tested as needed for: HIV 1,2; HTLV 1,2; Hepatitis
   C Antibody; Hepatitis B surface antigen; Tuberculosis (PPD);
   Syphilis (RPR or VDRL); CMV.
8. I understand that I am responsible for any costs related to the
   blood testing listed in #7 above.

Signature: _____ Date: ___/___/___ Time: ___:___ AM/PM

Print Name: _____

Witness: _____ Date: ___/___/___ Time: ___:___ AM/PM

Best Medicine: Human Milk in the NICU

INFORMATION REQUEST AND MEDICAL RELEASE
FROM DONOR'S HEALTHCARE PROVIDER
TO MEDICAL DIRECTOR OF LACTATION SERVICES

Date: __/__/__

To: _____
             (Donor's Healthcare Provider)

_____ has volunteered to be a donor for one of our babies at the Neonatal Intensive Care Unit at Mary Birch Hospital for Women. To comply with the Human Milk Banking Association of North America guidelines, we need certain information for our records.

If you have not done the tests listed below during this pregnancy, they will need to be done before she begins donating milk.

After you have completed this form, please ask your patient to return it in the enclosed envelope to the Medical Director, Lactation Services. All donor records are confidential, to be released only to the physicians caring for the infant receiving donor milk. Thank you for your assistance.

Sincerely, _____
               (Physician's Signature)

- -

TO BE COMPLETED BY POTENTIAL DONOR

I authorize _____ to release
               (Donor's Healthcare Provider)
the requested medical information to the Medical Director of Lactation Services at Mary Birch Hospital for Women.

_____   _____

Donor signature   Date/Time

TO BE COMPLETED BY POTENTIAL DONOR'S HEALTHCARE PROVIDER

To the best of your knowledge, does this patient have a history of:

	YES	NO
1. Genital herpes?	___	___
2. Blood transfusion in the last 12 months?	___	___
3. TB, hepatitis or prenatal viral infection?	___	___
4. Taking any medication on a regular basis?	___	___

5. Laboratory tests in the last 6 months:	Results:	Date:
a. HIV – 1, 2	_____	___
b. HTLV – 1, 2	_____	___
c. Hepatitis C antibody	_____	___
d. Hepatitis B surface antigen	_____	___
e. Tuberculosis (PPD)	_____	___
f. Syphilis (RPR or VDRL)	_____	___
g. CMV	_____	___

To the best of my knowledge, _____

(Potential donor)

is in good health and would be an appropriate donor of human milk.

_____   __/__/__

Signature of Donor's Healthcare Provider   Date

Recipient Infant Name:
MR #
D.O.B.

Attachment E

INFORMATION REQUEST AND MEDICAL RELEASE FROM DONOR'S INFANT'S HEALTHCARE PROVIDER TO MEDICAL DIRECTOR OF LACTATION SERVICES

Date: ___/___/___

Dear Dr. _____

       (Infant's Healthcare Provider)

The mother of your patient _____ has volunteered to be a breastmilk donor to one of the babies in the Neonatal Intensive Care Unit at Mary Birch Hospital for Women. To comply with the Human Milk Banking Association of North America guidelines for safe use of donor milk, we request a review of your records to verify that this donation will not compromise the health status of your pediatric patient.

After you have completed this form, please ask the mother of your patient to return it in the enclosed envelope to the Medical Director, Lactation Services.

Thank you.

Sincerely, _____

       (Physician's Signature)

- -

TO BE COMPLETED BY POTENTIAL DONOR

I authorize _____ to

       (Infant's Healthcare Provider)

complete this form.

_____   _____

    Baby's Name   Mother's Signature

TO BE COMPLETED BY DONOR'S INFANT'S HEALTHCARE PROVIDER

Date last seen in this office: ___/___/___

I am aware of no contraindications for baby _____
if his/her mother donates milk to the Neonatal Intensive Care Unit at
Mary Birch Hospital for Women.

_____   ___/___/___
Signature of Infant's Healthcare Provider   Date

Recipient Infants' Name _____

MR# _____

DOB#_____

POLICY & PROCEDURE: BREASTMILK MISADMINISTRATION POLICY

I. Purpose

To provide guidelines for action when an infant is fed "unprocessed" human milk from a mother in the NICU other than his/her own mother.

II. Definitions

Misadministration - An infant given the wrong mother's milk "i.e., any mother's milk other than his/her own mother's milk"

Recipient Infant - The infant given the wrong mother's milk

Source Mother - Mother whose milk is fed to the wrong infant

Recipient Mother - Mother of infant who receives the wrong milk

III. Text

Despite significant prevention efforts, infants are still occasionally fed another mother's milk in error. This misadministration of human milk results in anxiety for both family and staff. Much of this anxiety is the result of misinformation about the potential infectious risks to the recipient infant and uncertainty as to how to evaluate the risk. In most cases the risk of transmission of infectious disease is extremely low. With increasing Joint Commission on Accreditation of Health Care Organizations (JCAHO) focus on patient safety and medical error reporting by hospital systems, a plan of care should be available in the (hopefully) rare instance when a mother's milk is given to the wrong infant.

IV. Procedure

If an infant receives the wrong breastmilk:

1. The RN/LVN will notify the Charge Nurse and the MD/NNP of both the source and recipient infants' identities.

2. The Charge Nurse will notify the source and recipient parents or legal representatives. Do not identify Donor Mother or Receiving Infant by name.

3. The MD/NNP will review the source mother's chart for maternal history and order appropriate lab work <u>on the source mother</u> which includes:

   a. HIV I and 2 Antibody

   b. Hepatitis C Antibody

   c. Hepatitis B Surface Antigen

   d. Syphillis Serology (RPR or VDRL)

   And <u>may</u> include:

   e. CMV Antibody Screen and/or breastmilk CMV culture

4. MD/NNP will obtain source mother's Informed Consent for HIV Test and Authorization for Disclosure of the Results if the result is not available in the source mother's chart.

5. The MD/NNP will notify the primary physician of the recipient infant to provide follow up care as needed.

   a. The misadministration of breastmilk should be part of the recipient infant's discharge summary.

   b. Follow-up laboratories at 3 months, 6 months and 1 year may include:

      i.   HIV antibody (HIVAB)

      ii. Hepatitis B Surface Antigen (HBSA)

      iii. Hepatitis C Antibody (HCVAB)

      iv. CMV antibody or PCR

6. The RN will complete and obtain signatures on the Consent for HIV Test form and Authorization for Disclosure of the Results of HIV Test form if needed.

7. The RN/LVN will process any ordered lab tests on the source mother or recipient infant.

8. Lab personnel will hand deliver test results in a sealed envelope marked "Breastmilk Workup" to the NICU Charge Nurse.

9. The Unit Charge Nurse will relay the sealed envelope marked "Breastmilk Workup" to the ordering/covering physician and/or Epidemiologist.

10. If the Source Mother refuses to give consent for HIV test or authorize release of the test results to the recipient's physician, notify the physicians for both the source and recipient patient to encourage counseling of both.

11. Note on the Recipient Infant's chart the date of the occurrence and laboratory studies sent. Also note that follow up lab on the infant may be needed.

12. The Infection Control Practitioner will notify the Recipient Infant's attending physician of the need for follow up laboratories as appropriate.

13. RN discovering misadministration will complete a quality variance report.

VI. References

American Academy of Pediatrics. 2003 Redbook: Report of the committee on infectious diseases. Pickering LK (ed). American Academy of Pediatrics, Elk Grove Village, IL, 2003, 26th Edition pgs 118-121, 2003.

Warner BB, Sapsford A. Misappropriated human milk: fantasy, fear, and fact regarding infectious risk. NBIN4(1): 56-61,WB Saunders. www.medscape.com/viewarticle/472406_print.

Lawrence RA, Lawrence RM, Breastfeeding: A guide for the medical profession. 5th Ed. 1999, Mosby: St. Louis, Chapter 16, pg 563-616.

V. Cross References

Breastfeeding Policy

Handling of Milk for the Hospitalized Infant Policy

Attachments:

Approvals:

Replaces:

History:

POLICY AND PROCEDURE: ALTERNATE FEEDING METHODS FOR BREASTFEEDING NICU INFANTS

I. Purpose

To provide guidelines for safe feeding of preterm infants by methods other than at the breast.

II. Definitions

Bottle-feeding - feeding with a bottle and nipple

Cup-feeding - feeding with any size cup

Finger-feeding - feeding with a feeding tube attached to a syringe attached to the pad of a finger inserted into the infant's mouth.

SNS - Supplemental nursing system (tube attached to the nipple attached to a reservoir of milk)

III. Text

A. Any method other than direct breastfeeding is an "alternate" feeding method.

B. Although bottles have become the predominant method of feeding in the U.S., most other cultures use cups for supplementary feedings when transitioning an infant from gavage to oral feedings at the breast.

C. Mothers may request, or a lactation consultant may recommend, alternate methods of feeding for preterm infants in order to limit exposure to the rapid flow through a bottle nipple or to facilitate long term breastfeeding.

D. Some feeding methods (e.g., finger-feeding) may also be recommended to help pattern or "train" an infant's immature or dysfunctional suck.

E. Until research as to the best way to feed preterm infants as they transition from gavage to breast is available, every effort should be made to accommodate mothers' preferences as long as appropriate weight gain is maintained and the infant remains physiologically stable with the method chosen.

IV. Procedure

1. Ask the mother of the baby if she has any preference regarding feeding method when she is unavailable to breastfeed, or if supplementary oral feeding is needed. (RN)

2. Document the mother's preferences. (RN)

3. **Bottle-feeding:** Artificial nipple with wide base and slow flow (long term use)

    i.   Swaddle infant and hold in semi-upright position.

    ii. Tickle the infant's lips with the nipple and allow infant to draw the nipple into the mouth by him- or herself.

    iii. Observe for signs of milk flow.

    iv. Allow the infant time to swallow, to pace the feedings, and stop to burp from time to time.

4. **Cup** (short or long term use)

    i.   Swaddle infant and hold in semi-upright position.

    ii. Fill the 30mL medicine cup at least ½ full and place cup up to infant's mouth touching upper lip (and not pushing down on lower lip).

    iii. Tip cup so supplement just touches infant's lips.

    iv. Infant usually laps or sips it. (Do not pour into baby's mouth.)

    v.   Allow the infant time to swallow, to pace the feedings, and stop to burp from time to time.

5. **Finger-feeding with dropper or syringe** (short term use) or with feeding tube **or commercial finger-feeding device** (longer term use)

    i.   Perform hand hygiene and ensure nail length is less than ¼ inch long. Gloves may be worn, if desired.

ii. Gather supplies (dropper, 20 mL syringe, or #5 Fr. feeding tube and a 20 mL syringe).

iii. Place infant on a pillow on your lap, facing you, and in a semi-upright position.

iv. Draw up desired amount of supplement into syringe, attach feeding tube, and push plunger to prime the tube.

v. Line tube with the end of your index or small finger on the top or lateral aspect of your finger pad. You may tape the tube to your finger towards the knuckle area, away from the end of the finger.

vi. Using the finger with the tube, gently tickle the infant's lips until the infant opens his mouth enough to allow the finger to enter.

vii. Insert your finger with the tube with your nail bed down on the tongue and the soft part facing the palate. Your fingertip should be raised to rest where the soft palate meets the hard palate.

viii. Ensure both lips are flanged outwards around your finger. The suck should be strong enough to pull down the fluids with no assistance.

ix. When fingerfeeding with a dropper: follow the same positioning and place dropper in the corner of the mouth to introduce the fluids.

6. **Spoon** (short term use)

i. Swaddle infant and hold in semi-upright position.

ii. Place expressed colostrum on the spoon and place spoon up to infant's mouth, touching upper lip (and not pushing down on lower lip).

iii. Tip spoon so supplement just touches infant's lips.

iv. Infant usually laps or sips it. (Do not pour into baby's mouth.)

v. Allow the infant time to swallow, to pace the feedings, and stop to burp from time to time.

7. **At the breast with a syringe or dropper** (short term use)

   i. Perform hand hygiene. Gather supplies (medicine cup, 20mL syringe or dropper), fill the 30mL medicine cup, and draw up supplement into dropper or syringe.

   ii. Position and properly latch baby at breast

   iii. Put the dropper or syringe to the corner of baby's mouth then gently and slowly drip the milk in and allow baby to swallow before more is given.

   iv. Refill dropper when empty.

8. **At the breast with a feeding tube/syringe or Supplemental Nursing System** (longer term use)

   i. Gather supplies (medicine cup, 20 mL syringe and #5 Fr. Feeding tube or SNS, and tape).

   ii. Fill appropriate container with supplement and prime tubing.

   iii. Place tubing on the nipple, making sure it extends about ¼ inch beyond nipple, and secure it with a piece of tape.

   iv. Position and properly latch baby at breast. You may need to adjust placement of tubing for infant comfort and optimal milk.

9. Document the volume and feeding technique used, including estimates of spillage.

V. References

Marinelli KA, Burke GS, Dodd VL. A comparison of the safety of cupfeedings and bottlefeedings in premature infants whose mothers intend to breastfeed. J Perinatol 2001;21(6):350-5.

Collins CT, Ryan P, Crowther CA, McPhee AJ, Paterson S, Hiller JE. Effect of bottles, cups, and dummies on breast feeding in preterm infants: a randomised controlled trial. <u>BMJ.</u> 2004 Jul 24;329(7459):193-8. Epub 2004 Jun 18.

Cloherty M, Alexander J, Holloway I, Galvin K, Inch S. The cup-versus-bottle debate: a theme from an ethnographic study of the supplementation of breastfed infants in hospital in the United kingdom. J Hum Lact 2005;21(2):151-62; quiz 63-6.

Biancuzzo M. Creating and implementing a protocol for cup feeding. Mother Baby Journal May 1997; 2(3): 27-33

Lang S, Lawrence CJ, L'eorme R. Cup feeding: An alternative method of infant feeding. Arch Dis Child 1994; 71: 365-9.

Nyqvist KH, Strandell E. A cup feeding protocol for neonates: Evaluation of nurses' and parents' use of two cups. J Neonatal Nurs 1999; 5(2):31-36

Cross References

POLICY & PROCEDURE: TEST-WEIGHING

I. Definition

Test weighing - Weighing the infant before and after breastfeeding to determine intake at the breast.

II. Requirements

A digital scale with the following features:
1. Digital read-out
2. Integration function that allows for movement of the infant
3. Accurate to 2 grams

III. Procedure

If leads can be disconnected for weights:

1. Place scale up against infant bed/warmer/isolette on flat, level surface.

2. Suspend alarms and disconnect leads.

3. Wrap infant tightly so he/she will not move around on scale. No leads should be hanging off the scale.

4. Turn on and zero scale.

5. Before breastfeeding, place baby on the center of the scale and weigh him/her. No need to undress or remove or hold up leads. This is the "before" weight. Leave scale on during breastfeeding.

6. Reconnect leads.

7. Mother breastfeeds infant. DO NOT CHANGE DIAPER YET.

8. Suspend alarms and disconnect leads.

9. Reweigh the infant, on the center of the scale with the EXACT SAME CLOTHES, DIAPER, BLANKET, LEADS, ETC. This is the "after" weight.

10. Subtract the first (before) weight from the second (after) weight. The difference in grams is considered the "intake" in milliliters (mL).

11. Some scales automatically store the values and compute the difference for you. Refer to manufacturers' instructions.

If leads or tubing cannot be disconnected for weights:

1. Place scale up against infant bed/warmer/isolette on flat, level surface.

2. Wrap infant tightly so he/she will not move around on scale.

3. Place the baby on the scale with scale turned off.

4. Tape lead connection and other tubes to side of crib or isolette. There should be no tension on wires/tubes and they should not touch the scale.

5. Lift infant off scale.

6. Turn on and zero scale.

7. Before breastfeeding, place baby on the center of the scale and weigh him/her. You may place a hand under the leads to relieve any pulling. This is the "before" weight.

8. Untape leads, tubes, etc., but leave tape on crib/isolette/warmer/etc.

9. Remove infant from scale and turn off scale.

10. Mother breastfeeds infant. DO NOT CHANGE DIAPER YET.

11. After breastfeeding, replace infant on center of scale with the scale turned off.

12. Retape leads/tubes in same spot as before (on crib/isolette/warmer).

13. Lift infant, turn on and zero scale.

14. Replace the infant on the center of the scale and reweigh the infant, with the EXACT SAME CLOTHES, DIAPER, BLANKET, LEADS, ETC. You may place a hand under the leads to relieve any pulling. This is the "after" weight.

15. Subtract the first (before) weight from the second (after) weight. The difference in grams is considered the "intake" in milliliters (mL).

16. Some scales automatically store the values and compute the difference for you. Refer to manufacturers' instructions.

POLICY & PROCEDURE: NON-NUTRITIVE ("DRY") BREASTFEEDING IN THE NICU

I. Purpose

To provide guidelines for non-nutritive ("dry") breastfeeding for preterm and ill infants in the NICU.

II. Definitions

Non-nutritive breastfeeding (NNB) - also called "dry" breastfeeding is breastfeeding done after a mother has completed her routine pumping to empty her breasts before putting the infant to breast.

LC - Lactation Consultant

III. Text

A. Infants are put to an "emptied" breast as a transition from kangaroo care to nutritive breastfeeding. It allows the infant to stimulate the mother's breasts while protecting the infant from a rapid flow of milk from a full breast before the infant is physiologically ready to handle it because of an immature suck/swallow/breathe pattern. It also allows the mother to practice positioning and latching on her fragile infant, without having to worry about volume of intake.

B. Non-nutritive breastfeeding improves mothers' milk supply and improves duration of breastfeeding post-discharge.

C. Infants may be simultaneously gavage fed during the NNB.

D. Infants eligible for NNB include:

1. stable (see G) premature

2. no weight or gestational age limitations

3. respiratory status stable:

a. minimal A&B's

b. O_2 acceptable

c. stable NCPAP

d. stable ventilated infants

4. PICC, Broviacs, or UVC are permissible

5. UAC/PAL require an MD/NNP order

E. Infants doing NNB will have continuous cardiorespiratory and oximetry monitoring with the following exception. If the infant is stable off oximetry, it is not necessary to restart oximetry for NNB.

F. NNB may be attempted before, during and/or after a gavage feeding, whichever works best for the infant.

G. "Stable" is defined as infants who are not requiring frequent changes of respiratory support, with stable vital signs in normal ranges, who will tolerate brief handling with no change, or brief changes, in oxygen saturation. Infants on low dose dopamine may be considered stable, if frequent adjustments of the dosage are not required.

IV. Procedure

A. Position as follows:

1. Mother may remove or wear bra and open blouse as if to breastfeed.

2. Infant may be swaddled or with only hat and diaper, as for Kangaroo care. If only hat and diaper, place warm blanket over infant and mother once infant is latched on. A heat source, such as an overhead warmer or heat lamp, may also be used.

3. RN or LC to assist mother in positioning the infant for breastfeeding. The "football hold" (infant placed under mother's arm, facing her, level with nipple) is often the best tolerated initially.

B. Provide privacy as requested.

C. Record temperature prior to and upon return to isolette. Monitor continuous skin temperature of infant <1000 grams via electronic skin temperature reading on isolette.

D. Start with 30-60 minutes, once daily and increase as tolerated.

E. Document:

1. Temperature before/after

2. Length of time actively suckling on each breast

3. Any milk noted in the infant's mouth

4. Any adverse reactions/cold stress

5. Parent interaction

V. References

Pinelli J, Symington A. Non-nutritive sucking for promoting physiologic stability and nutrition in preterm infants. Cochrane Database Syst Rev. 2001;(3):CD001071. Update of: Cochrane Database Syst Rev. 2000;(2): CD001071.

Narayanan et al. Sucking on the "emptied" breast: non-nutritive sucking with a difference. **Arch Dis Child** 1991; 66(2):241-244

VI. Cross References:

Kangaroo Care Policy

VII.   Attachments:

VIII.   Approvals:

IX.   Replaces:

X.   History:

POLICY & PROCEDURE: KANGAROO CARE: SKIN TO SKIN CONTACT IN THE NICU

I. Purpose

To provide guidelines for Skin-to-Skin Contact (STSC) in the NICU.

II. Definition

Skin-to-skin contact (STSC) - when the infant, dressed only in a diaper and a hat, rests against the parent's chest, or other person designated by parent, skin to skin in a prone, upright position. A warm blanket or cloth diaper is used to hold the infant against the chest.

III. Text

A. Infants eligible for STSC include:

1. stable premature

2. no weight or gestational age limitations

3. respiratory status stable:

   a. minimal A&B's

   b. O₂ acceptable

   c. stable NCPAP

   d. stable ventilated infants

4. PICC, Broviacs, or UVC are permissible

5. UAC/PAL require an MD/NNP order

B. Infants receiving STSC will have continuous cardiorespiratory and oximetry monitoring with the following exception. If the infant is stable off oximetry, it is not necessary to restart oximetry for STSC.

C. STSC is ideal before or during a feeding, but may be attempted before, during and/or after feeding, whichever works best for the infant and parent.

D. "Stable" is defined as infants who are not requiring frequent changes of respiratory support, with stable vital signs in normal ranges, who will tolerate brief handling with no change or brief changes in oxygen saturation. Infants on low dose dopamine may be considered stable if frequent adjustments of the dosage are not required.

IV. Procedure	Responsibility
A. Position as follows:	RN/LVN

   1. Mother may remove or wear bra and open blouse as if to breastfeed.

   2. Father opens shirt.

   3. Infant, wearing hat, is placed prone vertically or angled across chest.

   4. A warm blanket is placed over infant.

   5. Parents may close clothing over infant.

B. Provide privacy as requested.

C. Record temperature prior to and upon return to isolette. Monitor continuous skin temperature of infant <1000 grams via electronic skin temperature reading on isolette.

D. The length of time spent in STSC is as tolerated by the infant, usually at least 30 60 minutes and up to 3-4 hours as tolerated, once daily, and increase as tolerated.

E. Document:

   1. Temperature before/after

   2. Any adverse reactions/cold stress

   3. Parent interaction on Family Interaction Screen

V. References

Cattaneo A, Davanzo R, Uxa F, & Tamburlini G for the International Network on Kangaroo Mother Care. (1998). Recommendations for the implementation of kangaroo mother care for low birthweight infants. Acta Paediatrica, 87(4), 440-445

Kirsten GF, Bergman NJ, Hann FM. Kangaroo care in the nursery. Ped Clin NA 2001 April; 48(2):443-452

Ludington-Hoe SM, Ferreira C, Swinth J, Ceccardi JJ. Safe criteria and procedure for kangaroo care with intubated preterm infants. J Obstet Gynecol Neonatal Nurs 2003 Sept-Oct; 32(5):579-88

Ludington-Hoe SM, Anderson GC, Swinth JY et al. Randomized controlled trial of kangaroo care: Cardiorespiratory and thermal effects on health preterm infants. Neonatal Netw. 2004 May-June; 23(3):39-48

VI. Cross References

VII. Attachments

VIII. Approvals

IX. Replaces

X. History

SAMPLE LETTER: EXPLANATION OF MEDICAL NEED FOR BREAST PUMP

Date:

Insurance Company
Insurance Address
Insurance Address

Infant:
Medical Record #:
Insured:
Policy No:
Address:
Phone:

To Whom It May Concern:

The following explanation of medical need is provided in order to expedite insurance coverage for the rental of a full size, hospital grade, electric breast pump and purchase of necessary accompanying supplies.

Mrs./Ms. _____ delivered a high risk infant on___. The infant is too _____ (ill/immature) to nurse directly at breast. However, it is well established that breastmilk provides optimal infant nutrition, important growth and developmental hormones, significant protection against infection and other illness, as well as long term benefits.[1, 2] Breastfeeding promotes strong families by improving the health of the mother, promoting optimal child spacing, and establishing a close bond between mother and infant.[1, 3] Breastfeeding also provides significant economic benefits to the family, the community, and the healthcare system by reducing unnecessary expenditures for infant formula, reducing health care costs, reducing employee absenteeism to care for a sick child, and decreasing scarce resource use and waste.[4, 5] Breastfeeding cost effectiveness studies, using extremely conservative estimates, reveal that as little as three months of exclusive breastfeeding can save between $200 - $400 per child in health care cost during the first year of life.[6]

Recent research has revealed that preterm infants fed human milk:

- Establish full enteral feedings sooner, thereby needing less IVs and expensive parenteral nutrition[7, 8]

- Have a much decreased risk of necrotizing enterocolitis and sepsis[7-10]

- Spend fewer days in the hospital[7]

- Have an IQ advantage over formula-fed infants[11]

- Tend to have less, and less severe, retinopathy of prematurity[12]

- May have less allergies, better vision, and less disease as older children and adults[4]

Each mother's breastmilk is specifically tailored for her own infant. Thus, we encourage mothers of our sick and premature infants to pump their breasts in order to supply milk for their hospitalized infants, and to maintain lactation until the infant can ultimately nurse completely at breast. Many times these infants are not completely on the breast at the time of discharge and a breast pump is necessary in the home for a few weeks to a few months after the infant is discharged.

The automatic, intermittent suction, full-scale electric breast pump is by far the most efficient, effective, and physiologic means of simulating the suckling action of a normal infant. Inexpensive manual, battery operated, or small electric breast pumps are sometimes helpful for intermittent pumping, but cannot establish or maintain adequate milk production. A piston type full-scale electric breast pump is essential to establish and maintain an adequate breastmilk supply whenever the infant is unable to breastfeed normally for a week or more. Such pumps cost $1,000 or more, and are thus more economical to rent.

The electric breast pump will be necessary until the infant is able to take all required nutrition by nursing at the breast. Artificial formulas are **not** an adequate substitute. **An electric breast pump is not a convenience for the mother; rather it is a medical necessity in the best interest of the child.** It is also a cost effective measure for the health care or insurance plan. Please feel free to call upon me should you have any questions about the medical requirement for the breast pump.

Sincerely

_____ MD

Address
Phone
FAX
Pager

References:

1. The American Academy of Pediatrics, Workgroup on Breastfeeding. Breastfeeding and the use of human milk. Pediatrics 1999; 100(6):1035 – 1039.

2. Heinig MJ, Dewey KG. Health advantages of breast feeding for infants: A critical review. Nutrition Research Reviews 1996; 9:89-110.

3. Heinig MJ, Dewey KG. Health effects of breast feeding for mothers: a critical review. Nutrition Research Reviews 1997; 10:35-56.

4. Breastfeeding promotion Committee Report. Breastfeeding: Investing in California's future. California Department of Health Services, Primary Care and Family Gealth, Sacramento, CA, January 1997

5. Riordan JM. The cost of not breastfeeding: A commentary. J Hum Lact 1997; 13(2):93-97

6. Ball T, Wright AL. Health care costs of formula-feeding in the first year of life. Pediatrics 1999; 103(4 Pt 2):870-876.

7. Schanler RJ, Shulman RJ, Lau C. Feeding strategies for premature infants: beneficial outcomes of feeding fortified human milk verses preterm formula. Pediatrics 1999; 103(6):1150 – 1157

8. Lucas A, Cole TJ. Breast milk and neonatal necrotising enterocolitis. Lancet 1990; 336:1519-1523

9. Narayanan I, Prakash K, Gujral VV. The value of human milk in the prevention of infection in the high-risk low-birth-weight infant. J Pediatr 1981 Sep; 99(3): 496-8

10. Hylander MA, Strobino DM, Dhanireddy R. Human milk feedings and infection among very low birth weight infants. Pediatrics 1998; 102(3): e38 (www.pediatrics.org/cgi/content/full/102/3/e38)

11. Anderson JW, Johnstone BM, Remley DT. Breast-feeding and cognitive development: a meta-analysis. Am J Clin Nutr 1999; 70:525-535

12. Hylander MA, Stobino DM, Dhanireddy R. Human milk feedings and retinopathy of prematurity among very low birthweight infants. Abstract NPA Mtg Nov 1995. J Perinatol 1996; 16(3):236

SAMPLE LETTER: EXPLANATION OF MEDICAL NEED FOR DONOR HUMAN MILK

Date:

Insurance Company
Insurance Address
Insurance Address

Infant:
Medical Record #:
Insured:
Policy No:
Address:
Phone:

To Whom It May Concern:

The following explanation of medical need is provided in order to expedite insurance coverage for pasteurized donor human milk.

Mrs./Ms. _____ delivered a high risk infant on_____. The infant is too _____ (ill/immature) to nurse directly at breast. However, it is well established that breastmilk provides optimal infant nutrition, important growth and developmental hormones, significant protection against infection and other illness, as well as long term benefits.[1-3] Breastfeeding promotes strong families by improving the health of the mother, promoting optimal child spacing, and establishing a close bond between mother and infant.[1, 4,5] Breastfeeding also provides significant economic benefits to the family, the community, and the healthcare system by reducing unnecessary expenditures for infant formula, reducing health care costs, reducing employee absenteeism to care for a sick child, and decreasing scarce resource use and waste.[6,7] Breastfeeding cost effectiveness studies, using extremely conservative estimates, reveal that as little as three months of exclusive breastfeeding can save between $200 - $400 per child in health care cost during the first year of life.[8]

Recent research has revealed that preterm infants fed human milk:

- Establish full enteral feedings sooner, thereby needing less IVs and expensive parenteral nutrition[9,10]

- Have a much decreased risk of necrotizing enterocolitis (NEC) and sepsis[9-12]

- Spend fewer days in the hospital[9]

- Have an IQ advantage over formula-fed infants[13]

- Tend to have less, and less severe, retinopathy of prematurity[14]

- May have less allergies, better vision, and less disease as older children and adults[1-3,6]

Although we encourage mothers of our sick and premature infants to pump their breasts in order to supply milk for their hospitalized infants, **some mothers are unable, because of their own illness or medications, to provide sufficient milk for their ill infants.** Pasteurized donor human milk caries no risk of infection (it is sterile) and maintains many of the advantages of mothers' own milk in terms of growth hormones, enzymes and infection-fighting factors, as well as ease of digestion as noted above. Pasteurized donor human milk is also cost-effective, reducing expenditures for preventable NEC, sepsis, hyperalimentation, and extra hospital days.[15]

Pasteurized donor human milk is not just nutrition, it is a vital medicine for ill or preterm infants. Human milk banks will not release pasteurized donor milk without a physician's prescription. Donor human milk is also a cost effective measure for the health care organization or insurance plan. Please feel free to call upon me should you have any questions about the medical requirement for pasteurized donor human milk for this infant.

Sincerely,

_____ MD

Address
Phone
FAX
Pager

References:

1. The American Academy of Pediatrics, Workgroup on Breastfeeding. Breastfeeding and the use of human milk. Pediatrics 1999; 100(6):1035 – 1039.

2. Heinig MJ, Dewey KG. Health advantages of breast feeding for infants: A critical review. Nutrition Research Reviews 1996; 9:89-110.

3. Koletzko B, Michaelsen KF, Hernell O. Short and long term effects of breast feeding on child health. Advances in Experimental Medicine and Biology, Vol 478, Kluwer/Plenum Publishers, New York, 2000 (Proceedings of the 9th International Conference of the Society for Research in Human Milk and Lactation (ISRHML), held October 2-6, 1999, Bavaria.

4. Heinig MJ, Dewey KG. Health effects of breast feeding for mothers: a critical review. Nutrition Research Reviews 1997; 10:35-56.

5. Labbok MH. Health sequelae of breastfeeding for the mother. Clin Perinatol 1999; 26(2):491-503.

6. Breastfeeding promotion committee report. Breastfeeding: Investing in California's future. California Department of Health Services, Primary Care and Family Health, Sacramento, CA, January 1997.

7. Riordan JM. The cost of not breastfeeding: A commentary. J Hum Lact 1997; 13(2):93-97.

8. Ball T, Wright AL. Health care costs of formula-feeding in the first year of life. Pediatrics 1999; 103(4 Pt 2):870-876.

9. Schanler RJ, Shulman RJ, Lau C. Feeding strategies for premature infants: beneficial outcomes of feeding fortified human milk verses preterm formula. Pediatrics 1999; 103(6):1150 – 1157.

10. Lucas A, Cole TJ. Breast milk and neonatal necrotising enterocolitis. Lancet 1990; 336:1519-1523.

11. Narayanan I, Prakash K, Gujral VV. The value of human milk in the prevention of infection in the high-risk low-birth-weight infant. J Pediatr 1981 Sep; 99(3): 496-8.

12. Hylander MA, Strobino DM, Dhanireddy R. Human milk feedings and infection among very low birth weight infants. Pediatrics 1998; 102(3): e38 (www.pediatrics.org/cgi/content/full/102/3/e38)

13. Anderson JW, Johnstone BM, Remley DT. Breast-feeding and cognitive development: a meta-analysis. Am J Clin Nutr 1999; 70:525-535

14. Hylander MA, Stobino DM, Dhanireddy R. Human milk feedings and retinopathy of prematurity among very low birthweight infants. Abstract NPA Mtg Nov 1995. J Perinatol 1996; 16(3):236

15. Wight NE. Commentary: Donor human milk for preterm infants. J Perinatol 2001; 21:249-254 (83 references)

MOTHER'S DISCHARGE CHECKLIST

(Courtesy of Jane Morton MD and CPQCC)

Maternal Discharge Check List

For mothers of sick or preterm infants who choose to provide breastmilk for their infant(s):

Dear Mother: Please initial this form after receiving/understanding each of the following:

1. Breastfeeding benefits discussed with my baby's doctor (date: _____)   _____

2. Began assisted pumping by nursing staff (time and date: _____)   _____

3. Began pumping independently

   (time and date: _____)   _____

4. Learned how to record in diary my pumping frequency (minimum, 8 times per day)   _____

5. Learned how to clean pump and collecting equipment   _____

6. Learned about labeling, storage, and transport of my milk (including small vials for colostrum)   _____

7. Toured the NICU and saw pumping facilities and supplies   _____

8. Learned what to expect when milk comes in   _____

9. Learned about breast massage and manual expression   _____

10. Received my own copy of the video:

A Premie Needs His Mother, First Steps to Breastfeeding Your Premature Baby (for mothers of preterm infants only)   _____

11. My rental pump for home use will be available
the day of discharge.   Yes__ No __

If no, please give date of rental_____.
(Rental site_____)

12. I received contact information for breastfeeding issues and an invitation to the breastfeeding class for mothers of NICU babies.   _____

Signature of discharge nurse assisting mother complete her educational objectives:

_____   _____
          name   date

Staff Attitude/Knowledge Survey

Breastfeeding and the Use of Human Milk for Preterm/Ill Infants

I. Purpose

Although education is important, changing attitude is a pre-requisite to changing practice. The following brief survey will reveal areas of significant perinatal health care provider attitudes and concerns requiring attention. The survey may be repeated after significant educational and systems change efforts to assess progress.

II. Target Population

Many different perinatal professionals and support personnel interact with each mother-infant dyad and influence both a mother's decision to provide breastmilk for her NICU infant and her success at doing so.

Obtain completed questionnaires from at least 5 individuals in **each** of the following units:

- High Risk Antepartum Unit
- Labor & Delivery
- Post-Anesthesia Care Unit
- Post-Partum (Mother-Baby) Unit
- Newborn Nursery (if one exists in your hospital)
- Transition Nursery (if one exists in your hospital)
- Intermediate Care Nursery
- NICU/ICN

Although most of your responses may come from physicians, and nurses (RNs), do not forget:

- Social workers
- Nurse practitioners and physician assistants
- Physicians in training
- LVNs, nursing assistants
- Ward secretaries
- Occupational and physical therapists
- Respiratory therapists
- Doulas

SURVEY: Breastfeeding and the Use of Human Milk for Preterm/Ill Infants

Unit	Specialty	Position
☐High Risk Antepartum	☐Ob-Gyn	☐Attending MD
☐L & D	☐Perinatology	☐MD in training
☐Post-anesthesia care	☐Family Practice	☐RN Midwife
☐NICU	☐Pediatrics	☐NNP/PNP/PA
☐Intermediate care nursery	☐Neonatology	☐RN
☐Post-partum (mother-baby)	☐Anesthesia	☐LVN/Nursing assistant
☐Newborn nursery	☐Other	☐Social worker
☐Transition nursery	_____	☐Ward secretary
		☐Other_____

I am: ☐ male ☐female **I was born in** (year) _____

I have personal/partner breastfeeding experience (longest time with any 1 child):

☐None ☐< 2 months ☐2-6 months ☐7-12 months ☐>12 months

Are you familiar with the WHO/UNICEF Baby-Friendly Hospital Initiative?

☐Very familiar ☐Somewhat familiar ☐Not at all familiar

Please check the most appropriate box:	Strongly Agree	Agree	Unsure	Neither/	Disagree	Strongly Disagree
Breastmilk and formula are equally acceptable for preterm / ill infants.						
Physicians should actively encourage breastfeeding.						
Obstetricians have an important role in the decision to breastfeed.						
Healthcare professionals should not stress breastfeeding because it might make mothers feel guilty.						
Wearing formula lanyards and badge-holders tells mothers I endorse that formula.						
Almost all mothers can be successful at breastfeeding if they are supported and encouraged.						
Human milk is sterile.						
Premature infants fed human milk have less NEC and sepsis.						
In the long run, formula-fed babies are just as healthy as breastfed ones.						
I feel responsible for helping a mother be successful at breastfeeding.						
The PDR is the best source of information on drugs and breastfeeding.						

RESOURCES

Academy of Breastfeeding Medicine (ABM)
www.bfmed.org

American Academy of Pediatrics (AAP)
www.aap.org

American Dietetic Association (ADA)
www.eatright.org

Association of Women's Health, Obstetric and Neonatal Nurses (AWHONN)
www.awhonn.org)

Australian Breastfeeding Association
www.breastfeeding.asn.au/

Breastfeeding Medicine – Journal of the Academy of Breastfeeding Medicine
www.liebertpub.com/publication.aspx?pub_id=173

Breastfeeding Pharmacology – Thomas Hale PhD
http://neonatal.ama.ttuhsc.edu/lact/

Breastfeeding Pharmacology - National Library of Medicine (NLM)
- US - Toxnet - LactMed
http://toxnet.nlm.nih.gov/cgi-bin/sis/htmlgen?LACT

California Department of Health Services – WIC Branch- Breastfeeding
www.wicworks.ca.gov/breastfeeding/BFResources.html

California Perinatal Quality Care Collaborative
www.cpqcc.org

Centers for Disease Control and Prevention (CDC-US)
www.cdc.gov/breastfeeding/

Global Breastfeeding
www.global-breastfeeding.org

Human Milk Banking Association of North America (HMBANA)
www.hmbana.org

International Breastfeeding Journal
www.internationalbreastfeedingjournal.com

International Lactation Consultant Association
www.ilca.org

International Society for Research in Human Milk and Lactation
www.isrhml.org.umu.se/

Kangaroo Mother Care
www.kangaroomothercare.com

La Leche League International
www.lalecheleague.org

March of Dimes (US) – PeriStats
www.marchofdimes.com/peristats

National Association of Neonatal Nurses (NANN)
www.nann.org

PubMed – National Library of Medicine (US)
www.ncbi.nlm.nih.gov/PubMed

UK Association for Milk Banking
www.ukamb.org

UNICEF
www.unicef.org

United States Breastfeeding Committee
www.usbreastfeeding.org

World Health Organization (WHO)
www.who.int

Glossary

------------ A ------------

AAFP – American Academy of Family Physicians

AAP – American Academy of Pediatrics

ABM – Academy of Breastfeeding Medicine

ABM – abbreviation for Artificial Baby Milk (formula)

AGA (appropriate for gestational age) - a baby who weighs between the 10th and 90th percentile by weight for his gestational age on standard growth curves.

ACOG – American College of Obstetricians and Gynecologists

ADA – American Dietetic Association

Alveoli – 1. tiny sacs in the lungs where the exchange of oxygen and carbon dioxide take place, OR 2. tiny sacs in the milk glands of the breast where breastmilk is made.

Amniotic fluid - the fluid surrounding the fetus in the uterus, which serves to protect the fetus during pregnancy.

Anemia - an abnormally low number of red blood cells, which carry oxygen to the tissues. In preemies, anemia can cause breathing problems, low energy, and poor growth.

Antepartum - before birth.

Antibodies - proteins produced by the body that fight infections caused by bacteria and viruses that have entered the body. Many helpful antibodies are found in a mother's breastmilk, and can be passed into a baby through breastmilk feedings.

Apgar score - a score first introduced by Dr. Virginia Apgar to assess the newborn's need for resuscitation. Apgar scores range from 0 to 10. Points are assigned beginning at one minute after birth, and at five-minute intervals thereafter, for heart rate, respiration, reflexes, muscle tone, and color, until an infant is stable.

Apnea - a pause in breathing that lasts for more than 20 seconds, or is accompanied by a slow heart rate (Bradycardia) or a change in skin color. Apnea is common among preemies, who still have immature control of their breathing.

Arachidonic acid – an omega-6 fatty acid.

Areola – the dark area on the breast surrounding the nipple.

AWHONN – Association of Women's Health, Obstetric and Neonatal Nurses

Bacteria – one-celled organisms that can cause infection.

B.I.D. – the abbreviation for the Latin words meaning "twice a day".

Bili lights (phototherapy) - special lights used to treat neonatal jaundice.

Bilirubin - a substance produced when red blood cells break down. When excessive amounts are present in the bloodstream, jaundice, a yellowing of the skin and whites of the eyes, can occur. When very high levels are present, brain damage can result. See kernicterus.

Blood glucose - a test used to determine the baby's blood sugar.

Blood pressure – the pressure the blood exerts against the walls of the blood vessels. It is this pressure that causes the blood to flow through the arteries and veins. The blood pressure measurement is given in the form of two numbers. The top number, the systolic pressure, is the measurement of the pressure exerted when the heart contracts and sends blood to the body. The lower number, the diastolic pressure, is the measurement of the pressure exerted during the relaxation between heartbeats.

Bonding - the process by which parents and baby become emotionally attached.

Bradycardia ("brady") - a heart rate that is slower than normal.

Brazelton Neonatal Assessment Scale (BNAS) – tests of a newborn's reflexes, behavior, and responses to his environment.

Breastfeeding jaundice – a type of jaundice caused by low intake of breastmilk in the first week after birth.

Breastmilk jaundice – a common type of jaundice thought to be caused by a substance in the mother's milk.

BUN (blood urea and nitrogen) – a blood test for liver and kidney function.

CDC – Centers for Disease Control and Prevention

Charge nurse – the nurse in the unit who is in charge of nursing care for that shift.

Chronic lung disease (CLD) - chronic injury or scarring in a premie or sick infant's lungs thought to be caused by the action of oxygen and mechanical ventilation on immature or very ill lungs over time. Formerly called "bronchopulmonary dysplasia."

Chylomicrons – large lipoprotein particles that are created by the absorptive cells of the small intestine.

CMV – see Cytomegalovirus.

Colostrum - breastmilk produced in late pregnancy or in the first 3-5 days after delivery. This milk is usually yellowish in color and is especially rich in nutrients and antibodies.

Continuous Positive Airway Pressure (CPAP) - pressurized air, sometimes with additional oxygen, that is delivered to the baby's lungs to keep them from collapsing as the baby inhales and exhales. Usually delivery by nasal prongs or face mask.

Corrected age – 1. the age of a premature baby determined by adding his postnatal days to his gestational age at birth. A baby who is fourteen days old and was born at twenty-six weeks would have a corrected age of twenty-eight weeks. 2. the age a premature baby would be if he had been born on his due date. For example, a baby born 3 months early is, at the actual age of 7 months, only 4 months old according to his corrected age.

Cortisol – corticosteroid hormone, sometimes referred to as the "stress hormone." It increases blood pressure and blood sugar levels, and has an immunosuppressive action.

Creamatocrit – the percentage of cream in mother's milk. Using a technique that estimates the lipid concentration and caloric density of mother's milk based on the centrifugation of milk in a hematocrit centrifuge. The percentage of fat is read from the hematocrit capillary tube and is linearly related to the fat and energy content of the milk.

Cup-feeding – an alternative feeding method in which the infant is allowed to "lap" milk from a small cup.

Cytomegalovirus (CMV) - a type of virus that may infect a baby either before or after birth. In some cases, if the infant is infected in utero, CMV causes severe illness and birth defects. Infants can be infected through breastmilk, and if extremely immature, they may develop a sepsis-like syndrome.

Denver Developmental Screening Test (DDST) – a screening test to help identify infants and children with developmental delays.

Developmental delay – a delay in reaching certain developmental milestones, relative to most other children of the same age. In preemies, developmental delays may be temporary or permanent.

DHHS – United States Department of Health and Human Services

Dilatation – the process of enlargement or expansion.

Docosahexaenoic acid - an omega-3 essential fatty acid, commonly known as DHA.

Donor human milk – heat-treated milk donated by tested volunteer mothers.

Ductus arteriosus – a blood vessel in the fetus that joins the aorta with the pulmonary artery in order to divert most blood away from the fetal lungs. This blood vessel must close after birth so that blood can flow properly to the lungs to receive oxygen.

--------------- **E** ---------------

EBM – abbreviation for expressed breastmilk. Milk that is expressed by hand or with a breast pump to be fed to a mother's own baby.

Embryo - the term used to describe the early stages of fetal growth, approximately the fourth to ninth week of pregnancy.

Enteromammary system – the ability of a lactating mother's immune system to make specific antibodies against pathogens in her infant's environment.

Epidermal growth factor – plays an important role in regulation of cell growth, proliferation, and differentiation.

Epigenetics – term used to refer to changes in gene expression that does not involve changes in the underlying DNA.

Erythrocyte – a red blood cell.

Erythropoietin – this is a natural hormone that stimulates the body to produce red blood cells. It can be made in the laboratory, and given to preemies to help prevent or treat anemia.

Extrauterine – outside the uterus.

Extrauterine growth restriction – a marker of severe nutritional deficit during the first weeks of life. The risk is greatest for infants < 1500 g at birth.

Extremely low birth weight (ELBW) – Infants born at less than 1000g (<2 lb 3 oz).

Extubation – the removal of the endotracheal tube.

--------------- **F** ---------------

Failure to thrive – medical term which indicates poor weight gain and physical growth failure over an extended period of time in infancy.

Fetus - the developing baby from approximately the ninth week of pregnancy until birth.

Finger-feeding – an alternative feeding method in which a tube connected to a milk reservoir is attached to a finger. The infant sucks on the finger to feed.

Football hold – a way of positioning the baby at the breast so that his legs and body are along the side of your body and under your arm and your hand is at the base of his head and neck as if you were holding a football.

Foremilk – the first milk taken at a feeding. It is more plentiful, but has a relatively lower percentage of fat and calories than hindmilk which comes at the end of the feeding.

Full-term (FT) - an infant born between the thirty-eighth and forty-second weeks of gestation.

------------- *G* -------------

GA - see gestational age.

Galactogogue – material that stimulates milk production, usually a food, herb, or medication.

Gavage feeding - a method of feeding breast milk or formula through a small tube passed through the baby's mouth or nose into the stomach.

Gestation – the length of time between the first day of the mother's last menstrual period before conception and the delivery of the baby.

Gestational age - the length of time from conception to birth. A full-term infant has a gestational age of 38-42 weeks.

GI priming - feeding in the early days of life to stimulate gut maturation, hormone release, motility, and support the immune system.

Glucose – the type of sugar that circulates in the blood and is used by the body for energy.

Gram - a unit of measuring weight. 30 grams = 1 ounce. Each baby is weighed daily and the weight is measured in grams.

------------- *H* -------------

Hand expression – an effective method of expressing milk from the breasts using the hands instead of a pump.

Hands-on pumping – the use of breast compression, massage, and hand expression while using a breast pump to increase the amount of expressed milk.

High-Temperature Short Time (HTST) milk processing – heating milk to 72°C for 5-15 seconds. Heating for 5 seconds destroys all bacteria; heating for 15 seconds makes CMV activity undetectable.

Hindmilk – the fat-rich, higher calorie milk that is produced at the end of a feeding. Expressed hindmilk can be used to increase the infant's caloric intake.

Holder pasteurization – heating milk to 62.5°C (144.5°F) for 30 minutes. This treatment reliably inactivates HIV and CMV and will eliminate or significantly decrease most other viruses.

Human milk fortifier – a fortifier added to human milk to boost the nutrient content.

Hyperbilirubinemia - excess bilirubin in the blood. A condition common in newborns.

Hypoglycemia - a condition when not enough glucose (sugar) is in the baby's blood to use as a fuel for energy.

Hypothermia - abnormally low body temperature, a frequent problem with low-birth weight premature babies.

ICEA – International Childbirth Education Association

Intestinal submucosa – the layer of loose connective tissue that supports the mucosa and joins the mucosa to the underlying muscles.

Intrauterine – in the uterus (womb).

Intrauterine growth restriction (IUGR) - refers to a baby who is smaller by weight than normal for her gestation age at birth. This can be caused by various fetal or maternal complications.

Intravenous (IV) – a tube or a needle placed into a vein to allow the infusion of fluids into the blood stream.

Intubation - the insertion of a tube into the trachea (windpipe) to allow air to reach the lungs to assist with breathing.

In utero - within the womb.

Isolette (Incubator) - a transparent plastic box, equipped with a heating system, to keep premature babies warm. Isolettes used to be known as incubators.

IUGR - see intrauterine growth restriction.

Jaundice - a yellowish discoloration of the skin and whites of the eyes caused by a buildup of bilirubin in the body.

Kangaroo care – a way to hold your baby skin-to-skin, against your bare-chest, inside your shirt or covered by a blanket, like a baby kangaroo in his mother's pouch.

Kernicterus - damage to nervous system caused by very high levels of bilirubin in the blood. Also called bilirubin encephalopathy.

Ketone body – by-products of the breakdown of fatty acids in the liver and kidney. Ketone bodies are used by the heart and brain for energy.

Kilogram (kg) – unit of weight of the metric system that equals 1000 grams or 2.2 pounds.

Lactation - production of milk by the breasts.

Lactation Consultant - a person who is trained to assist mothers with breast pumping or breastfeeding.

Lactoengineering – Adjusting human milk content to meet the needs of an individual or a certain population of infants, e.g., premature infants.

Lactogenesis I – the hormonal preparation and growth of breast tissue that starts during pregnancy.

Lactogenesis II – the onset of copious milk production which occurs after the infant is born and the placenta is gone.

Lactose – sugar found in human milk.

Large for gestational age (LGA) – newborn infant who is above the 90th percentile in weight at birth for his gestational age.

Late preterm infant – infants born between 34 0/7 and 36 6/7 weeks.

LBW – see low-birthweight infant.

Let-down reflex – release of milk into the milk ducts and down to the nipple, sometimes accompanied by a tingling sensation.

LGA – see large for gestational age.

Lipids – any fat-soluble, naturally- occurring molecule.

Low birthweight infant (LBW) – baby who weighs less than 5½ pounds (2500 gm) at birth; can be premature or full-term.

Mastitis – an inflammation of the mammary gland or breast.

Metabolic acidosis – an excess of hydrogen ions in the blood or tissues which interferes with normal cell functions.

Microbiota – microorganisms that normally live in the digestive tract and perform useful functions for their hosts.

Microflora – means the same as microbiota, but microbiota is the more preferred term since flora refers to plants and biota refers to microbial life.

Milk ejection reflex – the process initiated by oxytocin in which milk is released from the breasts.

Motility – the sequential contraction and relaxation of the muscular part of the gastrointestinal tract that propels ingested material forward.

NANN – National Association of Neonatal Nurses

NAPNAP – National Association of Pediatric Nurse Practitioners

Nasal CPAP – continuous positive airway pressure administered to an infant through nasal prongs.

Necrotizing enterocolitis (NEC) - an intestinal disease, most common in young preemies, in which portions of the bowel are damaged or destroyed because of poor blood flow, inflammation, or infection.

Neonatal nurse practitioner (NNP) – a registered nurse who has received additional training, usually through a master's degree program, and who is qualified by this training to provide certain aspects of the baby's medical care under the supervision of a physician.

Neonate – a baby during the first month of life.

Neonatologist - a pediatrician who specializes in the care of premature or sick newborn infants. A neonatologist has special training and certification in neonatal intensive care.

Newborn Intensive Care Unit (NICU NBISU, NBIC, ICN) - section of a hospital with trained staff and special equipment to care for critically ill newborns. See NICU.

NG tube – see Nasogastric tube.

NICU – short for Neonatal Intensive Care Unit. An NICU is a hospital ward where preemies that require complex medical care are taken care of, along with other critically ill or medical unstable newborns.

Nipple shield – a very thin, flexible silicone sheath worn over the areola and nipple while nursing. The nipple shield has holes at the end to allow milk to pass through.

Nippling – sucking on a bottle filled with formula or breast-milk.

NMA – National Medical Association

Non-nutritive tasting at the breast (dry breastfeeding) – the infant is allowed to suckle at a previously pumped breast to get used to breastfeeding and to stimulate milk production. This process has been shown to lengthen the time of breastfeeding post discharge.

Nosocomial infections – infections as a result of treatment in a hospital that appear 48 hours or more after hospital admission or within 30 days after discharge.

NPA – National Perinatal Association

Nutritional assessment – an assessment which includes growth parameters (weight, length, head circumference) and biochemical measurements (phosphorus, alkaline phosphatase, urea nitrogen, and transthyretin/prealbumin).

Osteopenia – a condition like rickets, in which the bones lose minerals (demineralize), become weak, and break easily. This condition is sometimes seen in prematures who receive hyperalimentation for long periods.

Oxytocin (Pitocin) – a hormone that stimulates uterine contractions and the "let-down response" in lactating mothers.

Parenteral nutrition – nutrition that is given intravenously, rather than through the stomach and the intestines.

Patent ductus arteriosus (PDA) – a blood vessel present in the fetus that allows blood coming from the placenta that is rich in oxygen to bypass the left side of the heart and lungs and flow through this blood vessel to the rest of the body. It usually closes in the first two weeks of life in term infants but may remain open in the preterm infant, requiring treatment to close it.

Pediatrician - a doctor who specializes in the care of infants and children.

Perinatal – the period from the twentieth week of gestation through the first twenty-eight days after delivery.

Perinatologist – a physician who has completed training in obstetrics and takes further training in the care of high-risk pregnancies.

pH – the symbol for hydrogen ion concentration. It expresses the degree to which a solution is acid or alkaline. The lower the pH, the more acid the solution.

Phototherapy - a treatment for jaundice by placing fluorescent (blue or green) lights over the baby's bed to help break down bilirubin into a water-soluble form that can be eliminated in the kidneys.

Postpartum – after delivery.

Postpartum depression – depression that occurs after having a baby. It may be a brief period (80%) when women are tearful or extremely sensitive and moody (baby blues) which lasts only a few weeks or a woman may have more significant symptoms of depression (12 – 15%) lasting weeks or months after delivery. In the most extreme cases, suicide or infant homicide is a possibility. Mothers experiencing depression should contact their health provider.

Prebiotic – food intended to promote the growth of certain bacteria in the intestines.

Premature infant – an infant who is less than thirty-seven completed weeks' gestational age at birth.

Prenatal – before birth.

Preterm milk – milk from mothers of preterm infants which appears to have a higher concentration of growth factors, hormones, anti-inflammatory factors, immunomodulators, immunoglobulins, and live infection-fighting cells than term milk.

Probiotics – living non-pathogenic microbial preparations that colonize the intestine and provide benefit to the host. They normalize intestinal microflora, increase mucosal barrier function, reduce intestinal permeability, enhance immune defenses, and improve enteral nutrition.

Prolactin – a hormone that stimulates breast development and milk production.

Pumping diary – log maintained in the NICU for mothers to record their pumping history. This log, if regularly recognized by NICU staff, may encourage mothers to visit, pump, and hold their premature infants frequently.

------------ ℛ ------------

RBC – red blood cell.

RDS (respiratory distress syndrome) - also called hyaline membrane disease, it is the result of a premie having immature lungs. A baby with RDS is not able to breathe well on his own as small air sacs (alveoli) tend to collapse (atelectasis).

RSV (respiratory syncytial virus) – a common virus that gives most people a cold, but can be more serious in premature babies, causing infections such as pneumonia or bronchiolitis.

Residuals - the amount of undigested food left in the stomach after a reasonable length of time has elapsed for digestion.

Retinopathy of prematurity (ROP) - a disease affecting the retina of a preterm baby's eye. ROP can lead to serious eye complications and even blindness. Formerly called retrolental fibroplasia.

------------ 𝒮 ------------

Sepsis - an infection of the blood.

SGA – see small for gestational age.

SIDS (sudden infant death syndrome) – crib death, the death of an infant during sleep from unknown causes.

Skin temperature probe – a small soft wire taped to the baby's skin to allow us to know the baby's temperature at all times.

Skin-to-skin care – see Kangaroo care.

Small for gestational age (SGA) – a newborn is considered small-for-gestational age if her birth weight is below the tenth percentile on the standard growth curve for her age.

Supplemental nursing system – an alternate feeding method in which a tube is taped to the breast. The other end of the tube is connected to a bottle. The infant sucks at the breast to feed. This method encourages latch-on because of the immediate reward, encourages correct infant suckling technique, allows baby-led pacing of the feeding, stimulates the mother's milk supply, and allows measurement of the amount taken.

Symbiotic – the living together of unlike organisms in a relationship where both organisms benefit.

---------- *T* ----------

Term infant – an infant born between approximately thirty-eight and forty-two weeks of gestation.

Test weighing – weighing the infant before a feed and after a feed. The difference in weights is the amount the infant consumed during a feeding.

Total parenteral nutrition (TPN; hyperalimentation) – a type of nutrition that is administered through intravenous infusion. TPN provides all of the essential nutrients needed.

TPN – see total parenteral nutrition.

Triple feeding – the practice of breastfeeding, supplementing with previously pumped milk or artificial milk, then pumping to remove residual milk.

Trophic factors – endogenous or exogenous proteins or other substances that stimulate growth and development of a tissue or organ.

Trophic feeds – small feedings starting soon after birth to prevent atrophy of the gut.

Trophic feeds – small feedings starting soon after birth to prevent

---------- *U* ----------

UAC/UVC (Umbilical Artery Catheter/Umbilical Vein Catheter) - a soft plastic tube inserted into an artery or vein in the baby's naval in order to give IV fluids or medications, to monitor blood pressure, and obtain blood for tests.

------------- 𝒱 -------------

Very low birth weight (VLBW) – an infant, of any gestational age, who weighs less than 1,500 grams at birth.

Villus – tiny, finger-like projections that protrude from the wall of the intestine. They increase the absorptive area and surface area of the intestinal wall.

-------------  -------------

Warmer - an open bed with an overhead heating unit allowing several people to care for the baby at the same time. A temperature probe taped to the skin measures and controls the baby's temperature. See radiant warmer.

Wean – to slowly decrease and then stop an intervention. This could be used when stopping a medication, when removing certain technological support such as a ventilator, or when stopping breastfeeding.

Wet nurse – a woman who breastfeeds a baby that is not her own.

White blood cells (WBCs) – WBCs are a part of the body's blood responsible for fighting against infection. See leukocyte.

------------- 𝒳 -------------

X-ray - a diagnostic technique when an electromagnetic wave produces an image of internal body parts.

Index

Volume of human milk 62

———— w ————

Weekly meetings 193
Wet nursing 1
World Health
        Organization (WHO) 21

Biographies

NANCY E. WIGHT MD, IBCLC, FABM, FAAP

Neonatologist at Sharp Mary Birch Hospital for Women and Rady Children's Hospital San Diego, and Medical Director, Sharp HealthCare Lactation Services. President and web editor, San Diego County Breastfeeding Coalition. Past President Academy of Breastfeeding Medicine. ILCA & HMBANA Advisory Boards.

JANE A. MORTON MD, FAAP, FABM

Clinical Professor of Pediatrics, Stanford University School of Medicine. Executive board member of the American Academy of Pediatrics' Section on Breastfeeding. Past Director of Breastfeeding Medicine, Stanford University. Producer of Breastmilk Solutions, educational breastfeeding videos.

JAE H. KIM MD, PHD, FRCPC, FAAP

Assistant Clinical Professor of Pediatrics, Divisions of Neonatology and Pediatric Gastroenterology, Hepatology and Nutrition, University of California, San Diego and Rady Children's Hospital San Diego. Research Director of Supporting Preterm Infant Nutrition (UCSD). Past Medical Chair of the Toronto Human Milk Bank Initiative.

ORDERING INFORMATION

HALE PUBLISHING, L.P.

1712 N. FOREST ST.

AMARILLO, TEXAS, USA   79106

8:00 AM TO 5:00 PM CST

CALL ... 806-376-9900

SALES . 800-378-1317

FAX 806-376-9901

Online Web Orders...

http://www.ibreastfeeding.com